TARTAN
REDS

by Iain McCartney

foreword by Tommy Docherty

a britespot publication

Foreword by Tommy Docherty

There has been a tartan thread running through the shirts of Mancester United since 1902 when the club changed it's name from Newton Heath and the shirts from green and gold to the famous red shirts they still wear today.

Since that time the scottish influence at Old Trafford has been considerable bothe on the pitch and in the Manager's office. Over 150 Scotsmen have played for the club and under the stewardship of Sir Matt Busby and Sir Alex Ferguson, Manchester United have accumulated more trophies than any club in the history of football.

I also like to think I contributed to the scottish success at the club, and becoming manager of Manchester United was certainly one of the proudest moments of my footballing career.

Many of the players in this fascinating book bring back wonderful memories from my playing and managerial days.

Players like George Mutch; who I knew at Preston North End. Jimmy Delaney, like myself, a former Glasgow Celtic player. David Herd, from my days at Arsenal. Jim McCalliog, a youngster I had at Chelsea, and of course all the other scots that I signed for United.

Reading through the papers of this book, reveals how big an impact players from north of the border have made on Manchester United and without their contribution, the list of honours would certainly not have been so great.

I consider it a privilege to have been asked to write the foreword for this book, and I hope you will find the story of the 'Tartan Reds' as enjoyable and interesting as I have.

Tommy Docherty

Tartan Reds
A Britespot Publication

First Published in Great Britain by
Britespot Publishing Solutions Limited
Chester Road, Cradley Heath, West Midlands B64 6AB

August 2002

ISBN 1 904 103 05 7

Cover design and layout:
© Britespot Publishing Solutions Limited

Printed and bound in Great Britain by:
Cradley Print Limited, Chester Road, Cradley Heath, West Midlands B64 6AB

Acknowledgments:
(in no particular order)
John Fitzhugh - for his help in supplying many of the photos,
Gareth Dukes - for his superb book 'The United Alphabet',
Phil Martin - for the use of the lithography on p. 10 copyright
Peter Holme - National Football Museum
John Lister, David Allan, Andrew Hoggan, John Henderson, James Thomas Photography,
Roger Marshall, Paul Burns, Linda Perkins, Chris Ivens, James Cadman, Tommy Docherty,

CONTENTS

Dedicated to:
All the 'Tartan Reds' with his special memories of Jim Holton.

PREFACE

On November 8th 1745, Prince Charles Edward Stuart, the 'Young Pretender' led his 16,000 Jacobite Army into England, crossing the River Esk, north of Carlisle.

Twenty one days later, to the utmost fear of many, but also to the delight of others, the strange, bedraggled assortment of 13,000 foot soldiers and 3,000 horse arrived in Manchester, following a stop at Preston.

Their stay in Manchester was brief, and with a few unemployed locals joining the ranks for a bit of an adventure and something to do, the army headed south, with the man at their head hoping to reach London and claim the throne of England.

Some 241 years later, almost to the day, another Scot journeyed South to Manchester, but this one had no vast following, nor indeed had he any aspirations to continue southwards to London.

The 'Young Pretender', however, he could well have been, as for a number of years a successor to Sir Matt Busby had been sought and following Alex Ferguson's success in Scotland, with Aberdeen, he could certainly be regarded as the ideal choice to take over the mantle of the great man and claim the Old Trafford throne. In time, he took Manchester United through the most successful period in their long and colourful history.

From the days of Newton Heath, in the late 1800's, to the present day Manchester United, Scots have served the club in various capacities. Some nondescript individuals, such as John Aitken, played only one game, while others like Arthur Albiston saw their appearance record run into hundreds. Names like Cairns, Grassam, Lochead and Brown mean nothing to the present generation of supporters, but mention Delaney, Law, Crerand and McClair and the eyes light up as the matches and goals are recalled.

Sir Matt Busby created three great post war sides, spanning three decades, while Sir Alex Ferguson emulated the Bellshill miner in the nineties with a cabinet full of trophies, cumulating with the treble success in 1999. But what of the other Scottish managers A.S.Duncan and John Chapman?

Within the pages of this book, the history of Newton Heath/Manchester United is traced and the career of every player and manager from north of Hadrians Wall covered in detail.

Up until the end of season 2000-2001, there had been a Scot involved in some way, with every success. This is their story.

THE EARLY YEARS

Rugby was the favoured sport of the Mancunians in the latter years of the 1880's, with each district seemingly having, at least, one team. Newton Heath was no exception and surprisingly, the area could boast of two rugby teams – the Wasps and the Wanderers. Football, on the other hand, was slowly gaining in popularity, the Lancashire Football Association being founded in 1878, with teams such as Turton, Darwin, Blackburn Rovers and Accrington Stanley well to the fore. In Manchester itself, teams such as West Manchester, Fairfield, Gorton Villa, Hurst and Hurst Nook Rovers were competing regularly between each other and against any eleven individuals who fancied to participate in a game. Despite there being no organised Leagues or whatever, games were enthusiastically played out, with players having to provide their own playing kit and also help with the upkeep of the pitch.

With the popularity of the round ball game gaining momentum, it is not surprising that the sports loving people of the Newton Heath area of Manchester should get together and form a team of their own.

And so it was, the Dining Room Committee of the Carriage and Wagon Works of the Lancashire and Yorkshire Railway, situated in that north east area of the city, got together and formed Newton Heath (Lancashire and Yorkshire Railway) Football Club. Sadly, there is no definitive record of the club's formation, but the 'History Of The Lancashire Football Association', published in 1928, mentions that the club was formed in 1878, so this date is generally taken as the beginning of the clubs' history.

Early details of Newton Heath and its players are few and far between, but one of the earliest reports appear in the 'Bolton Evening News' of November 26th 1880, where brief details appear of the Wanderers reserve side defeating Newton Heath 6-0 some six days earlier at their Pike Lane ground. A return match in Manchester on January 22nd resulted in a similar score line. Other fixtures around this time were as equally unrewarding for those connected with the club, although a 2-0 victory against Bootle's reserve side was recorded, with goals coming from Cramphorne and Minchley.

With the recently formed club still in its infancy, fixtures were played on an irregular basis, often with little notice to players and public alike, against such teams as Manchester Arcadians, Blackburn Olympic, Haughton Dale, Earlstown, Greenhays and Ougtrington Park.

By 1882, the team of that time comprised of Fulton in goal, Black and Rigby the backs, Edmonson and Charlton the half backs, Latham and Thompson on the right wing, Jarratt and Jones on the left wing, with Thomas and Kenyon playing in the centre, were what could be considered 'locals'. However, with the legalisation of professionalism in 1885, the make up of the Newton Heath side began to change. Employment on the railways and the added incentive of payment for playing football enticed players from further afield, particularly from Wales, to join the ranks.

With the organisation and day to day running of the club still very much in its infancy, there were numerous hiccups along the way, ranging from results, personnel and travel. Reading through newspapers of that time and their reports on the fixtures, reveal much about the life and standards that the footballers of Newton Heath had to endure in the mid to late 1880's and early 1890's.

A report of the Newton Heath – Accrington fixture of September 3rd 1887 mentioned that the match had been due to kick off at 3pm, but due to the Accrington team "being delayed on their journey", the game did not get under way until 4.15!

Following another fixture, played almost a year before, on November 5th 1886, away to Fleetwood Zingari, it was mentioned that an irate Fleetwood spectator assaulted one of the Newton Heath players after the game.

One another occasion, a game was altered to thirty minutes each way due to poor weather, whilst in November 1981, the enterprising Lancashire and Yorkshire railway organised a special "fast excursion" to Blackpool for the English cup tie against South Shore. Those who made the journey must have been rather annoyed, to say the least, upon their arrival at their destination around half time!

Fixtures were not confined solely to local League and Cup competitions, with the name of Newton Heath appearing on the list of fixtures for the Lancashire Senior Cup competition in 1883-4 and the Manchester Senior Cup in 1884-85. In the former, an early exit was made, losing on their own ground 7-2 to Blackburn Olympic, while in the former, victories over Eccles, Manchester and Dalton Hall earned a place in the final against Hurst. There was to be no after match celebrations as the match ended in a 3-0 defeat.

The F.A.Cup was first entered in 1886-87 and a creditable 2-2 draw was earned against Fleetwood Rangers on October 30th. For some strange reason, the Heathens refused to play extra time and the match was awarded to the Lancashire coast club.

Friendlies continued to be arranged against numerous teams, many out with the Manchester area, with reports of games against Heart of Midlothian and Third Lanark in January 1889 and Cambuslang in January 1890. Whilst enjoying refreshments following such fixtures, conversation would move from the ninety minutes just played to numerous other topics, with players of other clubs learning of the exciting prospects to be had in Manchester, with the opportunities of both steady employment along with the added attraction of football. It soon became a well-known fact, that a good footballer could always obtain employment at the Newton Heath depot.

Football developed almost simultaneously in Scotland and England, however, in Scotland it was soon considered as not only an after work, recreational activity, but something which could be pursued as an alternative to numerous backbreaking hours down the pit or some menial form of employment in the ear splitting factories.

In the likes of Dundee, the major jute manufacturing centre of Britain in 1913, many men actually stayed at home 'dry nursing', with the women out earning the weekly wage, while Ayrshire saw mining and farming as the main areas of employment. Miners in the early 1900's earned 6/8d (approximately 33p) per day, while labourers in a brick factories could earn 4/4d (approximately 21p). Young boys, working as milkmen, from 6.30am, for twelve hours, would take home the pricey sum of 1/6d (approximately 8p).

The length of the working day varied considerably in the 1800's, with carters in Glasgow putting in a 98 hour working week – 4.30am until 9.30pm, Monday to Friday and 5.30pm on a Saturday, for 5d (approximately 2p) per week.

It is a wonder that many found time, or the energy, for any recreational activities and with money to be made from football it is of no surprise that so many teams began to spring up around the country and an easier life was looked for.

One of the earliest Scotsmen to decide that Manchester was the place for him, was **Pat McDonnell** who, in August 1887, set off from his Glasgow home on foot and walked all the way to Manchester to seek a job at the Newton Heath works and a place in the football team.

Another of the early Heathens to hail from Caledonia was **William Tait**, a Glaswegian born in August 1863.

Some nine years earlier, whilst living in the Crosshill area of the city, "Wully" Tait developed an active interest in football and joined Granville Parkside, a local Junior side of that time. In a later magazine interview, he was quoted as saying, "I played in nearly every match for the Granville side, over a ten year period. When I left, they had the best Junior side in Glasgow".

Leaving Granville Parkside in 1882, he was next noted as a member of the Glasgow Pilgrims side of 1883-84 and made an appearance for them against Preston North End, who at that time were beginning to develop into the best club side in England

In 1894, he joined Third Lanark R.V. and following three practice (trial) games was included in the first eleven.

During his second season, he "played in every position on the field" and suffered a dislocated ankle playing against Aston Villa at Perry Bar.

In the magazine article, he also recalled, "Last year but one (1885-86), I played full back in the Scottish Cup semi-final versus Queens Park (this was on January 16th), which Queens Park won 3-0, in the so called 'snow semi-final'". This match was apparently over by half time due to a

A rare pencil illustration of William Tait

heavy fall of snow and the Third Lanark players, being numb with cold, more or less refused to continue the game. Queens Park did come out for the second half and to indicate their willingness to continue the game, kicked off and walked the ball through the unattended goal and were duly awarded the tie.

During 1884 and 1886, he was selected to play for Glasgow against Sheffield and in the match in Sheffield, he was later recorded as being a 'Glasgow Rangers player'.

His appearance within the pages of the magazine continued with him saying " I came to Manchester early in 1887 and was agreeably surprised to find a club at Newton Heath, which I joined".

To be honest, I find this rather surprising, as having played football on a regular basis for a number of years, having also played against English clubs, it difficult to believe that the name of Newton Heath was not known to him. The previously mentioned Pat McDonnell had heard of them, so why hadn't the more experienced Tait? Had he been illegally approached at some point or other and did not want to readily admit it?

The committee of the Lancashire and Yorkshire Railway side must have been suitably impressed by the new arrival to the city, as he was quickly installed in the first team, making his debut against Macclesfield on February 5th. He was then to appear frequently for the Heathens throughout the next season and a half, when it was normally friendly fixtures that were played. He was also a member of the side upon its election to the Football League.

Surprisingly, as the initial Alliance season progressed, the name of Tait no longer featured in the Newton Heath line up, never to re-appear. His whereabouts in football after this remain unconfirmed.

Another Scotsman in the early days of Newton Heath was Robert Milarvie.

One of only four ever presents in the Newton Heath side for their second season in the Football Alliance was **Robert Milarvie** who filed the inside left berth, scoring four goals in his twenty two appearances.

A former Pollockshields man, Milarvie had assisted Stoke City during 1888 (the first season of the Football League), joining their near neighbours Burslem Port Vale the following year.

From there, he joined Derby County, before coming to Manchester to assist the Heathens in 1890-91 season. Making his debut on the opening day of season 1890—91against Darwen on September 6th, he scored his first goal at the end of that month in the 2-1 defeat by his former club Stoke City.

At the end of this season, he crossed Manchester and joined Ardwick (soon to become Manchester City), where he played until 1896.

In the 'Sporting Chronicle' of August 13th 1891, an article on Scottish football contained the following — "This weekend, the Scottish League will resume operations, the following being there list of matches — Heart of Midlothian v Celtic: Renton v Glasgow Rangers; Third Lanark v Leith Athletic; Clyde v Vale of Leven and Cambuslang v Dumbarton.

"The news of men who take part in these games will doubtless be perused with anxious curiosity by officials of a good many English clubs, though not a few of the Scottish pro. Have already arrived in this country (England) to practise for the season, which does not commence until Tuesday September 1st".

The Newton Heath team of the late 1880's was predominately Welsh, with the likes of Burke, Davies, the Doughty brothers, Powell and Owen all representing the land of the dragons between 1888 and 1893. By season 1892-83, however, the red and white halved shirted Newton Heath had gained promotion to the Football League, having spent three seasons in the Football Alliance, finishing runners up in 1891-92. Prior to that, they had competed in the Football Combination, a competition played by teams who had failed to gain entry into the Football League.

The competition was poorly organised, with the twenty competing clubs only playing eight fixtures, some not even managing that. At what was considered the end of the season, Newton Heath were adjudged to be winners, having a slightly better record than Notts Rangers, a club that they had not played!

By now, the Welsh predominance had been replaced by an influx of Scotsmen, (although the team relied frequently on the goals of the brothers Doughty), with seven in the line up for the opening fixture of that memorable campaign in the top flight against Blackburn Rovers at Ewood Park. Brown, Erentz, Coupar, Carson, Mathieson, Stewart and Donaldson the players concerned. All but the latter two having been signed in June 1892. Unfortunately, they could not stop the home side recording a 4-3 victory. Coupar, Donaldson and Farman scoring for the visitors, in front of 8,000 spectators.

William Stewart had moved from Warwick County in the close season of 1899, having previously served Dundee Our Boys, a club that was to provide the Heathens with a number of players in those early years and a club, formed in 1877, that was later to amalgamate with Dundee East End to form the Dundee FC of today.

Born in Coupar Angus, Perthshire in1872, Stewart was a notable individual who had appeared in Newton Heath's initial match in the Football Alliance, scoring in the 4-1 victory over Sunderland Albion at North Road on September 21st. Plating as an inside forward, he recorded a total of 19 appearance in that first Alliance season, ending the season as the club's leading scorer with 10 goals.

Against Small Heath, at North Road, on April 7th 1890, he scored the first hat trick by a Newton Heath player in the 9-1 demolition of the club who were later to become Birmingham City. The following season, he played in all but one of the fixtures, scoring 5 goals in the 21 games, again mainly in a forward position. However, in the final Alliance season of 1891-92, he was switched to centre half where he was an ever present, tightening up the defence which conceded 22 goals less than in the previous season, and still managing to contribute 3 goals himself.

During that feet finding debut First Division season of 1892-93, he scored a hat trick, playing at centre half, against Wolverhampton Wanderers in the 10-1 victory on October 15th. A match that still holds the record of the club's highest scoring league win.

The week prior to that Wolves fixture, whilst training for the match against West Bromwich Albion, William Stewart was involved in a bizarre incident. For some unknown reason, hammer throwing was included in the training schedule and to his, and his team mates horror, he could only stand open mouthed as one of his attempts soared through the air in the direction of team mate Bob Donaldson. This unfortunate individual was unable to get out of the way, before being knocked to the ground unconscious.

Fortunately for both players, Donaldson made a quick and full recovery and he was able to face the Albion a couple of days later and actually score.

The visit to Wolves the following week, was expected to see the dismal run of two draws and four defeats in the opening six fixtures continue, as the visitors had won four of their opening half dozen games. However, much to the surprise of the 4,000 drenched spectators gathered at North Road, Wolves, somewhat handicapped by the dreadful playing conditions, put up little resistance.

The Athletic News correspondent of the time was to write, "If one may venture to criticise even the winners of such a day, we should say that Billy Stewart came first, Billy Stewart came second and Billy Stewart came third".

Later that season, on January 7th, at Stoke, Stewart showed his dedication, by playing in goal for the Heathens, who had travelled to the Potteries with only ten players, all for outfield positions, in the party. Unfortunately, his ability between the posts did not match his normal outfield performances, with the home side winning 7-1.

As his appearance and goal scoring record showed, he was a more than able player, however, his esteem increased considerably following the switch to defence. Opponents seldom outplayed him, and his footballing skills, something relatively rare in a defender's make up at that time, enabled him to support his forwards time and time again. Not content with just playing football, Stewart would return to his native Scotland during the close season and play cricket for Forfar and Perthshire.

His association with Newton Heath came to an end in may 1895, when he moved south to join Luton Town, where he enjoyed three seasons before moving to Millwall Athletic. After only one season there, he returned to Luton for a year before signing for Thames Iron Works in January 1900. At the end of that year, he returned north and saw out his career with Dundee.

The unfortunate victim in the previously mentioned hammer-throwing incident, **Bob Donaldson**, became a Newton Heath player in August 1891 after having previously been with Airdrie and Blackburn Rovers. His signing, however, caused some dispute between the two clubs, with the Football Association having to step in and sort the matter out. The 'Sporting Chronicle' of August 13th mentioned that "Newton Heath L. & Y. F.C. have secured the Scottish player Donaldson, about whose registration with the F.A. there has been a dispute with Blackburn Rovers. He practised with the Newton Heath team on Thursday night".

In those early days of professionalism it was believed that in order to secure Donaldson's signature from Airdrie, Blackburn Rovers had to pay the player a £50 signing on fee and the considerable sum of £2.10/- (£2.50p) per week.

Donaldson made his Heathen's debut on September 12th 1891 against Burton Swifts, scoring in the 3-2 defeat. He went on to make a telling contribution in what was to be the final season in the Football Alliance, scoring 20 goals in 22 games from the centre forward position.

The stocky built individual continued his fine scoring rate in the First Division campaign of 1892-93, with 16 goals in his 26 appearances. This included two hat tricks, against Wolves in the record breaking 10-1 match and against Derby County on the last day of 1892. He also enjoyed the distinction of scoring the club's first ever League goal, against his old club, Blackburn Rovers in the opening match of that season.

Donaldson was a typical centre forward of the period, who played the game hard, giving as much out as he took from defenders. Goalkeepers were also to bear the brunt of much physical attention from the 5'8", 12st 10lb individual. The physical side of the game was something that was generally accepted in those bygone days, but Donaldson's performance against Derby County on October 7th 1893, and that of his team mates Perrins and Clements, did not escape the attention of the referee. In the aftermath of the fixture, they were all reported to the Football Association and subsequently suspended for fourteen days.

The Lanarkshire born player's Newton Heath career came to

an end in December 1897, moving to Luton Town, where he enjoyed one season, before moving to Glossop North End. He was to finish his playing days with Ashford in Kent.

Of the other five Scots who made up the back bone of that initial Football League side on the opening day of season 1892-93, only one enjoyed a prolonged and successful career with the club. He was **Fred Erentz**.

Born in Dundee, in 1870, he moved south to take his place in the Newton Heath side as a 22 year old from Dundee Our Boys. His early appearances were as a half back, but was later to play at full back and the noted athlete's career in Manchester went on to span some ten seasons and 310 games. In a periodical of the time, he was described as a "consistent, cool and effective player who was rarely out of form". As a player who missed few games during the course of a season, it was rather ironic that his career should be brought to an abrupt end in the summer of 1902 due to a knee injury. Upon retiring, he took over the licence of a hotel in Miles Platting.

Two other Dundee Our Boys players followed Erentz south in June 1892 to seek fame and fortune. They were James Coupar and James Brown.

James Coupar was the third of the trio of West Craigie Park players to be signed by Newton Heath officials, who had spent a few days in the Tayside town, attending the 10th Annual Amateur Athletic Sports held by the Dundee club. He was signed on June 12th 1892, a day after Erentz put pen to paper and two days after James Brown did likewise. Slimly built, but a very effective individual who played in three of the five forward positions during that first season of League football, earning the distinction of scoring the first ever Football League goal against Blackburn Rovers on September 3rd 1892.

Missing half a dozen games through injury during October and November did not help his Newton Heath career, but he soon returned to the side and missed only three more fixtures during the remainder of the season. An injury received during 1892-93 proved troublesome and he was advised to rest for twelve months. It was later reported that due to his popularity and the director's disappointment at losing a player of such prominence, that he would be paid the sum of £1.5/- (£1.25p) per week while he recovered.

He recovered sooner than expected and it was mentioned in the 'Athletic News' prior to the commencement of season 1893-94 that "James Coupar is also here once more, his leg having improved". It was therefore to come as something of a shock to the club and its followers when the player decided to return north and sign for St Johnstone prior to the commencement of season 1893-94. This transfer must have been arranged during his period of recuperation.

Coupar was only to spend one year back in Scotland, before returning south in October 1894 to assist Rotherham Town. June 1897 saw him move to Luton while season 1898-99 found him at Swindon Town. A brief spell at Linfield followed before he returned to Swindon to see out season 1899-00.

During September 1901, he returned to Clayton and managed a further 11 appearances for Newton Heath, scoring 4 goals, three of these coming against Doncaster Rovers in a 6-0 victory in only his second game back. This was to be his last season in professional football, as during the close season of 1901-02 he made an appeal to the Football Association to be reinstated into the amateur ranks. Perhaps James Coupar's Newton Heath career was not as notable as that of numerous others, but he at least had the distinction of scoring in his first and last games for the club.

His former Dundee Our Boys team mate **James Brown** had a less eventful time in Manchester and returned home after only one season. His career with the Heathen's began well, turning out at left back in the first six fixtures of season 1892-93. None of the games were won, however, and he was one of three players dropped from the team for the next

fixture. This happened to be the first victory of the campaign, the 10-1 defeat of Wolverhampton Wanderers and he failed to reappear in the first team again until January 26th. Even then, it was just for the one match.

Possibly one of the reasons for Brown's omission from the team was his state of mind rather than his playing ability. On October 19th 1892, in a Lancashire Combination fixture against Darwen, he was involved in an accidental collision with a Darwin forward called Joseph Aspden, who was carried from the field of play. Although feeling well enough to travel home with his team mates, he collapsed and died some four days later.

An enquiry was held at Darwin Coroners Court and in his evidence, Brown said "I went to meet the ball, slipped and missed it, and struck one of their players in the stomach". He continued to say that he was uncertain, but thought that it was his knee that had made the contact and that he waited beside the player until he had came round and had picked him up from the ground.

As the referee had not seen fit to give a foul and all the other statements taken into consideration, a verdict of 'accidental death' was recorded.

Other Scots in that opening league fixture against Blackburn Rovers were the left wing pairing of Adam Carson and William Mathieson, making outside right Farman the odd man out in what was a predominately an all-tartan forward line.

Adam Carson was a product of Glasgow Thistle and had caught the eye of numerous clubs with a notable performance in a Scottish League versus the Scottish Alliance fixture, when he was considered to be "the best forward" on show.

Like his other fellow countrymen, he put pen to paper for Newton Heath in June 1982, receiving a £20 signing on fee and the weekly sum of £3 during the season and £2 in the summer. The

latter payment never came into effect, as he failed to complete one season with the club, moving to neighbours Ardwick, (later to become Manchester City), in March 1983, having made only 13 appearances for the Heathens. Twelve of those had come in a run at the start of the season. The following February, he joined Liverpool, but was to remain with the Merseyside club for only three months.

His partner on the left flank, **William Mathieson** was another Glaswegian and had previously been with Clydeside FC, before moving south. He joined Newton Heath in the latter stages of season 1891-92 and played in the final three games of that particular season at outside left, scoring in the second of those, against Lincoln City.

Like Carson, he was not cut out for the more physical English game and soon found things a bit tougher south of the border. He was unfortunate to miss the record breaking 10-1 victory against Wolverhampton Wanderers in October 1892 through injury and after that, he was to find it difficult to get back into the team, making only two other first team appearances during that season.

1893-94 saw his opportunities even more limited with his first appearance of that campaign not coming until February 3rd at Aston Villa, with his only other outing on the final day of the season at home to Preston North End. Ironically, he scored United's only goal on both occasions. In the close season of 1894 he moved to Rotherham Town.

Tommy Docherty's reign as manager of Manchester United in the 1970's saw the signings of eight of his fellow countrymen, with tartan scarves a not too unfamiliar sight on the Old Trafford terraces. It might come as a surprise to many though, to discover that during Newton Heath's first season in League football a total of thirteen Scotsmen made appearances in the first eleven. The previously mentioned Brown, Stewart, Erentz, Coupar, Donaldson, Carson and Mathieson, were joined by Mitchell, Fitzsimmons, Hendry, Cassidy, McFarlane and Colville.

Andrew Mitchell did not appear in the opening match of 1892-93 against Blackburn Rovers, but replaced Clements at right back the following Saturday against Burnley and retained his place for the rest of that season, with Clements returning to the side at left back at the expense of the previously mentioned James Brown.

He had been signed from Airdrie in September 1892 in what could be considered strange circumstances. The regular Newton Heath right back during the successful Alliance season of 1891-92 was **Bob McFarlane**, a fellow Scot who had began his career at Airdrie, turning out for Bootle and Sunderland Albion between 1888 and 1891, before joining Newton Heath for that 1891-92 campaign.

During the close season, he had returned home for what was meant to be a holiday, (whilst being paid by Newton Heath) and was approached, and successfully signed by his former club. During his second spell with Airdrie, he played in sixty-seven League games, scoring once and one Scottish Cup tie, over a five season period between 1894-95 and 1898-99. His final appearance for the club was on October 8th at Cappielow, against Morton, and tragically he died before the end of that month having caught pneumonia.

Whether out of spite or whatever, Newton Heath officials immediately signed Andrew Mitchell, the player he would have partnered at Airdrie, as his immediate replacement.

The 22 year old Mitchell made an early impression on all who saw him play, with his firm tackling and fine distribution, making an unbroken 49 game League and Cup run in the team. Following the club's relegation into the Second Division at the end of season 1893-94, Mitchell moved to Burton Swifts.

Few players could have made a more eventful league debut than **James Hendry**, Signed from Alloa Athletic in the close season of 1892, he was drafted into the side to face

Wolverhampton on October 25th, following a difficult start to the season. With many spectators still making their way into the ground and less than one minute played, the Newton Heath outside left put the home side in front with what was practically his first kick in League football, paving the way for the record 10-1 score line.

October 1892 and was given his debut on November 12th at home to Notts County, in what resulted in a 3-1 defeat. Two games later, he scored what was to be his only goal for the club, in a 2-2 draw at Accrington. Unfortunately for the player, he received an ankle injury at Bolton on December 3rd, his fifth game, which was to

Fig: i

NEWTON HEATH 1892/3

		HENRYS,	CLEMENTS,		
TIMMONS (TRAINER),	COUPAR	PERRINS,	STEWART,	ERRENTZ,	MITCHELL,
FARMAN,	HOOD,	DONALDSON,	FITZSIMMONS,	COLVILLE	

Sadly, he was to make only one other appearance for the club, seven days later and left at the end of the season. Outside left seemed to be something of a problem position during season 1892-93, with seven different players tried, in an effort to find the right man. One of those given a run was **James Colville** (see Fig: i pg 16), whose seven appearances wide on the left failed to secure him the position on a permanent basis.

Born in Ayrshire, a notable area for producing footballers, Colville was signed from Annbank in

keep him out of the side for a few weeks. He returned for the 4-0 FA Cup defeat at Blackburn and played in only a further four games during 1892-93.

In the summer of 1893, he dropped down into the Manchester Amateur League, signing for Fairfield, spending a couple of years there before returning home to Annbank following an unsuccessful trial with Notts County.

In James Colville's second League outing, against Aston Villa at home, he found himself forming a left wing partnership with his former Annbank team mate **Tommy Fitzsimmons**, (see Fig: i pg 16) with the latter scoring one of the goals in the Heathens 2-2 draw. Perhaps if Colville had not suffered his ankle injury, this partnership might have flourished.

In his eighteen League outings during 1892-93, Fizsimmons looked an impressive player, scoring five goals, and the following season he played in nine of the opening twelve fixtures, scoring in the last of these at Sheffield United. This was sadly to be his last first team appearance with the club. He remained with Newton Heath, however, until the end of season 1893-94, when he, like Colville, returned to Annbank.

The former Celtic trialist enjoyed a further two years with his home town club before moving to St Mirren for one month in October 1894, returning again to Annbank where he was to see out the season. In September 1895, he decided once again to try his luck south of the border, returning to Manchester to join Fairfield in the Manchester League. He spent three years in the area, playing for the likes of Glossop North End, Oldham County, Chorley and Wigan County, with a second spell at Fairfield sandwiched in between, before once again returning to Annbank in September 1899.

One player who was more or less a regular in the Newton Heath line up between October and March of that initial Football League season was William Hood, the only player within the pages of this book where a question mark appears over his inclusion.

Football in the 1880's was certainly (and obviously) no where near as comprehensively covered as it has been in more recent times, so in many cases information is sketchy to say the least. Newspaper reports can be very conflicting and records can vary accordingly.

Information from one source gives Hood's birthplace as Ashton, while a contemporary magazine of the time gives his previous club as Dundee Our Boys, a source of regular contributions to the Newton Heath cause. If the latter is correct, then there is a very strong possibility that he was

from that area, rather than having been born in Ashton and moved north, before returning to Manchester.

Possible, but......?

Anyway, if he is a Scot, he has to be included here, so to be on the safe side, the inside forward, who was a big favourite with the North Road supporters, makes an appearance.

William Hood (see Fig: ii pg 16) made his Newton Heath competitive debut against Lincoln City on November 21st 1891, scoring twice in the 10-1 victory. He retained his place the following week and for the remainder of season, scoring a further three goals as the team pushed for promotion from the Alliance to the Football League.

Missing from the line up for the first four games of that initial Football League season, Hood reappeared, at outside right, against West Bromwich Albion on October 1st, scoring once in the 4-2 defeat. Finding the net again seven days later, when for the second season in a row a 10-1 score line was recorded. This time Wolves were the victims of the Heathens onslaught.

The following season, 1893-94, saw him make only a dozen appearances, scattered through the campaign, playing in a variety of positions from right back to inside right and by the summer of 1894, he left Clayton for pastures new.

Having finished bottom of the First Division in 1892-93, Newton Heath maintained their position in the top flight for the following season by means off a 5-2 Test match victory over Small Heath at Bramall Lane, Sheffield on April 27th, following a 1-1 draw at Stoke five days earlier.

One of the scorers in the 5-2 win was **Joe Cassidy**, (see Fig: i pg 18) a recent acquisition from Blythe on a loan deal, secured purely with possibility of Newton Heath's involvement in the end of season Test Matches. Whether the signing of Cassidy was a major reason for the end of season improvement in form is debatable, but only one of the final four League fixtures, in which he played, were lost and he did indeed make a major contribution to the defeat of Small Heath in the Test Match.

Lanarkshire born Cassidy, had begun his career with Motherwell Athletic before moving to the north East of England to join Blythe in 1890. Following his six game spell on the left wing with Newton Heath at Bank Lane, he returned to Scotland in May 1893, signing for Celtic on what was again initially a loan deal.

He remained with the Glasgow side until March 1895, however, scoring seventeen goals in thirty six appearances, winning four Scottish caps and a Charity Cup medal in 1893. Also a League Championship medal and Glasgow Cup medal in 1894, before returning to Manchester and

dismayed by their headline making defeat, protested about the ground conditions at Clayton and had their appeal upheld, with the match being subsequently rescheduled for April 3rd, much to Newton Heath's annoyance.

The Saturday following the Walsall Town Swifts debacle saw Grimsby Town arrive in Manchester to visit the dismal surroundings of Clayton, without complaint, and Joe Cassidy's two goals secured another two points.

Fig: ii

NEWTON HEATH 1894/5

ALBUT(SEC), PALEY(TRAINER), DOW, DOUGLAS, PALMER (DIRECTOR), ERRENTZ, DAVIDSON, FAULKNER (DIRECTOR)
CROMPTON (PRESIDENT), PERRINS, MCNAUGHT, STEWART, JONES (VICE PRESIDENT)
CLARKIN, DONALDSON, CASSIDY, SMITH, PETERS

Newton Heath in March 1895, due to some disharmony in the Celtic dressing room.

By now, the Heathens were back in the Second Division and having a reasonable season. Once again, however, the appearance of Cassidy in the line up, this time at centre forward, produced a noticeable improvement. In his 'return' match, against Walsall Town Swifts on March 9th, he scored four in a 14-0 trouncing. Unfortunately, this score line does not appear in any of the record books as the visitors,

A fortnight later, following a 3-2 defeat at Woolwich Arsenal, Walsall Town Swifts returned to Bank Street and with something of a point to prove, Cassidy and his team mates ran up a 9-0 score line, this time without complaint, with the former Celtic forward notching another double. April 6th brought another two goals, against Newcastle United, and with two more added to his total by the end of the season, Joe Cassidy's record read eight goals from eight games.

Cassidy was indeed an outstanding individual and a firm favourite with the club's supporters. He was a well built forward, possessed a strong shot and was a difficult individual to knock off the ball. His second spell with Newton Heath stretched over six seasons, during which the talented forward scored ninety goals in one hundred and fifty two League games and a further nine in fifteen FA Cup appearances.

In his five full seasons – 1895-96 to 1900-01, after scoring eight in eight games during 1894-95, he was leading scorer in four of those, on two occasions with nine more goals than his nearest rival and on another with eight more. These included fifteen doubles and five hat tricks. In April 1899, he was awarded a benefit match for his services to the club.

At the end of season 1899-00, despite his contribution to the club by way of goals scored and also his undoubted popularity with the supporters, the Newton Heath directors were forced to sell him due to the financial difficulties surrounding the club, and he was subsequently sold to neighbours City for the pricey sum of £250.

On the other side of Manchester, he failed to enthral the crowds as much nor did he endear himself to the club hierarchy who felt he was not worth his weekly wages of £4 and he was sold to Middlesbrough for £75 twelve months later.

Up in the North East on Teeside, he had the distinction of scoring the club's first goal at their new Ayresome Park ground against Sunderland on September 9th 1903 and went on to notch up thirty-four goals in his one hundred and thirty-five appearances.

Having survived the embarrassment of being tagged one season wonders in the First Division of 1892-93, thanks to the 5-2 Test Match victory over Small Heath, (with two of the five goals coming from Cassidy and Coupar), secretary A.H.Albut had hopes that he could recreate the attacking play of the last Alliance season when the team scored 60 goals in 22 games, during the following campaign. Unfortunately, it wasn't to be, despite getting off to an ideal start.

In the opening fixture of season 1893-94, the first match to be played at the new ground at Clayton, a Farman hat trick

secured a 3-2 win over Burnley, with the team showing four new faces compared to that which had played last season. Two of whom were Scots.

Into the side on the opening day at left half back came newly signed **William Davidson**, (see Fig: ii pg 18) a position he made his own, only missing two games in March through injury. Unfortunately, it was another injury, received the following season against Crewe on December 1st 1894, that was to force him out of the game for good. Another of the numerous signings from Annbank in Ayrshire, Davidson quickly settled in the English game and enjoyed the support of the sometimes fickle Bank Street crowd. Such was his popularity, that upon his retirement from the game, he was awarded a benefit match in the form of a 'Scottish X1 versus English X1'. Sadly, the promised support from neighbouring clubs failed to materialise, with only Bury and Fairfield obliging, with the attendance only totalling a disappointing few hundred.

Filling the inside right berth that same afternoon when William Davidson made his debut was **James McNaught**. (see Fig: ii pg 18) Unlike his fellow countryman, McNaught had joined the club towards the end of season 1892-93 and like the previously mentioned Joe Cassidy, it had been hoped that his presence would boost the end of season fight for survival. As it turned out, McNaught injured his shoulder in a friendly against Ardwick shortly after signing and missed the vital fixtures.

McNaught began season 1893-84 at inside right as mentioned, he was soon moved to inside left, then back to inside right for a couple of games. A run of half a dozen games switching between outside and inside right followed, before enjoying a somewhat settled run of ten games back at inside left. Then came two games at left half, before he was finally switched to centre half.

Known as 'the little wonder', the former Dumbarton and Linfield man was one of the finest ball players ever seen at Clayton. Although only 5'6", he preferred to play at the back and in his second season he played all but two of the League fixtures in the centre half position.

His versatility, however, caught up with him during 1896-97, when he made only one appearance in his favoured position, in the last game of the campaign at Loughborough, with the other thirty split almost evenly between left half and inside left, with a handful at inside right. The signing of Caesar Jenkyns, a notable centre half, also played a significant part in McNaught switching positions.

In what was to be his final season with Newton Heath, he again featured mainly as a centre half and at one point was considered a possibility for international recognition. Sadly such honours passed the player, considered to be a gentleman footballer, by.

At the end of season 1897-98 Tottenham Hotspur, then in the Southern League, made a move for his services, offering him a £50 signing on fee and £4.10/- (£4.50p) per week, a 10/- (50p) per week increase on his Newton Heath wage. Much to the despair of the Heathens support and directors he accepted the terms and went on to enjoy a successful nine years in the South, winning a Southern League Championship medal in 1900, but missing out on an F.A. Cup medal a year later. In the summer of 1898, the Daily Post wrote that 'McNaught who could not resist the temptation from the south, will be greatly missed at centre half by Newton Heath'.

With Tottenham, he played mainly as a centre half and made ninety-nine Southern League appearances, thirteen F.A. Cup appearances and scored one goal. He also came close to winning Scottish international honours, being selected to represent the Anglo Scots against the Home Scots in 1899.

In 1907, he left the Spurs for Maidstone, but retired soon afterwards.

He was also a highly intelligent and respected individual, who played a major part in the early days of the Professional Footballers Association, which was formed in January 1892 in the Spread Eagle Hotel, Corporation Street, Manchester.

It must have been something to do with the name, as five players called Thompson played with Newton Heath/Manchester United and they only made a total of nineteen appearances between them. Three making three each, with the other totalling up six and four.

One of those who made three appearances was **William Thompson**, who had begun his professional career with Dumbarton, before journeying south to join Aston Villa in April 1893. His stay in the Midlands was brief, six months to be more exact, as he joined Newton Heath in October that same year, but had to wait a couple of weeks for his debut due to an injury received in training.

Unfortunately for Thompson, his three consecutive appearances, beginning at Burnley on October 21st, also coincided with three defeats and he was omitted from the side for the home fixture against Wolves on November 11th, which was won 1-0 and he subsequently drifted into obscurity.

Perhaps the unfortunate Thompson should not have been the only one to suffer the loss of his first team place during 1893-94, as only four of the nineteen fixtures between September and January resulted in victories. One of those was a draw, with the others lost.

Another individual, who was to enjoy only a brief interlude in the Newton Heath side of season 1893-94, was **William Campbell**. A player who had served a number of clubs's, before finding his way to Clayton in November 1893, to begin what was only to be an association of only a few weeks.

Campbell's professional playing career had begun in London with Royal Arsenal, but he was never to feature in the first eleven for a competitive fixture.

December 1890 saw him move to Lancashire, signing for Preston North End, but by the beginning of season 1891-92, he was a Middlesbrough player, spending only one season in the north-east before moving on again, back to the land of the cotton mills and joining Darwen.

It was here that his playing career finally took off and he was to achieve some minor success with the Lancashire club, as they challenged for promotion from Division Two and had an impressive run in the F.A.Cup during 1892-93. His services were then claimed by yet another of the Football League's biggest club's of that time, Blackburn Rovers, but following his signing in August 1893, he was to make only one appearance before joining Newton Heath. Campbell made his debut against Sheffield United on November 25th at inside right, in a 3-1 defeat. This did not bode well for the much travelled Scotsman, as by the end of December he was gone.

In his five appearances for the Heathens, they failed to record a solitary victory, with the only plus point from his outings being a goal against Sunderland, in his third match. Leaving Manchester, in March 1894 he moved to Nottingham to join Notts County. True to form, his stay was again for only a limited period and by the end of the year he had moved to Newark. The non-League side were to be his final club, as the Football Association handed out a two year ban following an investigation into an attempt to offer a cash inducement to a former Blackburn Rovers colleague if he would sign for Notts County

Following the seventh consecutive League defeat, losing 2-0 at Everton on January 6th 1894, an effort was made to save what was left of the season. In an attempt to avoid the Test Matches, a flurry of transfer activity took place, with the Scots once again being heavily relied upon to rescue the club from its troubles. A move, which was to reoccur time and again as the years rolled by.

Into the side as a right wing partnership came **John Clarkin** (see Fig: ii pg 18) and Samuel Parker, signed from Glasgow Thistle and Hurlford respectively. Outside right Clarkin made an immediate impression, scoring five goals in the remaining twelve games of that season, but his endeavours were not enough to save the club as nine of those games resulted in defeats. One was drawn. Surprisingly, the two victories saw score lines of 5-1 and 6-2, against Blackburn Rovers and Stoke City respectively, Clarkin scoring in both.

Born in Nelston, Renfrewshire, John Clarkin began his career with his home town club before joining Glasgow Thistle in July 1893. His level of consistency continued following Newton Heath's drop down into the Second Division, missing only one game and scoring eleven goals from the outside right position. The following season, 1895-96 continued on a similar vein, with seven goals from twenty-six outings and it came as something of a surprise when he was allowed to leave in the close season to join Blackpool, a club who were only beginning their career as a League club.

His right wing partner, **Samuel Parker** an Ayrshire man from Hurlford, failed to make a similar impression on club officials and spectators alike, with his eleven appearances failing to produce any of the much hoped for goals. Season 1894-95 saw him as a member of the reserve side and with only a few weeks of the season played, he was transferred to Burnley in October. By the end of that season he was a Southport Central player and in the summer of 1895, he returned, somewhat disillusioned, to Hurlford.

The signing of two forwards in the crisis torn season of 1893-94 could be considered strange, as it was clearly defensive problems which beset the team and this should have been the number one priority when it came to changes in personnel.

Following the debuts of Clarkin and Parker in the 2-1 home defeat by Sheffield Wednesday, goalkeeper **William Douglas** (see Fig: ii pg 18) was introduced into the line up as a replacement for local lad Joe Fall in the next League fixture against Aston Villa away on February 3rd.

Another former member of the Dundee Our Boys side, Douglas arrived at Clayton via neighbours Ardwick, where he had enjoyed playing for almost four years. His seven league appearances during the last few weeks of season 1893-94 brought little improvement in way of results, but the following season, when he made the position his own, saw a dramatic change in fortune, with the team finishing third in the Second Division.

Season 1895-96 again saw him as the club's number one custodian and he was an ever present between the start of the season and January 4th. The 3-1 defeat at Leicester that afternoon was to be his last League appearance for Newton Heath, as the following match, a Manchester Cup tie against Fairfield resulted in a disastrous 5-2 home defeat.

Douglas had received the brunt of the criticism and had suffered as much from the crowd behind his goal as he had from the Fairfield forwards. Being something of a sensitive soul, he took much of the abuse hurled towards him to heart and packed his bags and disappeared back

T / R

to Dundee. In the furore that followed, Douglas, and the Newton Heath trainer were suspended sine-die.

The unfortunate goalkeeper, who was considered a first class player, did not have long to wait for a new club, with Derby County stepping in almost immediately. Here he remained only to the end of the season, before joining former team mate and fellow countryman John Clarkin at Blackpool, for their inaugural Football League season. His stay with the Seasiders lasted two seasons and he was later to return home to Dundee in August 1899, following a brief spell in the southern league with Warmley.

Another Dundonian, **Jack Dow**, (see Fig: ii pg 18) joined the Newton Heath ranks in February 1894, making his debut at right back versus Bolton Wanderers at home on March 24th. Some of the newspapers of the time, however, list a M.J.Wood as the Heathens right back that day, and in the following fixture against Blackburn Rovers, but this was merely a pseudonym to keep Dow''s identity under wraps for some unknown reason.

Those two late season appearances were all he made that term, but in their pre-season report on the club, the 'Athletic News' wrote, "Dow is likely to turn out a very useful man, as he can play in any part of the field". Quite a prediction, as when season 1894-95 got under way, Dow could be found at centre forward, a position that he held for all but two of the opening fourteen fixtures, making a telling contribution, with five goals. Midway through the season, he reverted back to defence and remained there, more or less, for the remainder of his Heathens career. His versatility, however, was not always appreciated, with many preferring the defenders of the day to merely boot the ball clear rather than dribble it from the defence.

Jack Dow played his last game for the club as an outside right on March 18th 1896 at Burton Wanderers and following a brief stay at Fairfield and Glossop North End, he returned to League football as captain of Luton Town and then enjoying spells at Middlesbrough and West Ham United before returning to Luton in 1903, where he finished his career in 1905.

Relegation to the Second Division at the end of season 1893-94, following the 2-0 Test Match defeat by Liverpool at Ewood Park, Blackburn, gave the club the opportunity to re-organise themselves. Despite an opening day setback against Burton Wanderers with a 1-0 defeat, a settled side, with only fourteen players used in the opening eighteen fixtures (compared to twenty-four throughout the previous season) results improved, with only two further defeats. Captain of the new look Heathens side, was right back **John McCartney**, a solidly built individual, of whom it was once written that "charging him would be like a ball going against a billiard cushion".

McCartney, was a distinguished professional before his arrival in Manchester, having been a member of the Glasgow Rangers side who had reached the semi finals of the F.A.Cup in 1887. Cartvale, Thistle F.C. and Cowlairs were also former employers.

Despite being given the captaincy, his spell at Clayton was brief, despite taking the Heathens to within touching distance of possible promotion, with his playing record showing only eighteen appearances in the League, one F.A.Cup and one Test Match, before joining Luton Town, in April 1895, where he again became club captain.

His career following his departure from Newton Heath is well worth noting, as few individuals since can have put so much into the game. Following his three years at Luton, he returned north, joining Barnsley in August 1898.

With the Yorkshire side, he played in their first ever Second Division Two match against Lincoln City on September 1st 1898, which they lost 1-0, as they did their second at Burslem Port Vale, this time 2-0. However, on September 8th, he was to score Barnsley's first ever League goal, from the penalty spot, in the 2-1 home win over Luton Town. He later became trainer with the Yorkshire side in August 1900 and during the close season of 1901 Barnsley's secretary, Arthur Fairclough offered to resign as long as the committee appointed McCartney in his place. Not only did they appoint their former player as secretary, they also gave him the title of manager, giving him complete control over the running of the club.

A similar position with St Mirren took him back to his native Scotland in August 1904, spending just over five years with the Paisley club, during which time he introduced many fine young players. In January 1910, he moved across central Scotland to become secretary-manager of Heart of Midlothian, a challenge he found too hard to resist.

On a salary of £5 per week, McCartney set about attempting to make Hearts a force in Scottish football and within four years had created a side, considered by many, as the best the club had had for many a year. They finished third in the First Division on goal average in 1912-13 and 1913-14 and runner-up in 1914-15. Unfortunately, the outbreak of war brought to an end all hopes of going one step further.

In a strange patriotic sense, upon the start of the First World War, he declared that the complete Hearts team (worth around £12,000 at that time) would be joining the Army.

He was something of a new breed of managers, always talkative to the press, eager to get Hearts as much publicity as possible, while showing much flexibility over his team selection and tactics.

Popular with the supporters, he was a figure who always stood out in a crowd, dressed immaculately in a three-piece suit, with the accompanying bowler hat and his moustache neatly waxed.

Despite the lack of top domestic honours, under McCartney Hearts did win the East of Scotland Shield and the Roseberry Charity Cup, as well as reaching the semi-finals of the Scottish Cup two seasons in a row.

On the 18th of October 1919, he left Tynecastle, following a disagreement over club policy with the directors and was somewhat surprisingly succeeded by his son William.

Following a short spell out of the game, he resumed his secretary-managerial career with Portsmouth in May 1920, a position he held for some seven years.

With the Fratton Park club, he took them from the Third Division South to the First Division in a mere seven years. Promotion to the Second Division as Champions in 1923-24 and from the Second to the First as runners-up in 1926-27.

In September 1927 he returned to Luton Town for a second spell in charge, and despite severe financial restraints helped them maintain a place in the Second Division.

His involvement with the club and indeed football came to an end in 1929 and he returned to Edinburgh, taking up an engineering post, spending much of his spare time writing to newspapers, often under the pseudonym of "Sir Gorgonzola" also writing a history of the Scottish League. He also became greatly involved in local council affairs. In latter years, his health suffered following an amputation of a leg, curtailing his energetic activities and in January 1933, he died, at the age of sixty-seven.

With Jack Dow being used as something of a makeshift centre forward, a proven leader of the front line was obviously required by Newton Heath if they were to reach the status that they considered themselves worthy of and the signing of George Millar, from Glasgow Perthshire towards the end of 1894, looked to have filled the void.

Making his debut against Lincoln City on December 22nd, **George Millar** scored with a header after only ten minutes, making an instant impression. A goal in each of the following two games, against Burslem Port Vale and Walsall Town Swifts, followed by a double two games later in the return match against Burslem on January 1st gave everyone associated with the club a boost. Surprisingly, however, he disappeared from the first team starting line ups, re-surfacing on only one other occasion that season in what was the second last fixture. During the close season he was released by the club and joined Chatham, where he continued to score on a regular basis.

In the final match of season 1894-95, against Notts County at Clayton, the centre half position was filled by **William Longair**, yet another Dundonian, but one who was not destined to enjoy a career similar to others from the city of jute, with this outing his sole appearance for the club.

A former centre forward, Longair signed for Newton Heath from Dundee (who had been recently formed with the amalgamation of Dundee Our Boys and Dundee East End) in the early weeks of 1894, having previously played for another local side, Rockwell.

The Scottish internationalist, who had won one cap against Northern Ireland that same season (playing alongside goalkeeper Frank Barrattt who was also to play for Newton Heath), missed out on adding to this, with appearances against England and Wales, due to injury. He then became rather disillusioned with life in Manchester, refusing terms for season 1895-96 and promptly returned home to re-join Dundee.

Eight months later, in February 1896, he decided to give the English game a second chance, joining Sunderland, but before the end of the year he was on the move again to Burnley. At the end of the season, he once again signed for Dundee, but stayed only one season before taking his boots to the south coast for a season with Brighton United.

In May 1899, he began a fourth spell with Dundee for what was to be his final season as a player, hanging up his boots to become the club's trainer in August 1900, a position he was to hold for 22 years before continuing his association with the club as groundsman between 1924 and 1926.

A 3-0 defeat in the Test match against Stoke City, (who had also knocked them out of the F.A.Cup), at Burslem on April 27th ended any hopes and aspirations of returning to the top flight. "A bit down on their luck" was how the Athletic News described the Heathens season of 1894-95 but expectations of an improvement in the following seven months were soon to rise.

Four new signings were made in the hope of boosting the squad, with three of these from north of the border, maintaining the attraction of Scottish players with English clubs. The trio of Scots, Fitzsimmons, Kennedy and Aitken were all to make their Newton Heath debuts in the opening match of the new season against Crewe on September 7th, playing inspired roles in the 5-0 victory.

David Fitzsimmons joined his fellow countrymen Douglas, Dow, Erentz and McNaught in the Newton Heath defence, with a sixth new signing, Cartwright being something of the odd man out, hailing from nearby Nantwich.

Fitzsimmons had followed in the footsteps of his brother Thomas, who had appeared for the club during 1892-93 and 1893-94, having also moved south from Annbank. A determined and excellent team player, he missed only four appearances, playing in both half back positions, however,

once again the financial situation of the club came to the fore with the lack of funds to pay close season wages resulting in his signing for Fairfield. A route taking by numerous other Heathens in the past.

One season with the Manchester side was followed by spells with Chorley and Wigan County, before a surprise return to Newton Heath for season 1899-1900. Although age was still in his favour and despite being judged to have put on a bit of weight, he was considered along with Cartwright, Morgan and Griffiths as making up a "capital quartet" and to being "a very efficient player". Following his appearance in the opening fixture of the season, at centre half, he made only one other appearance in the first team, before disappearing from League football.

Coming into the side at inside right at the start of season 1895-96 was **William Kennedy**, who marked his debut against Crewe with a goal.

The former Ayr Parkhouse player quickly settled into life in Manchester and enjoyed a progressive season at Clayton, playing in all but the final League fixture, scoring eleven goals, including a hat trick against Darwen, a total which made him the club's second highest goalscorer that season. A re-shuffle of the team the following season saw Donaldson move to inside right, with Kennedy finding himself in the reserves, making only one appearance all season, in the 2-0 defeat at Gainsborough Trinity on October 24th. His opportunities were clearly limited, with the addition of Matt Gillespie to the ranks in mid November, so a move was considered the best option and a few weeks later he joined Stockport County, where he was to play for three seasons. At the beginning of season 1899, he returned to Scotland and joined Greenock Morton, after being reinstated as an amateur.

The third of the opening day debutants on that September afternoon back in 1895 was **John Aitken**, an outside left, signed from the strangely named 5th Kings Rifle Volunteers, a local Dumfries side, where his last appearances were at outside right in the Final and replay of the Southern Counties Cup against Maxwelltown Thistle on May 25th and 29th of that same year. Considered "a valuable signing", with "an abundance of speed and good shooting powers", he had played with his local side for a number of years, mainly as a forward, but proved to be a versatile player by turning out at right back against Renfrew Victoria a month prior to his transfer. He also scored a number of goals, with two in a notable friendly in Dumfries on New Years Day 1895 against London Casuals, which the visitors won 5-2. While on October 13th 1894, in a third round Scottish Cup tie against St. Cuthberts Wanderers a newspaper correspondant wrote "Aitken sent in a stinging shot which it was almost impossible for any man to keep out". Aitken's promise in Manchester, however, failed to materialise, or ensure him of first team football with the Heathens. Despite scoring against Crewe on that opening day, he was dropped for the following two fixtures, but returned for the away match at Crewe on September 28th, only to be omitted again the following week. Indeed, he was never to appear in the Newton Heath first eleven again. In comparison to the opinion of the Scottish press as to his attributes, a local Manchester newspaper correspondent wrote, "Aitken was uncertain in his work and needs to put more practice into his shooting and passing". He saw out the season in Manchester, but then disappeared into footballing obscurity.

At the turn of the year, the Newton Heath officials decided to strengthen the side once again with their thoughts more than likely on a second half of the season push for promotion via the 'test matches'.
One of the players brought to the club was **James Vance**, yet another player from the Ayrshire side Annbank. How many signings from Robert Burns country was that now? The nineteen year old stepped straight into the first team, making his debut on February 3rd 1896, against Leicester Fosse, at Clayton, in a 3-0 defeat. Five days later, he opened his scoring account with the Heathens netting the only goal in the 4-1 defeat by Burton Swifts.
Despite missing the next match, he returned to the side for the final eight games of the season, but failed to score, or indeed lend any inspiration towards the team earning a 'test match' place.
He was re-signed for season 1896-97, but with only one start in the first eleven by the end of October, a 3-0 win

against Burton Wanderers on the 24th of the month. Such inactivity at first team level made him decide that he would be better off elsewhere and left for Fairfield, the Heathens 'vulture' club, just before the end of the year. The Manchester side always seemed to be happy to sign any discarded individuals or anyone deciding to leave their more illustrious neighbours.

Having spent two seasons in Division Two, a more determined push for promotion had to be high on the agenda for season 1896-97. The club's financial position had improved, with players retained and signed, along with a social club being formed to provide the stars of the day with a place to relax and also spend time amongst the supporters. Despite winning four of their opening five fixtures at the start of the season, a new goalkeeper was introduced for the match against Newcastle United at home on September 26th, with Ridgway being replaced by **Frank Barrett** (see Fig: iii pg 26).

Barrett had been signed at the start of the season from Dundee, where he had spent three years, having joined them from Dundee Harp. With the Tayside club, he had won two Scottish caps, against Northern Ireland in 1894 and Wales a year later, playing behind former Dundee team mate William Longair in the former and earning himself an excellent reputation in the process.
Despite his confidence between the posts, he was a rather sensitive individual and criticism directed towards him, on more than one occasion, saw him return to Dundee with the Newton Heath officials hot on his trail in an effort to entice him back to Manchester.
During his spell with Newton Heath, he missed only 4 League games out of a possible 122, quite a record, with four clean sheets in a row on more than one occasion. Somewhat unorthodox at times, a report from season 1897-98 covering the home match against Arsenal included - "tricks by the home goalkeeper were suddenly put to a stop, when White nearly scored".
At the end of season 1899-1900 he signed for New Brighton Tower and by the end of his one season there, he had chalked up a total of 153 League appearances out of a possible 162, spread over a five year period with his two

English club's. Following his solitary season on the south coast, he returned north for what should have been another twelve month stint, this time at Arbroath, but joined Manchester City a couple of months later.

In November 1902, it was back to Dundee, where he was to spend two seasons, before seeing out his playing career with a further two year spell at newly formed Aberdeen.

Frank Barrett could certainly be considered a first class custodian and the first in a long line of great goalkeepers who served the club over countless decades.

such an impressive initial performance, as he managed only two goals in his seventeen outings during season 1896-97. His record failed to improve any during season 1897-98, with only three from nineteen outings, but he surprisingly held down a regular place in the first team line up the following season despite scoring only seven goals in twenty eight games. It was, however, Gillespie's work rate which saw him hold onto his place in the side, something that was not always appreciated by the Clayton faithful.

LANCASHIRE CUP WINNERS 1897/8

A. NORRIS (TRAINER),   H. ERRENTZ,   F.C. ERRENTZ,   F. BARRETT,   H. STAFFORD,   W.L. DRAYCOTT,   J.R. McNAUGHT,   W. MORGAN
W. CARTWRIGHT,   J. COLLINSON,   H. BOYD,   M. GILLESPIE,   W. BRYANT,   J. CASSIDY

Two months after the arrival of Barrett, **Matthew Gillespie** (see Fig: iii pg 26) was signed from Lincoln City. The twenty five year old, had turned out for Strathclyde and Leith Athletic, prior to moving south in September 1895 and upon signing for Newton Heath immediately made his League debut against Small Heath, following an excellent display in a friendly against Fairfield. A match that saw him score thrice.

Sadly, his scoring ability seemed to desert him following

In March 1899, Gillespie, along with team mates and fellow Scot's Henry Boyd and John Cunningham, was suspended by the club for "extra curricular activities". The latter two were subsequently placed on the transfer list, while Gillespie, having served his suspension, apologised to the club officials and re-appeared in the first team for the final five games of the season, scoring twice.

Season 1899-1900 saw his appearances somewhat limited to only ten, scattered throughout the campaign, but surprisingly, he scored a creditable five goals.

In the summer of 1900, he was to leave the club, with the Heathens officials beginning their search for new players to aid their push for promotion the following term. Perhaps the memories of his mis-endeavours were also still fresh in their minds.

As we have seen in the past, new signings were regularly made at the turn of the year, if the management committee considered that there was a possibility of a productive end to the campaign.

Season 1896-97 had begun well, with only one defeat in the opening nine games, but four defeats in the six League fixtures between the end of November and the beginning of January had brought panic to the club office bearers. It was obvious to all, that someone to boost the goals for column was desperately required.

So, it was into the transfer market once again, with **Henry Boyd** (see Fig: iii pg 26) being signed from Arsenal.

Boyd, born in Pollockshaws in 1868, had begun his professional career with Sunderland Albion, before joining Burnley prior to the commencement of season 1892-93 after the north-east side went into voluntary liquidation. His stay with the Lancashire side, however, was brief to say the least, as he was transferred to West Bromwich Albion two months later.

At the end of season 1893-94, he was on the move again, journeying further south through England, to join Royal Arsenal on May 14th, making a goalscoring debut two days later against Grimsby. Unfortunately, his career in the capital did not get off to the best of starts, as he suffered a broken leg in October of that first season, whilst playing against Newton Heath.

This, however, was treated only as a minor set back, as the name of Boyd soon became prominent on the Arsenal score sheets, scoring 32 in 40 League games, plus a further 47 in 32 friendly fixtures, before moving north to join Newton Heath for a fee of £45 on January 18th 1897.

He made his Heathens debut at centre forward against Loughborough Town on February 6th, scoring once in the 6-0 victory and his goals, four in the remaining nine games, along with his persistent and unselfish play, took the club into the end of season Test Matches as runners

up to Notts County, in the Second Division.

The first of the nail biting ninety minutes produced a 2-0 defeat at one of Henry Boyd's previous club's, Burnley on April 19th, but two days later, in the return fixture, the score was reversed with Boyd and Jenkyns the goal scorers. Against the other of the First Division's bottom two club's, Sunderland, it was a Boyd goal which earned Newton Heath a draw, keeping their hopes of promotion faintly alive. But a 2-0 defeat in the north-east, at Sunderland, saw them finish bottom of the group, with Notts County claiming the vacant spot in the First Division. Abandoning the now familiar green and gold shirts for a new strip of white shirts and blue shorts during the season had perhaps, brought them bad luck!

The following season, 1897-98, saw Henry Boyd an ever present in the team at centre forward, finishing the campaign as leading scorer with 22 goals from the 30 League games, six goals in front of his striking partner Cassidy. This goal tally included two hat tricks in the opening two fixtures against Lincoln City at home and Burton Swifts away, with a third hat trick following, against Loughborough Trinity in March. His 22 goals also saw him enter the record books as the first Newton Heath player to score more than 20 in one season.

He had now set himself a standard, with much expected from the player by both the supporters and management the following season. It was, however, to be a season of despair and disappointment.

No sooner had the new season, 1898-99, got under way, with Boyd scoring two goals in the opening five fixtures, when he was suspended for seven days after missing training, sending his Newton Heath career on a downward spiral. Upon being told of the club's decision, he immediately disappeared and the first anyone knew of his whereabouts was following a telegram to club secretary Mr A.H.Albut, from Scotland, requesting leave of absence.

On Christmas Eve, he made a surprise return to the fold in the 9-0 thrashing of Darwin, surprisingly failing to score.

Goals on the last day of the year in the 6-1 win over Gainsborough and on the 2nd of January, a 2-2 draw against Burton Swifts, gave the club's officials and supporters hope that things were returning to normal with the player. Another goal against Small Heath on February 25th added to the reassurance. However, in mid-March, he was suspended again, for further indiscretions, placed on the transfer list and subsequently never played for the club again.

Perhaps the behaviour of Henry Boyd could not be entirely unexpected, as he had disappeared on a previous occasion, whilst with West Bromwich Albion, prior to a scheduled court appearance.

At the start of season 1899-1900, he was registered with Falkirk and immediately set about the job in hand, with two goals on his debut.

An injury to club stalwarth Harry Stafford early in 1898, saw the unique pairing of Harry and Fred Erentz filling the two full back positions against Woolwich Arsenal on January 8th, with the former making his League debut and the latter of the two marking the occasion with United's only goal of the game.

The pairing was not able to flourish, however, due to the presence of Stafford, but **Harry Erentz**, (see Fig: iii pg 26) who had been signed from Oldham County in the close season of 1897, having joined the Lancashire side from Dundee a year earlier, did manage other occasional appearances together before the end of that particular season. His only significant contribution to the Newton Heath cause came at the end of March 1898, when he was a member of the side that beat Blackburn Rovers 2-1 in the Final of the Lancashire Senior Cup at Goodison Park, to win the trophy for the first time.

With Stafford and his brother well in command of the two full back positions, his appearances were always going to be few and far between, so when the opportunity arose to join Tottenham Hotspur, being offered a good financial package, he decided to take the chance and move south.

As things turned out, it was certainly the correct decision, as he helped Tottenham to the Southern League Championship in 1899–1900 and the F.A. Cup the following season, with his career at Tottenham spanning six years and some 300 odd games.

In 1904 he moved to Swindon Town, but a broken leg on March 25th 1905 at Millwall, in what was only his sixteenth game for the Wiltshire side, forced him to retire. Returning to his native Dundee, he, like many other footballers of the period, became a publican, regaling the locals with tales of his footballing exploits south of the border.

Harry Erentz's last appearance for Newton Heath was on April 16th 1898, playing left half against Loughborough Town and as he contemplated his future with the club, another Scot had already made a decision regarding his career and left Lincoln City to try his luck in Manchester .

James Cairns, unlike Erentz, made the wrong choice as his career took something of a backward step. Having begun his playing career in local Ayrshire football with Stevenston Thistle in 1895, he subsequently played for Glossop North End, before joining Lincoln City in September 1897. Although having signed for the Heathens in April 1898, he had to wait until October 8th of that year before making what was not only his debut, but his last appearance for the club, against Burslem Port Vale.

Having been given his first team opportunity due to injury to the regular inside right James Collinson and the failure of Owen Jones to grasp his opportunity in that position when given his chance seven days earlier, Cairns, despite the Heathens victory found himself ousted by the return of Collinson.

One month later, he was off the Newton Heath pay role and a player with Lancashire league side Berry's and Brookes, who were based in the Stalybridge area.

Considering that he had been at the club since the previous April and was only given the one opportunity, James Cairns could perhaps have felt himself rather badly done by, especially as he had performed favourably in the second team.

Two other debutantes followed Cairns into the Newton Heath League side during 1898-1899, they were James Connachan and John Cunningham. Both, ironically making their initial appearances in the same match, against Grimsby Town at home on November 5th, playing right half and inside right respectively.

Of the two, **James Connachan** made the least impression, despite having played north of the border for Glasgow

Pertshire, Duntocher Hibs, Celtic and Airdrie. It was from the last named club that he had joined the Heathens on October 28th.

Not the most gifted of players, with many bemused at his actual signing and more so when his second appearance for the club saw him turning out at centre forward.

Only two other performances were to follow, both in December, and by the end of April he was a Glossop North End player, helping them towards the runners up place in Division Two, behind Manchester City. By the end of the following season, Glossop had found their way into the record books, but for all the wrong reasons, finishing bottom of the First Division with only four wins all season! Connachan, along with numerous others left the club with heads held low at the end of that campaign and joined Leicester Fosse, where he obtained the satisfaction of scoring his last Football League goal against Newton Heath at Clayton on March 20th 1901.

Upon leaving Leicester, he had a trial with Nottingham Forest, which came to nothing, and he decided to return to Scotland, joining Morton in October 1901. Spells with Renton, Brittania F.C. in Canada and Dumbarton Harp followed before he eventually hung up his boots in the close season of 1908.

Glasgow born **John Cunningham**, had covered countless miles whilst pursuing his playing career prior to joining Newton Heath from Aston Villa in October 1898.

He was a junior with Benburb, when offered trials with Glasgow Celtic, which he grasped with both hands, turning in note worthy performances against Bolton Wanderers and Preston North End in a two day period at the end of May 1889.

For one reason or another, an offer to sign for the Glasgow giants was not forth coming and in November of the same year he took his boots to Lancashire, joining Burnley.

Within a month, he was back in his home city, playing with Glasgow Hibernians, moving once again early in 1890, when he at last received the call he had always wanted from Celtic.

His career in the east-end of Glasgow failed to take off, despite being given a second bite at the cherry, with only seven League and two Scottish Cup ties to his credit as a first team player over a two year period.

In 1892, he joined Partick Thistle, spending only a few months there before moving to Edinburgh and Heart of Midlothian in October of that year.

By the end of 1892, he was back in Glasgow and a Rangers player, but again it was only for a brief period, three months to be exact and was then to be found in the colours of non-League Glasgow Thistle.

For a player who had spent so little time with a number of teams, it was difficult to see him ever making much of a name for himself or enjoying a lengthy spell with a prominent club of that period.

So, it came as something of a surprise that he should be signed by Preston North End in September 1893 and remaining with them until May 1897, during which time he did become something of a popular individual.

Upon leaving Preston in September 1893, he joined Sheffield United and a year later, Aston Villa.

With the Sheffield side, he came face to face with his former colleagues in the green of Celtic, facing them in the un-official championship of Britain (both teams being their countries First Division Champions) in March/April 1898, which Sheffield won 2-1 over two legs.

October 1898, while still only in his mid-twenties, he joined Newton Heath, making his debut the following month against Grimsby Town.

True to form, his time in Manchester was brief and during his five month career with the Heathens, he played in four of the five forward positions during his seventeen match spell, scoring two goals.

He was made available for transfer in March 1899, following an internal disagreement, subsequently joining Wigan County.

In August 1901, he lined up with newly formed Barrow, his final club, of a lengthy, but somewhat anonymous career, becoming something of an additional attraction in the Lancashire sides first ever fixture.

One other Scotsman was to make his debut in the final stages of season 1898-99, in the centre half position, which at that time was causing the selection committee problems, with four different players filling the void in consecutive games.

February 18th saw yet another former Annbank player **John Gourlay** given the chance to make a name for himself, but despite the Heathens winning 1-0 away from home, against Loughborough Town, this turned out to be his only first team outing, as he was no better than others who had been tried before him.

Much to his disappointment, he was released at the end of the season, giving him the unwanted distinction of one of the briefest careers at the club – just over two months.

Season 1898-99 once again finished in disappointment, with fourth place being the final position achieved in the Football League, or the second successive term. Although some five points more had been obtained.

The 1899-1900 campaign had something of a stuttered start, with three wins, two draws and three defeats in the opening two months, with the forward line causing the selectors something of a headache.

In order to open their options a bit more, Scotland was again invaded by Newton Heath delegates, with the jute town of Dundee their destination, rather than the rolling green fields of Ayrshire, with the expense sheet justified by the signing of James Bain and Joseph Clark.

It was **James Bain**, who made the first appearance in the side, with his debut against Loughborough Town on September 16th, scoring one of the goals in the 4-0 victory. He was, however, to become yet another of the many individuals to be signed by Newton Heath and then fail to recapture the form which lead to his signing.

A goal on his debut was an ideal start for the former Dundee player, but following a 0-0 draw at Burton Swifts seven days later, he lost his place and failed to make the starting line up again.

Rather ironically, it was **Joseph Clark** who took over the centre forward role from his former Dundee team mate, but an uninspired performance on his debut against Sheffield Wednesday on September 30th, saw him omitted from

the team for the next three outings.

Collinson and Blackmore were then tried at centre forward, in what seemed to be something of a problem position, as they were the fourth and fifth players to be tried there in the opening eight games. Neither managed to impress the Heathens committee over much and with Joe Cassidy stepping into the breach for one game and Bob Parkinson signed from Nottingham Forest, Clark must have thought that moving from Dundee to join Newton Heath had been a big mistake. However, he must have displayed some of his talents during his debut, as he was brought back into the side on November 4th as Parkinson's partner, at inside right, playing in eight of the following nine games. Although he failed to score, Parkinson found the net on four occasions. A constructive and intelligent player, he was unfortunate to suffer an injury to his knee against Bolton Wanderers on January 6th and was unable to play again.

The first season of the new century brought little in the way of great improvement for Newton Heath and the results of the opening weeks, with only four wins in thirteen games, did not provide much in the way of hope for a successful, promotion winning campaign.

Scoring goals once again appeared to be a major problem, with the end of season tally registering only forty two compared with sixty three in the previous season. A run of four wins in five games from the final three weeks of the year and the opening match of 1901, brought some encouragement, but this was immediately followed by six without a win and four in a row without a goal.

Some twenty-five players were used throughout what was to become a totally unmemorable season, with the influx of the ever dependable Scotsmen limited to only two, with both being able do little in the way of improving matters on the pitch.

The home match against Walsall, on October 20th, saw the introduction of **James Fisher** at inside right, a player signed from Celtic, earlier that month, having previously served Vale of Forth, King's Park, Aston Villa, St.Bernards and East Stirlingshire, where he began his senior career in June 1895.

"Cud" Fisher had returned north from a year with Aston Villa in August 1898 and joined Celtic, but by the end of January 1899, he had returned to England for a loan spell with Preston North End. In December of that same year he rejoined East Stirling, but after only two months, he was back with Celtic. Whilst with the Parkhead club, he was involved in a notable match with Clyde in November 1898, which saw him score to make it 6-2 in Celtic's favour. Considered by the Clyde players to be offside when he scored, they refused to re-start the game. Eventually they did change their mind, but when Celtic added a further three goals, the visitors walked off.

During his time with Celtic, he was clearly viewed as a disappointment and thought of as a "winger who could not cross the ball".

Seven days after making his Newton Heath debut, he found himself switched to inside left to face Burton Swifts, with his third appearance, against Woolwich Arsenal, finding him filling the outside right berth. The selection committee, content to play Leigh and Jackson at centre forward and inside left on a regular basis, happily juggled various others players around the other forward positions in an effort to bring an end to the goal drought. Fisher was therefore to find himself back at inside right for three games before enjoying some thing of a settled run in the team at outside left, scoring his only goal of the season in the 3-2 defeat at home to Leicester Fosse.

His game quickly developed as a wingman and he soon gained a reputation as being able to supply pinpoint crosses to his fellow forwards. Something of a surprise following the opinion of many in the Glasgow area and at a time when the turnover of the Newton Heath playing staff was quite numerous, he found himself retained for the following season, which he began again as first choice outside left.

Having played in the entire first half of the seasons fixtures, it came as something of a surprise to the regular supporters who had appreciated his determined

displays that his name failed to appear on the team sheet again. With financial problems prominent in the club's affairs at this time, the question of money could quite easily have played a major part in this departure from Clayton.

Upon leaving the Heathens, he rejoined Kings Park on March 14th 1902, moving to Vale of Leithen nine months later. He returned to England the following year for a spell with Fulham, before retiring in 1904.

The other Scot who arrived at Clayton around the end of 1900, was **Hugh Morgan**, a player with a CV better than most.

Having begun his career with the rather nondescript Harthill Thistle, he joined Airdrie in August 1896, but was snapped up by Sunderland four months later, where he played his part in the club securing the runners up spot in the Football League at the end of season 1897-98.

Bolton, attracted by his talents, paid the pricey sum of £250 for his signature in February 1899 and once again, his presence helped towards his club winning promotion, this time in the Second Division, with the Wanderers finishing in the runners up spot. It was nevertheless a notable achievement for the Lancashire side, having been relegated from the top flight at the end of the previous season.

It was from Bolton Wanderers that he joined Newton Heath, making his debut on December 15th against Lincoln City, scoring in the 4-1 win, their first victory in seven games.

For the remainder of the season, he filled the inside right spot in all but two of the fixtures, scoring four goals. In one of those, he played outside right, while he failed to appear at all in the final fixture against Chesterfield. During the close season, however, he moved across Manchester, joining City, with an Athletic News correspondent in his pre season assessment of Newton Heath writing – "The most notable absentee will be Hugh Morgan, who has gone over to Manchester City".

THE HEATHENS BECOME UNITED

In the latter days of the 1890's, Manchester was a million miles from the thriving metropolis that it is today, with poverty and hardship going hand in hand. Such financial difficulties also affected Newton Heath Football Club, with the players being uncertain as to whether or not they would receive their agrees weekly wage come pay day, as a number of debts hung over the club. By season 1901-02, the threat of extinction was not just a possibility, but very much a reality. Thankfully there were teams who were perhaps more financially sound than Newton Heath, but were not as competent on the field of play and the Heathens somehow escaped being pushed out of the Second Division by finishing above Gainsborough Trinity and Stockport County. They had, however, a much tougher off the field battle to fight.

Much of the club's debts had been accrued through ground improvements and on the signing of numerous players, with more than the odd one or two of those signed being somewhat haphazardly on the spur of the moment.

A bazaar, in February and March of 1901 had failed to produce the revenue that had been anticipated by the organisers and as 1902 began to unfold, creditors opened bankruptcy proceedings in a bid to reclaim as much of the £2,670 that was owed as they possibly could.

Somehow, part of the debt was paid off, mainly to local contractors for the ground improvements, but a shareholders meeting on March 18th in the new Islington Hall, brought revelations that some £2,000 was still required in order to save the club from extinction.

Harry Stafford, the club captain, had not been idle during the days and weeks prior to the meeting, as he promptly announced that he knew of four business men who were willing to put £500 of their own money into the football club. A further meeting was held at the end of April, when it was suggested that perhaps a change of name would bring about a new lease of life to the ailing club. Various titles were banded about, but it was only when a lone voice from the crowd uttered 'Manchester United' that an agreement was reached.

For the first year since the early days of the Heathens, no Scotsmen were added to the ranks. Whether a shortage in funds prevented the directors from making their seemingly annual sojourn to Dundee or the pleasant surroundings of the Ayrshire coast, or whether there was simply no cash available to tempt anyone from north of Hadrians Wall south is not known, but it is a good assumption that both reasons were not far off the mark.

Having finished season 1901-02 in 15th position in the Second Division, the lowest since relegation in 1894, and one which would certainly have been lower if three wins and a draw in the last five fixtures had not been achieved. Improvement was certainly required and twelve months later, some ten places had been jumped, finishing 1902-03 in a creditable 5th.

Some thirty-two players were used during the campaign, seventeen of those making their debuts. So with such an unsettled side, it was slightly surprising that any improvement was made at all, and a closer examination of the results show that there was indeed much inconsistency, especially in the latter half of the season. Of those seventeen debutants, there was of course a touch of tartan.

Into the side on the opening day of 1902-03 to face Gainsborough Trinity came **John Peddie**, a Glasgow born forward, who was described as "both a provider and a goalscorer, possessing a dynamic shot". Both attributes were first class, but he appeared to be something of an easy going, laid back individual, which throughout his career saw him receive both the praise and the scorn of the supporters. Despite this, the Newcastle fans were dismayed, when the man who had scored 80 goals in 137 appearances (including 17 in his first 20 games), was transferred from Tyneside to Manchester United in June 1902.

With goal scoring being the former Benburb and Third Lanark mans' forte, it is rather strange to note that it took him some eight games to get his name on the United score sheet for the first time – a double against Lincoln City on November 8th. Despite the delayed start, he still finished the clubs' top goal scorer that season, with eleven to his credit.

At the end of 1902-03, many were surprised to hear that he had been transferred to Plymouth Argyle and they were equally taken aback when Peddie returned to the

United ranks in the summer of 1904.

Once again, he was a regular in the side and he was to better his previous scoring rate, notching 17 in 32 outings. This included two hat tricks, against Leicester Fosse and Burton United.

Season 1905-06 also saw the player top the United scoring chart, 18 from 34 games, playing a big part in the club's promotion back into the First Division after two years of 'almost but not quite', with third place finishing. It was therefore quite surprising that other than selection for the Anglo-Scots whilst with Newcastle United in 1899 and 1900 and again in 1906 with Manchester United, he received no International recognition.

As season 1906-07 got under way, he was once again an ever present in the side, with half a dozen goals to his credit after sixteen appearances. However, shortly after the turn of the year, along with team-mates William Yates and Richard Wombwell, he was transferred to Heart of Midlothian.

He was later to emigrate to the USA, where he died in October 1928.

Back to season 1902-03 though, and November 22nd, with the fixtures showing United away at Leicester Fosse. Making his League debut that afternoon was Alex Downie, who marked the occasion with a goal, which gave his team a share of the points in a 1-1 draw.

Griffiths, the team's stalwart centre half for over three seasons had been missing since the end of September through injury with Vince Hayes and Bill Ball filling the breach without receiving too much in the way of acclaim. The introduction of twenty six year old Alex Downie, however, produced an immediate improvement and an unbeaten run of seven games, with Downie making a big impression in his first appearance. So much so, that he retained his place in the side the following week, this time in his more familiar position of right half.

Born in Dunoon, he was already an experienced player by the time he arrived at United in October 1902, having played for Glasgow Perthshire, Third Lanark, Bristol City and Swindon Town over a period of some five years.

His spell in the United side saw them scale to the heights of League Champions and F.A.Cup Winners, but unfortunately in the latter competition he failed to play in any of the ties

despite playing in twenty two of the League fixtures. Indeed, he had played in the League fixtures before and after both the quarter-final and semi-final ties and had played at right half against Leicester Fosse the Saturday prior to the Cup Final. Unlucky or what!

In February 1908, he was given a benefit match for his services to the club and a correspondent with the Manchester Evening News wrote in his pre season notes......"Alex Downie, takes a well deserved benefit during the coming campaign. A loyal servant, a terner at work and a right good player. All those compliments have been well earned by the right half back and Clayton people must make it their business to see that the benefit is a big success". Sadly, this was not to be, as the turnout was unexpectedly poor.

The disappointment of losing out on an FA Cup winners medal was something that Alex Downie did not really get over and in October of 1909, he joined Oldham Athletic for a fee of £600. Taking over immediately as their captain, he guided the Latics to promotion into the First Division as runners-up, the clubs' first League success just ten years after turning professional.

He remained with Oldham until season 1911-12, when he joined Crewe Alexandra as player coach and was later to serve in a coaching capacity with Manchester League side Old Chorltonians.

Returning to season 1902-03 and a 3-1 victory at Glossop on January 24th. This match marked the debut of an outstanding individual, who went on to make over 300 appearances for the club and feature in on of the most memorable half back lines in not only United's history but that of the Football League. His name was **Alexander Bell** (see Fig: iv pg 35).

He is included amongst the illustrious names of the other Scots who assisted both Newton Heath and Manchester United by default really, as he was born in South Africa. But, after much deliberation, I decided that he earned his inclusion as he had been born off Scottish parents and was also capped by Scotland in 1912 against Northern Ireland. One other point that swayed the quiet, unassuming individual's inclusion, was

Fig: iv

MANCHESTER UNITED 1903/4

BLACKSTOCK, READ, MR BACON, SAUNDERS, BONTHRON,
MR J. TAYLOR, STAFFORD, DOWNIE, GRIFFITHS, CARTWRIGHT, MOGER, A. ROBERTSON, BELL, VALENTINE, MR J.J. BENTLEY,
MR WEST, MCCARTNEY, PEGG, SCHOFIELD, MORRISON, SUTCLIFFE, ARKESDEN, A. ROBERTSON, T. ROBERTSON, HAYES.

his jocular nickname during his time with United – 'The South African Scotsman'.

His parents returned to their native land with young master Bell whilst he was still at an early age and upon leaving school, his early days as an amateur footballer saw him involved with Ayr teams Spring Vale and Parkhouse.

It was from the latter that the 20 year old joined United in January 1903 for a fee of £700, on the recommendation of former Newton Heath player Willie Donaldson.

In his debut against Glossop, he lined up at inside left, switching to centre forward and outside right in the following two fixtures. Missing nine games, he returned to the line up, again at centre forward, but was out again for the following match before playing his final ninety minutes of the season in the penultimate fixture, playing in the half back line for the first time, albeit at centre half.

His appearance record for season 1903-04 was also brief, managing only six outings which were once again spread over four positions. But, in the fourth match of the 1904-05 campaign, ironically against Glossop, he stepped into

the left half berth for the first time, the position in which he was to make his name, and never looked back. In December 1906, Dick Duckworth, who had only made fleeting appearances in a variety of positions, was given the right half slot on a regular basis. Thus was formed the classic half back line and the axis of the United side of that time, as the duo linked up with centre half Charlie Roberts, the third member of the legendary trio.

Bell, was the quiet man of the trio, which brought two Football League Championships, an FA Cup win and two FA Charity Shield successes to the club, but was as capable a player as any in those distant days. It is surprising that he only added a solitary Scotland cap to his list of honours.

By the end of season 1912-13, he had ran up a total of 278 League and 28 FA Cup appearances for United, scoring 10 goals and in July of 1913 he was transferred to Blackburn Rovers for £1000, after having been refused a second benefit match by the club.

A brief spell with Clackmannan in 1921 brought the curtain down on his playing career, but he remained in the game, taking up the post of trainer with Coventry City in the summer of 1922. Three years later, he took a similar post with Manchester City, a position he held until his untimely death in November 1934.

One interesting item of note, is that he was the City trainer when they met, and defeated United, in the 1926 FA Cup semi final at Bramall Lane. Inspiring his charges by showing them his own FA Cup winners medal which he proudly wore on a gold chain.

For season 1903-04, hopes were high as regards to promotion, with an almost complete new team signed. Needless to say, a fair sprinkling of Scots included, with R.Bonthron, W.McCartney and a trio, by a strange co-incidence, all with the surname Robertson amongst those signed. All five making their League debuts on the opening day of the season against Bristol City at home.

At right back that afternoon, was **Robert Bonthron**, (see Fig: iv pg 35) yet another player prized from the Tayside area. Although born in Dundee, he initially escaped the clutches of the local sides, beginning his career with Raith Athletic before signing for the more familiar Raith Rovers in the summer of 1900. Two seasons later, however, he returned to his hometown, signing for Dundee.

A well built player, he gave numerous wingers a difficult time during his days with United, with whom he made over 120 appearances during his four year spell.

During his first two seasons at Clayton, he missed only three games and made a telling contribution during the promotion-winning season of 1905-06.

Not a player usually associated with making headlines, his tough tackling certainly brought him to the fore, following the 5-1 victory over Bradford City on February 10th 1906. The five goal triumph would have normally have been captured on the back pages of the local and national newspapers with the likes of – "Five Star United" or whatever took the sports editors fancy on that particular day. Instead, the headlines screamed – "Manchester United Team Mobbed – Mud And Stones Thrown", with Bonthron's name a prominent feature in the report which followed.

The unsportsmanslike Bradford crowd were unhappy with their favourites having been defeated so comprehensively by

United and at the end of the match a large crowd assembled outside the changing rooms to vent their disapproval. Bonthron, having given the home forwards a hard and unrewarding afternoon was singled out by the mob for special attention and at one point was physically struck by one of the crowd, who was immediately arrested by the police.

The walk from the dressing rooms to the awaiting transport was no short distance and by the time the United players got to the safety of the vehicles, they had been hit by stones and mud. The United full back received much more of the mud than his team mates and was in a sorry looking state by the time he managed to get into a waiting cab.

Although highly commendable, the full back's displays did come in for some criticism, outwith Bradford, with the 'Cricket and Football Field' adding to this in their pre season review of United's prospects for seasons 1904-05 and 1906-07.

In the former, it was written – "Bonthron's abilities are great and if he could only be imbued with a little more steadiness and some of that recklessness taken out of him. It would be an advantage, both to himself and his side". Two years later, it carried the following – "While Bonthron, if he would only quieten down a bit, should prove a rare stumbling block to our opponents".

At the end of season 1906-07, despite having played in 28 of the 38 league fixtures, Bob Bonthron decided to leave United and after considering a number of options, chose to sign for Sunderland. He stayed on Wearside for only the one season before joining Northampton Town in the Southern League. A two year spell there ended in July 1910 and this was followed by a further two years with Birmingham City, his last English club. Upon leaving the Midlands, he returned north, joining Leith Athletic in the summer of 1912.

At outside left on that opening day of the 1903-04 season was **William McCartney**, (see Fig: iv pg 35) no relation to the previously mentioned John, captain of the Heathens back in 1894.

A Scottish international at both full and League level whilst with his previous club Hibs, McCartney was described as a "man of more than ordinary capability". His reputation, however, did not provide him with a regular place in the United starting line up.

Having served his time with Rutherglen Glencairn and Ayr, with whom he turned professional in 1898, he joined Hibs in January 1900 and soon became a firm favourite with the green side of the Edinburgh footballing public.

He played a predominant part in Hibs' Scottish Cup run of 1901-02, scoring in the first round 2-0 win over Clyde going on to give the Rangers defence a torrid time in the semi-final at Ibrox, scoring one of the goals in another 2-0 win. Such was his performance in the semi-final tie that he was subjected to some crude and unnecessary robust tackling from the frustrated Glasgow players.

One of those uncalled for, clumsy, challenges broke McCartney's leg, just above the ankle, and he was carried off the field in great pain, much to the disapproval of his disgusted team mates and to the unsportsmanship relief of the home club's players.

It was a sad blow for the individual, as not only did he miss out on a Cup Final appearance but also the distinct possibility of representative honours with Scotland at that particular time.

He was, thankfully, able to make a full recovery and returned to the Hibs team on September 15th 1902, almost six months exactly after the unsavoury incident at Ibrox. Ironically, his return to first team action was against Rangers and he showed little in the way of apprehension, as he once again tormented the Glasgow sides defence, gaining a small amount of personal satisfaction by scoring the only goal of the afternoon.

On December 20th, he was again on the score sheet as Hibs defeated Partick Thistle 2-0, a victory that gave them their first ever League Championship. The "ever tricky McCartney" also scored one of Hibs' four goals in the final match of that season, against Celtic, "with an incredible dribble, before walking the ball arrogantly into the net". Sadly, success did not follow the player south after his transfer to United in May 1903, as a mere 13 appearances and one goal (in the 1-0 victory over Leicester Fosse on April 2nd) was his contribution to his new club's 1903-04 season. During this time, he filled five different positions, including something of a surprise appearance at centre half.

In the summer of 1904, he took his leave of Manchester, moving to London to join West Ham United. Again, his stay was brief and he eventually returned to Scotland for brief spells with Broxburn and Lochgelly United before joining Clyde in September 1902, with whom he played in the Scottish Cup Final of 1910.

He was to finish his playing career with the Shawfield club in the summer of 1913, although the seven year run with them was interrupted by a few scattered appearances with Broxburn.

The inclusion of the three Robertson's in the opening day line up of 1903-04 would have been a nightmare for any newspaper correspondents of that time, with two of them being named Alexander not helping matters at all.

At right half was **Alexander Robertson** (mark 1, see Fig: iv pg 35), signed from Hibernian at the same time as the above mentioned William McCartney, where he had won both Scottish Cup and Scottish League honours in 1901-02 and 1902-03 respectively.

Although described as a "splendid class man, for whom a place would have to be found", his United first team career was, however, limited to only 33 League appearances, along with a couple of cup ties, despite being with the club for some four years.

Robertson had the appearance of a player who was slightly over weight, something which would often catch out opponents, as he could be quite fleet of foot when the occasion demanded and he also made considerable contributions to the work rate of the team.

Following the 2-2 draw in the opening match of 1903-04, Robertson found himself missing from the line-up for the next seven games, returning for the 3-1 win against Stockport County on October 24th and then remaining an almost permanent fixture in the side until the end of the season.

Season 1904-05 began with Robertson in possession of the left half position, playing in seven of the opening ten fixtures, but the emergence of Alec Bell more or less brought the former Hibs man's United first team career to an end. He was to feature only once more, despite remaining at the club until 1907, seemingly content to play in the reserve eleven, whom he captained during 1905-06.

The career of **Alex Robertson** (mark two, see Fig: iv pg 35), although taking an almost parallel course, was also almost over before it began.

In the opening month of the season, the United players had been taken to Lytham St Annes for some special training and Robertson, along with his namesake Tom, who was also a former team mate at Dundee, shocked officials and team mates alike by turning up at their hotel 'the worse of wear'. Both players were immediately dismissed for serious misconduct, but Alex Robertson was fortunate enough to be reinstated and was able to regain his first team place, going on to make 27 appearances, scoring 10 goals during that particular campaign.

Robertson (mark two) had begun his career in his hometown of Dundee, playing for both Dundee Violet and Dundee, before joining Middlesborough in May 1900. Eight goals in the final six fixtures of his second season with the North-East club, playing at centre forward, made a big contribution to Middlesborough claiming the runners up spot in Division Two and therefore promotion to the top League.

His ability to perform well in any of the forward positions made him an ideal addition to the United squad and in his first season at Clayton, he filled four of the five front line spots.

Season 1904-05 saw him make only one appearance, but like his aforementioned namesake, he was content to remain at the club until May 1907 when he moved to Bradford City.

The third of the similarly named trio was **Tom Robertson**, (see Fig: iv pg 35) who had arrived at Clayton as a Scottish internationalist and the owner of a League Championship medal, won whilst with Heart Of Midlothian. The medal coming his way in 1897, a year after he joined the Edinburgh club from Fauldhouse, with the cap being awarded the following year, against Northern Ireland. He was later to add to this a Football League Championship medal, won with Liverpool in 1901, where he made his name as an outstanding wing man.

The move to Liverpool in April 1898, was something that had been forced upon the club by their bankers and brought in £350 from a move that also included his team mate J. Walker.

Surprisingly, Hearts resigned him in May 1902 for a club record fee of £200, at a time when the earlier financial restraints must have been lifted. His return only lasted five months as he was swiftly sold to Dundee in October, for a fee of £185, after breaching the clubs' disciplinary code. With Manchester United, he had played in the opening three fixtures of 1903-04, before his involvement in the previously mentioned seaside incident. Obviously not having learned from his previous brushes with club authority. The record books go on to show that these were indeed all the first team appearances that he was to make for Manchester United.

Unlike his team mate, Alex Robertson, he was not reinstated to the ranks and his banishment remained a blot on his record. He duly returned to Scotland, under something of a cloud, but was later to resume his playing career with Bathgate at the start of season 1905-06.

The suspension of Tom Robertson and an injury to William McCartney left the team a little short up front, so moves were made to introduce new faces to the team. Northwards the United officials travelled once more, but the road to Dundee was, for once, avoided and with the coal fields of Ayrshire no longer a productive source for any players of note, Glasgow was the preferred destination, with Celtic's Billy Grassam, a goalscoring inside forward, their target.

Born in Larbert, **Billy Grassam** spent spells with junior sides Redcliffe Thistle and Glasgow Maryhill during 1896 and 1897, before being tempted south to join Burslem Port Vale in July 1899, as a nineteen year old.

The Scottish junior internationalist immediately settled in England and soon made his mark on the game. So much so, that he was soon attracting admiring glances from numerous other clubs, with West Ham United quickly making a move for his signature as he completed his first season in the Football League. The London club had just become a limited company and turned professional, having become members of the Southern League, so the recruitment of players was high on their list of priorities. In their opening fixture at this level, Grassam, on his debut, scored four goals, in the 7-0 trouncing of Gravesend.

After three seasons with the Hammers, whom he captained and also enjoyed his best spell as a player, he returned to Scotland in May 1903, moving to Glasgow and joining Celtic. His career in Celtic's colours never quite got of the ground, however, and he after a mere four months at Parkhead he was on the move again, joining United.

He made his debut for his new club on October 3rd at Woolwich Arsenal, but took a few games to settle in and find his feet in his new surroundings. Once he did readjust, there was no looking back and his 11 goals in 23 games, making him joint top scorer, helped United to a respectable third place in the League.

Prior to the start of season 1904-05, it was written in the 'Cricket and Football Field', "United had Grassam and Lyons to choose from in order to fill the inside right position, with the preference to the former when at his best".

Their assumption, however, was to be seen as being quite far out, as Lyons failed to make the starting line up at all throughout the season, whilst Grassam did not make an appearance until Boxing Day against Chesterfield. He was to make only a further five appearances in the latter half of the campaign and inevitably left during the summer, returning to London and joining Leyton F.C.

He re-joined West Ham six months later, before concluding his career with Brentford in 1909.

Another Scot, **Thomas Blackstock**, (see Fig: iv pg 35) also made his United debut against Woolwich Arsenal on October 3rd 1903, having joined the club from Cowdenbeath during the close season.

A knee injury to first choice left back Thomas Read gave Blackstock the break that he required, but following a run of seven successive games he was replaced by the fit again Read. His performances could not have been too impressive, however, as when Read suffered a re-occurrence of his injury, the left back spot went to Vince Hayes, a player who had filled numerous positions during his time at United.

The following season, with Hayes and later Fichett (following an injury to the former), filling the left back

slot on a regular basis, Blackstock's outings were restricted to two.

A broken leg suffered by Hayes in a reserve fixture prior to the start of the 1905-06 Second Division campaign enabled Blackstock to start as the first choice left back. Despite missing most of the fixtures between December and mid-April, he still managed 21 appearances as United claimed the runners up spot to gain promotion.

At the start of 1906-07, he was back in the reserves at the expense of Dick Holden and by the turn of the year had only recorded 3 appearances. The Kirkcaldy born defender, who had previously played with Dunniker Rangers, Blue Bell F.C., Raith Athletic and Leith Athletic, had certainly not enjoyed the best of luck during his career in Manchester, only making the first team through injuries to others.

To say that his bad luck continued through the latter half of 1905-06 is something of an understatement, as while playing for United in a Lancashire Combination fixture at Clayton against St Helens Reserves, he collapsed after heading the ball out for a throw in after only ten minutes play.

Attempts by the trainer to revive him failed and he was quickly carried from the pitch. Further attempts were made to revive him in the confines of the dressing room, but they were to no avail, as Thomas Blackstock was dead.

The inquest into his untimely death returned the verdict of "natural causes" and when his body was taken to the station for its final journey back to his native Kirkcaldy, his team mates followed the coffin and a large gathering of supporters were also present to pay their final respects.

Towards the end of season 1903-04, with the indifferent early season form making the difference between promotion and remaining in the Second Division, another Scotsman, twenty-two year old **Hugh Kerr**, found himself drafted into the team. Appearing at centre forward, on March 9th at Blackpool, in somewhat controversial circumstances.

Unfortunately for Kerr things did not improve, as he did not get his United career off to the best of starts, with the Seasiders winning 2-1.

Kerr had only spent half a season with Ayr, before joining United as an amateur early in 1904, but his transfer south had caused much displeasure in the town more associated with the poet Robert Burns than for producing footballers. The Ayr officials strongly insisted that representatives of United had made an un-official approach to their player, in an attempt to convince him that a move to Manchester would be favourable.

So strongly did they complain, that an International Board enquiry was set up, much to United's annoyance, but they were eventually cleared of any underhand dealings.

The verdict came a week or so after Kerr had made his second appearance for his new club (against Grimsby Town) and only a few weeks before he was released by United, despite his eager performances, especially at reserve team level.

Having finished season 1903-04 in third place in Division Two, it was felt that the team, as a whole, were quite capable of mounting a similar challenge for promotion the following year. These opinions were strengthened further with the signing of Charlie Roberts from Grimsby Town, along with a couple of lesser known players, giving the team a more formidable look.

One of those signings, was **Charles Mackie**, a centre forward, who had finished top scorer with Aberdeen in 1903-04. The 'Cricket and Football Field' at the time commented, "he was well made, speedy and young, with every promise of early improvement". Hopes that he could continue along a similar vein with Manchester United, were made even more favourable following an encouraging pre-season trial match performance whilst facing the above mentioned and more experienced, Charlie Roberts.

His display in the trial match earned him a place in the starting line up for the opening fixture of the 1904-05 campaign, away at Burslem Port Vale. His performance in the Potteries that afternoon, was considered satisfactory enough to enable him to retain his place in the side for the second match, at home to Bristol City.

Scoring the only goal of the match, in the third fixture of the new season, again at home, this time against Bolton Wanderers, looked to be the ninety minutes that Mackie required to give, not only himself a boost, but prove that he was worthy of his first team place. Sadly, it was not to be, as his appearance the following Saturday, in the 2-1 win at

Glossop, was his last until January, due to injury. His natural goalscoring ability had not deserted him during the enforced lay off, as he proceeded to score once in the 2-2 F.A.Cup draw against Fulham on January 14th at Clayton. Missing the replay, four days later, he returned to League duty the following Saturday, scoring a double in United's 4-1 League victory against Glossop. Hopes, however, of a continued run in the side were dashed, as he discovered that he was only seen as a replacement for Peddie, who had made the successful switch from inside left to centre forward, whilst his fellow Scot was on the sidelines.

The name of Mackie was missing when the team to play Lincoln City on February 11th was announced and a hat trick by Peddie seven days later against Leicester Fosse, spelt the beginning of the end for the young Aberdonian. When the previously mentioned Peddie had to miss a match a few weeks later, Mackie was overlooked in favour of playing Dick Duckworth out of position at centre forward.

At the end of the season, it was widely assumed that he would leave, as his first team opportunities were now severely restricted. During the close season, Queens Park Rangers were widely tipped to secure his services, but it was West Ham United who lured him to London instead. Half way through 1905-06 he returned to Aberdeen and played out his career a year later with Lochgelly United.

By the time season 1905-06 came around, the nucleus of United's first successful trophy winning side had emerged. With sixty-five goals spread between messers Beddows, Picken, Sagar and Peddie, backed up with only one defeat in the final sixteen games, promotion back to the First Division was achieved as runners up, four points behind Champions Bristol City and nine in front of third place Chelsea.

John Picken (see Fig: v pg 41) was leading goalscorer with twenty, all scored as an inside forward and he had caught the eye of many prior to the start of the campaign, with a noteworthy performance in the Attack versus Defence pre-season trial match, testing goalkeeper Moger on numerous occasions.

He was, a very experienced individual, having spent his early days in Ayrshire with Hurlford Thistle and

Kilmarnock Shawbank, before signing for Bolton Wanderers in August 1899, as a nineteen year old.

By the end of his first season south of the border, he had helped Bolton to promotion and played a prominent part in their return to the First Division. A broken leg in November 1902, however, brought a temporary halt to what was certainly becoming a promising career.

Plymouth Argyle took something of a gamble when they signed him at the end of season 1902-03, as he had not played for some six months. Their gamble did, however,

City and despite not finding the back of the net again for some ten games, still managed to end the season with twenty goals to his credit.

The following season, 1906-07, his goals surprisingly dried up, with only four in twenty six games and as United strode to the League Championship a year later, his appearances were few and far between, managing only eight, scoring one goal, as Sandy Turnbull kept him out of the team.

Fig: v

MANCHESTER UNITED 1905/6

BURGESS,   BANNISTER,   BERRY,   WALL
F. BACON, MENZIES, MEREDITH, MOGER, J. TURNBULL, MILLS, STACEY, WILLIAMS, BROOMFIELD, McGIILIVARY, J.E. MANGNALL
DUCKWORTH, DALTON, PICKEN, WHITESIDE, HOLDEN, THOMSON, BELL, A. TURNBULL

pay off, as Picken scored 46 goals in 89 appearances for the Pilgrims over a two year period.

When signed by United in the summer of 1905, he was described as " a bustler with a deadly shot, who had been playing some rare fine games down south" and was considered by many to be a "very good capture".

He got his scoring record off the mark during his debut, on the opening day of season 1905-06 against Bristol

Although not a regular, John Picken was content at Manchester United and whenever called upon gave his best, something that the Clayton regulars certainly appreciated. Not all supporters, however, felt the same way as, both he and Alec Bell were hit by stones thrown by supporters of Hungarian side Ferencvaros, following United's 7-0 victory. This fixture was one of a few arranged on the continent as something of a reward for winning the League Championship.

THE HEATHENS BECOME UNITED

Thankfully for the United players, this was the last to be played, as the treatment that they were subjected to by a vast majority of the 12,000 crowd was unsavoury to say the least.

Having missed out on a League Championship medal in 1907-08, he was delighted to make amends for this three years later, as United once again won the Championship, with John Picken contributing four goals in his fourteen outings.

His contribution to the United cause in general, was not forgotten, when the club set aside the match versus Newcastle United on October 15th 1910 as a benefit match for both himself and Dick Holden. Each man was guaranteed £300, and the attendance of over 50,000, paying gate receipts of £2,320 ensured that both players obtained that sum.

In December 1911, his connection with Manchester United was severed, when he joined Burnley, later moving to the team that he made his United debut against, Bristol City, in October 1913, where he saw out his professional playing career.

Although signed around the same time as John Picken, **Archibald Montgomery** had to wait until the fourth game of season 1905-06 before making his League debut, taking over in goal from Harry Moger against Glossop. He played in three consecutive fixtures, which were all won, conceding only two goals, but was dropped in favour of Robert Valentine and never turned out for the first team again.

Born in Chryston, Lanarkshire, he began playing with the local Chryston Athletic, strangely enough at centre forward. Like many before him and others since, he took over the goalkeeping position only to help out in an emergency and remained between the posts for the rest of his career.

In April 1894, the same year as he represented Scotland at junior international level, he joined Glasgow Rangers, but was encouraged to give football in England a try with Bury, a year later.

He was to make his Bury debut against Newton Heath on April 12th 1895 and went on to give the Shakers good service during his five years and 200 odd appearances with the club. Helping them clinch promotion to the First Division during that first season. This followed a rather inconsistent settling in period, which saw him sent off, shortly after signing, whilst playing in a Test Match against Liverpool.

Injury prevented him from picking up an F. A. Cup winners medal with Bury in 1903, when they defeated Derby County 6-0, but he soon recovered, regaining his confidence and earned himself a transfer to near neighbours United, along with team mate Charlie Sagar.

Due to his limited first team appearances with United, he returned to Gigg Lane Bury in the summer of 1906 and in February of the following year was appointed manager. A position that he held until April 1915.

Much uncertainty greeted the return to the First Division at the end of season 1905-06, following an unbeaten end of season run of nine consecutive games, cumulating with a 6-0 win over Burton United. A look at the record books also shows that the team suffered only two League defeats between January and the end of the campaign. Any doubts, were soon dismissed, as three wins in the opening four fixtures of the new season boosted the teams confidence for the weeks and months ahead.

Towards the end of November and the beginning of December, the team began to show signs of struggling, with only one win and two draws from nine games, conceding twelve goals in three of those. Results and confidence were soon to take an upward turn, with the signings of Meredith, Burgess, Bannister and Sandy Turnbull, from Manchester City. All four players had been suspended (along with another twelve of their team mates) after having been found guilty of receiving illegal payments in 1905.

By the end of season 1906-07, a creditable eighth position had been secured, mainly because of the new arrivals' contributions.

An early debutant during this season, was **Arthur Young**, but his flirtation with First Division football was to be brief.

Another signing from Hurlford Thistle, he was given his

first team chance, at outside right, against Birmingham City, shortly after his arrival in October 1906. He performed reasonably well in the 2-1 victory and retained his place the following Saturday at Everton.

A 3-1 defeat on Merseyside at the hands of the current League leaders, with the United forward line receiving much criticism in the national press, did little for his prospects and he was dropped for Arsenal's visit to Manchester seven days later, never to return and subsequently disappearing into obscurity.

On November 17th 1906, **Alexander Menzies** (see Fig: v pg 41), replaced Peddie at centre forward in the United line up and marked his debut against Sheffield Wednesday with a goal in a disappointing 5-2 defeat.

Lanarkshire born Menzies had begun his career north of the border with the notable junior side Blantyre Victoria in 1901, before signing for Heart of Midlothian in December 1902, specifically to play alongside the legendary Bobby Walker, a player reputedly to be the best the Edinburgh side has ever had.

A loan spell at Motherwell the following year and a season back in the junior ranks at Arthurlie, gave him the time to develop and gain the confidence required to make the grade at the higher level.

Returning to Hearts in May 1905, the gifted centre forward became something of a regular in the side second time around, winning a Scottish Cup medal in 1906, as well as selection for the Scottish international side to face England. United brought him south in November 1906, paying Hearts £500 for his services and following his excellent debut display, he should have went on to make a real name for himself. Instead, he drifted in and out of the side for the remainder of that season, only managing to add a further three goals to his debut strike.

He began season 1907-08 as first choice centre forward, playing in the opening five games, but his failure to score and the arrival of Jimmy Turnbull saw him demoted to the reserves.

The name of Menzies was only to appear in the first team line up on one further occasion, January 23rd against Chelsea, before leaving to join Luton Town. The road back to Scotland was retraced in the summer of 1909 when he

joined Dundee, who were to be his final League club, retiring at the end of the 1909-10 season. Bringing to a close a career that promised so much but in the end, delivered so little.

As mentioned earlier, January 1st 1907 marked the resurgence of form to what was becoming a rather testing season and what was in reality, the beginning of Manchester United/Newton Heath's most successful period to date, with a team of players who could hold their own at any level.

The merlinic Welshman, Billy Meredith, the first footballing superstar, was the lynch pin of this early 1900's side, but behind him, the half back line of Duckworth, Roberts and Bell were the backbone upon which the team was built, with Moger behind them a first class custodian. Alongside the charismatic winger from the land of the dragons were the likes Alex 'Sandy' Turnbull, George Wall, Jimmy Turnbull and Jimmy Bannister, giving the Manchester United supporters the team that they had craved for over the long dark years in the past.

Besides the aforementioned Alex Bell, there were two other Scotsmen in this notable side, the unrelated Sandy and Jimmy Turnbull.

Sandy Turnbull was yet another product of Ayrshire and the Hurlford club, but was a player who had been overlooked by the United scouting contacts in the area and had been signed instead by Manchester City, who enticed him south in January 1902. A transfer which cemented the basis of an eventful playing career.

Prior to City appearing on the scene to offer Turnbull a contract, the talented individual had agreed to sign for Bolton Wanderers. However, whilst awaiting the arrival of the necessary papers from Bolton, which required his signature, officials from Manchester City arrived on his doorstep. With them, they did have the necessary papers which upon reading, contained more attractive terms than that offered by Bolton. With little hesitation, or conscious reflections, Turnbull signed on the dotted line and became a Manchester City player.

It was certainly proved to be Bolton's loss, as Sandy Turnbull, scoring twelve goals in twenty-two games, helping City to the Second Division Championship in 1903. Twelve months later he added a F. A. Cup winners medal to this, scoring in every round up to the Final, with a further sixteen in the League, as City narrowly missed out on the First Division Championship.

1903-04 also saw the diminutive 5' 5" forward notch nineteen goals, which earned him selection for the Scottish international trial, representing the Anglo's against the Home Scots.

Controversy though, was never far away and following the allegation of violent play against Aston Villa in a tempestuous match on the final day of the 1904-05 season, he was suspended for one month.

Going into that final Saturday of the season, Manchester City had to defeat Aston Villa at Villa Park, whilst hoping that in the North-East 'derby', Midlesbrough would defeat Newcastle United, in order for them to be crowned Champions. If both won, then the Geordie's would claim the title on goal average.

As expected, City's match against Villa was a wholehearted affair, with the Birmingham versus Manchester aspect as much a factor as the footballing side of things.

With City 3-1 behind and the second half in progress, Sandy Turnbull was on something of a one-man crusade, with his opposite number Alec Leake finding his opponent an ever-increasing handful.

Following one collision between the two, the Villa captain threw a handful of dirt at Turnbull, which brought a two-fingered response from the offended player.

Not content to let it rest, Leake, with the referee following play, slapped Turnbull. Unable to restrain himself a second time, Turnbull retaliated with his fists, bringing the game to a halt as players from both sides attempted to restrain the two.

Much to the visitors and more so Sandy Turnbull's despair, the match ended in a 3-2 defeat and as the two teams left the field, police officers had to hold back the crowd as they made several attempts to reach some of the City players. Worse was to follow. Tempers, which had been frayed during the ninety minutes, suddenly bubbled over.

While making his way to the sanctuary of the dressing rooms, Sandy Turnbull was to his utmost surprise, dragged into the Aston Villa dressing room and the door held firmly shut. Minutes later, the shaken City player was thrown dishevelled into the corridor, his cheek scratched along with other marks to his face and bruising to his ribs.

Following a F.A. enquiry, Turnbull was suspended for one month. The referee was suspended for failing to control the match to the required standard, while Leake, the Villa player who had actually lit the blue touch paper so to speak was let off completely.

1906 found him once again in trouble, but on this occasion it was much more serious than previously, with the illegal payment scandal earning him and his team mates, a one year suspension.

Returning to football with City's Manchester neighbours, he went straight into the United side, along with his co-conspiritors, making his debut against Aston Villa on New Years Day 1907.

Some forty odd thousand packed into Clayton to see Turnbull and the other new arrivals – Meredith, Burgess and Bannister make their initial appearances in the red shirts and for Turnbull it was a memorable afternoon on the mudded, water strewn pitch, scoring the only goal of the match, from a Meredith cross in the sixtieth minute.

Season 1907-08 brought Manchester United their first major honour, in the form of the First Division Championship, with Sandy Turnbull the clubs leading goalscorer with 25 goals from 30 appearances. This included two hat tricks (one in the second match of the season against Liverpool, the other against Blackburn, the following month) and all four against Woolwich Arsenal in November. Despite taking his football very seriously, he was renowned as the club joker, always game for a laugh. During one game at Oldham, the referee spoke him to regarding a comment he had made and was told that if he repeated the remark then he would be sent off. At the final whistle, Turnbull walked past the referee and said " I've said it again, but you didn't hear me".

He was also known to play the game hard, as numerous defenders would testify and on December 21st 1907, he was sent off against Manchester City for "rough play" after having scored twice

Injury reduced his appearances during 1908-09, managing

only nineteen League outings, which produced meagre five goals. Despite this, he played his part in the F.A. Cup success of this season and despite scoring the only goal in the Final against Bristol City, scored a hat trick in the 6-1 win over Blackburn in the third round.

His appearance in the Cup Final was in some doubt up until half an hour before kick off, due to injury. With the final decision to play left up to him, he declared himself fit and his goal was a typical opportunist effort, latching onto the ball after a shot from Halse rebounded off the cross bar in the 21st minute.

In March 1909, he was once again selected for the Anglo Scots in an International trial match, but to the surprise of many, he was not selected for the full Scotland side. His previous career misendeavours playing a big part in this.

By the end of season 1909-10, he had resumed his top goalscorers mantle, with 13 from 26 appearances, being piped by one goal for the same accolade twelve months later by Enoch West, as United once again lifted the League Championship trophy.

Sandy Turnbull continued to find the net on a fairly regular basis during the next three seasons, but his career was to come to an abrupt end in 1915, almost a year after having received a benefit match against City, along with George Stacey.

Not having learned from his previous brushes with authority, which also included a serious dressing room argument with the United club secretary J.J.Bentley for which he received a suspension and almost instigated a players revolt, he was suspended for life for match fixing allegations.

These allegations surrounded United's match with Liverpool on Good Friday 1915, a game in which he took no active part, but was reportedly involved in attempting to fix the result.

Following a lengthy enquiry, the allegations were proved to be true and along with Enoch West, Arthur Whalley and four Liverpool players, who included former United players Miller and Sheldon, he was suspended.

By this time, however, he had joined the, army and upon the outbreak of war was quick to seek active service, enlisting with the Manchester Regiment. Sadly, it was a decision that was to prove fatal, as on May 3rd 1917, Sandy

Turnbull, the first United player to score at Old Trafford, was killed at Arras, in France, blown up by a shell.

One Turnbull in the United side would have been quite enough for most defences, but when Ernest Magnall signed **Jimmy Turnbull** (see Fig: v pg 41) for United in September 1907, the rearguard of every First Division side knew that they would really be up against it. As when this talented individual was not scoring goals, he would be setting them up for his team mates.

 Born near Bannockburn in Stirlingshire, Jimmy Turnbull, (no relation whatsoever to Sandy), signed his first professional contract as a thirteen and a half year old, with East Stirlingshire, having made his footballing debut as an amateur with Stenhousemuir

In those distant days of the late 1890's, players were paid a share of the gate receipts and Jimmy's first 'wage' as a footballer was 2/6d (12.5p). This was quite disappointing for the youngster, as he was receiving around 10/- (50p) per week for expenses!

In the summer of 1901, a £30 fee took him to Dundee, but he was soon to discover that he was suffering from an over strained heart and promptly quit the game.

Twelve months later, he went to Falkirk to watch a five-a-side competition and when one team reported a man short, he reluctantly made up the numbers. Much to his surprise, he suffered no reaction and being convinced that he was indeed fully fit, subsequently joined Falkirk, where he earned 30/- (£1.50p) per week.

His displays with Falkirk during 1903-04, in particular his five goals against Aberdeen in the semi final of the Dewar Shield, brought him to the attention of numerous club's. Such interest began to have an unsettling effect on the player and he eventually decided to seek a transfer, with no shortage of prospective buyers.

Without thinking too long and hard about his destination, he signed for Glasgow Rangers. A decision that he was too later regret, as he never managed to make an appearance in their first team.

Towards the end of January 1905, he was on the move again, disillusioned by his time at Ibrox, accepting an offer from Preston North End. Slowly, he was to return to his best form, pushing the disappointments of his time with

Rangers behind him. However, at the end of season 1905-06 he surprisingly left the Lancashire side and moved to Leyton F.C. who played in the Southern League.

This move turned out to be a wise choice, as he regained much of his early confidence and also his goal scoring touch with the London side.

The summer of 1907 saw Jimmy Turnbull forsake the rigours of the Southern League and sign for Manchester United, with the 'Cricket and Football Field' correspondent 'Mancunian' writing – "Our greatest capture is said to be James Turnbull, the centre forward who last season played for Leyton, having previously worn the colours of Preston North End and Glasgow Rangers. His transfer fee, I am told was a big one, as both Preston and Leyton had a finger in the pie and he was eagerly sought after by others.

"He is regarded as one of the very best centres in the south and if he will only play up to his reputation, we shall have a good man to fill what was undoubtedly our weakest spot in the front rank. His age is 22, his height 5' 9" and his weight 12st".

Jimmy Turnbull's League debut for United, at Chelsea on September 28th 1907, passed without note, but the following Saturday against Nottingham Forest, at home, he opened his scoring account with one of the goals in a 4-0 victory. A further five in the next four games were to follow. His United career continued to be an eventful one, containing a mixture of both highs and lows.

On August 29th 1908 at Stamford Bridge, he scored a hat trick against Southern League Champions Queens Park Rangers, which saw the name of Manchester United become the first to be engraved on the F. A. Charity Shield. The first match between the two sides, on April 27th 1908 had ended in a 1-1 draw, but Turnbull's hat trick in a 4-0 replay win determined the first destination of the trophy.

Although not renowned as a regular goalscorer for United, managing a total of twenty-seven during his first two seasons with the club (1907-08 and 1908-09), he could claim a scoring average of 0.577 per game, during his three years at Clayton, with 45 in 78 appearances. This total included the above-mentioned Charity Shield hat trick and also gave him one of the best averages in the club's history. Following the match against Everton on April 10th 1909, one in which he scored both United's goals in a 2-2 draw

having missed the two previous games, one of the regular scribes in attendance penned - " The presence of Jimmy Turnbull as the pivot of the forward line made a wonderful difference. His dash and well timed passes to either of the men on each side of him adding that jest to the game which is required".

Early in season 1909-10, he was amongst the headlines on the sports pages two weeks in a row, but for incidents that were to show a different side to Jimmy Turnbull.

In the last four minutes of the match against Aston Villa at Clayton, on October 16th, he was sent off, along with Villa's left half Hunter. Describing the scene, one reporter wrote - "The two men came into collision in front of the Villa goal. They went to the ground and there was a scene which was terminated by the interference of the other players and the referee, who immediately sent the two players off".

Seven days later, against Sheffield United away, he was once again seen to make an early exit from the field of play, sent off in the second half for kicking an opponent.

"Play had begun to get a little physical, with Sandy Turnbull being spoken to along with a Sheffield United player. Bell was kicked, while on the ground and had to go off injured. Shortly after this, Jimmy Turnbull and Sturgess got at loggerheads and it appeared that the referee had a word with the United man.

"Only a second or two later, there was another scene between the two and as a result of this, Turnbull was ordered off the field and both teams were given a word of warning".

Jimmy Turnbull was subsequently missing from the United line up for the following six games, returning for two before missing a further eight.

A week after his return, a reporter at the goal less draw against Woolwich Arsenal on March 12th wrote – "Jimmy Turnbull looks as though he has lost a lot of his old virility and vigour and possibly some of his pace". A report that the player himself must have read, as he bounced back in the following three games, scoring in each and following on with a double against Everton on April 6th, in what was to be his last appearance for United.

In the summer of 1910, he caused a surprise, by retiring from the game, having failed to agree terms with United and returned home to Scotland. Perhaps he was also feeling a bit aggrieved at Manchester United for not accepting a £200 bid for his services from strangely enough, Glasgow Rangers. This was a move that he would have readily agreed to, as he had intended going into business with his brother in the area. Such were his feelings on the subject that he took the matter up with the F.A., but to no avail.

September 1910 saw him repack his boots and return south to join Bradford, later joining Chelsea in June 1912, where he scored eight goals in nineteen games to help the Londoners escape relegation.

If the audacious move by Glasgow Rangers to resign their former player raised a few eyebrows, then the attempt by United to do likewise, in September 1914, created an even bigger surprise.

Turning out in a reserve team fixture, was as close to a return that the old live wire managed, as Chelsea were reputed to have asked for a £300 transfer fee. Such a sum was beyond the cash strapped United at that time.

Jimmy Turnbull was therefore to finish his career with Hyde United, before becoming a successful estate agent in the Stretford area of Manchester. Like his namesake Sandy, he could consider himself unlucky not to have gained full international honours, with an appearance for the Anglo Scots versus the Home Scots in March 1911 being all he could add to his League and F.A. Cup winners medals with United.

We have to return to season 1907-08 in order to find the next player from north of the border to make an appearance in Manchester United's first team and compared to Jimmy Turnbull, **Kerr Whiteside** (see Fig: v pg 41) is a complete unknown, as his solitary League appearance signifies.

Yet another Ayrshire man, Whiteside began his career with Irvine Victoria, with whom he won Scottish junior representative honours.

Moving from the Ayrshire club to United in the summer of 1907, he made a good impression in the pre-season fixtures and the early reserve games of 1907-08. But, with the form of the regular half-backs, the stalwarts Duckworth and Bell, it was a foregone conclusion that his first team appearances were going to be severely limited.

He was eventually reward with his League debut at Sheffield

United on January 18th 1908, replacing Dick Duckworth. However, an injury received early in the game curtailed his performance and also prevented him from making a second appearance the following week, with the regular wing half still out injured.

Other players might have given up in frustration as to making a career at Clayton, but Whiteside remained at the club for three years before finally moving to Hurst, at the end of season 1909-10, where he enjoyed five years with the Manchester non-League side.

The career of another Ayrshire player, **David Christie**, ran somewhat parallel to that of Kerr Whiteside.

Beginning as a junior, with the now over familiar Hurlford, Christie journeyed south in the close season of 1907-08. He made his debut in the second match of 1908-09, replacing Picken against Bury, but despite the 2-1 victory, the inside left berth was given to Harold Halse five days later.

It was to be reserve team football for Christie throughout the following weeks and months, but with only three League fixtures remaining, he once again made a surprise appearance in the line up, again replacing Picken (who himself had only made sporadic appearances over the previous eight months).

The 3-2 defeat against Leicester Fosse was widely reported as "a very poor match" and it was to mark the end of David Christie's Manchester United first team career.

Like his fellow countryman Kerr Whiteside, he seemed content to pursue his career in the United reserve side, but at the end of season 1909-10, he was placed on the transfer list and eventually left United for pastures new.

An emphatic start, of only one defeat in the first fourteen fixtures, with forty-eight goals scored, set the standard for the 1907-08 First Division Championship success, with what was virtually the same team as in the previous season. By Christmas, the name of Manchester United sat at the top of the table with thirty-three points, having lost only one other fixture. Had the second half of the campaign ran along similar lines, then who knows what records may have been set?

Following the 2-1 win against Bury on Christmas Day, United sat in pole position with 33 points from their 19 fixtures, but with 1907 blending into 1908 things began to take on a completely different look. Dropped points became commonplace, virtually every c her game and seven defeats, three coming in a four match spell during April, when only one goal was scored, caused some concern.

However, at the end of the day, United finished nine points ahead of Aston Villa and Manchester City, to lift their first Championship.

Season 1908-09 began in similar fashion, with the opening weeks producing only one defeat in eight games. Even a 6-1 reversal at Sunderland, followed by a 1-0 defeat at home to Chelsea, failed to knock the confidence as five of the next six games were won.

As it had been in the previous campaign, it was the latter half of the season which saw the slump in form and the retention of the championship was soon dismissed from the thoughts of players and supporters alike.

With only one victory in the final fifteen games, failing to score in four consecutive outings, it was little wonder that the team slumped to thirteenth in the table.

Another reason for the poor League form between January and April, might have been the involvement in the F. A. Cup, which saw Brighton, Everton, Blackburn Rovers, Burnley and Newcastle United defeated in the march to the Final for the first time in the club's history.

The draw for the first round had seen Brighton and Hove Albion venture from their fresh air surroundings of the south coast to the polluted atmosphere of Clayton. The visitors, however, were more put out by the physical aspect of the game than the conditions and it was a solitary goal from Halse which decided the game.

Meredith was sent off in the second half for kicking an opponent, while Jimmy Turnbull was perhaps fortunate not to follow towards the end, following a collision with a Brighton defender.

Round two again produced a home draw, with Everton following Manchester United out of the hat. Again, it was a solitary goal from Halse decided the tie.

Blackburn Rovers were the next visitors to Clayton for round three, in what was to produce a surprising outcome. In front of a packed Bank Street ground, a Sandy Turnbull goal gave United a ninth minute lead. Blackburn came

close on a couple of occasions, but as the team changed ends, the score remained at 1-0.

Shortly after the restart, United were 2-0 in front. Jimmy Turnbull out running the visitors defence to beat the 'keeper. Livingstone, soon after, added a third with a long range drive.

Blackburn did manage to pull a goal back, but with ten minutes remaining, Sandy Turnbull, recovered after a first half collision which saw him leave the field for attention, made it four. Blackburn were now totally demoralised and Jimmy Turnbull, with a fine solitary effort for his second goal of the afternoon made it 5-1. The rout was completed in the final minute when Sandy Turnbull scored a sixth.

It is said that you need luck to win the cup and this was certainly true in United's case in the fourth round tie at nearby Burnley.

In a report of the game, which appeared in the 'Umpire', C. E. Sutcliffe wrote – "The day was just about as bad as it could be. When the gates were opened at 12.25 pm, snow was falling and later it changed to sleet. The ground was covered in frozen snow, which gradually softened and in places churned up very soft making the surroundings, like the ground, dismal and miserable, but it could not stiffle the lively sparks in the crowd".

In the tenth minute, Burnley opened the scoring and with the players finding the going difficult play slithered from around the pitch. Just before the interval, United almost drew level, but Sandy Turnbull missed a good chance of scoring the equaliser.

As the second half progressed, Burnley were still well in command and as the minutes began to tick away, it looked as though United's progress in the competition was coming to an end.

With eighteen minutes left for play, the referee decided the conditions had deteriorated so much that the had no choice but to abandon the game, much to the relief of the United players, many of whom had not wanted the game to start.

To say the Burnley players and officials were disappointed was putting it mildly, with the home support equally vocal in venting their disapproval of the referee's decision.

In the re-arranged match, there were no complaints regarding the playing conditions, although the Burnley players and officials made their feelings widely known about having to play the game at all. A matter, which was brought up time and time again, when the two team's met. Things were certainly not helped with United winning the re-arranged fixture 3-2, thanks to a Jimmy Turnbull double and another from Halse.

It is interesting to note that the referee who abandoned the match at Turf Moor was a MR W. H. Bamlett, who in 1927 was to become manager of United!

So, onto the semi final and Newcastle United at Bramall Lane Sheffield.

It was always going to be a closely fought encounter, and in front of 40,118 spectators, a solitary Harold Halse strike in the 28th minute, was all that separated the two teams. Both Jimmy Turnbull and Wall had come close, while an injury to Sandy Turnbull curtailed his effect on the game, but it was his namesake Jimmy, who was considered by many to be the man of the match.

On April 24th, it was off to Crystal Palace for the Final against Bristol City and one again, a single goal was enough to decide the outcome of the game and the destination of the trophy.

In the early stages, play was relatively even, but in the twenty second minute, a shot from Halse, a constant thorn in the side of United's cup opponents, saw his shot hit the bar and the quick thinking Sandy Turnbull latch on to the rebound to shot past the helpless Clay in the Bristol goal. As the game progressed, the United defence managed to sustain any Bristol attacks despite an injury to full back Hayes and were worthy winners of the F. A. Cup for the first time.

The poor League form between January and April 1909 must have given new signing **George Livingstone** food for thought and led him to wonder if he had made the correct decision of leaving Glasgow Rangers and joining United.

Livingstone's move from the Ibrox club to United in January 1909 gave him the unique claim to fame as the only player to have turned out for both Glasgow club's and both Manchester club's.

Born in Dumbarton in 1876, George Livingstone's playing career began with the unusually named Sinclair Swifts and Artizan Thistle, two local sides, before joining Dumbarton in 1895.Less than twelve months later, on May 25th 1896, he was signing professional forms with Heart of Midlothian. Almost exactly four years later, he moved to Sunderland for what was to be the beginning of a whirlwind adventure, taking in five clubs over a nine-year period.

His spell in the north east of England lasted only a year, as he returned to Scotland to join Celtic, whom he was to help to the Scottish Cup Final of 1902. Whilst with Celtic, where he scored seven goals in twenty three appearances, he also won Scottish League representative honours and made an appearance for Scotland in the Ibrox Disaster match of 1902. Despite this success, he was soon off again at the end of the season.

Liverpool was his next port of call, but once again he only saw out one season with his new club.

Manchester City were the next club to employ the nomadic Scot, with the reputation of being a rather physical player and it began to appear that at long last, he had dispersed with his wanderlust. With City, he won a F. A. Cup winners medal in 1904, when they defeated Bolton Wanderers 1-0, adding a full Scottish cap to his increasing list of honours, lining up against England at Hampden Park.

Despite being somewhat settled in Manchester, his City career came to something of a premature end, as he was one of the players suspended following the illegal payments enquiry in the summer of 1906. But, unlike four of his team mates, he did not move across Manchester and join United, Instead, he returned to Scotland and joined Rangers, where he won a second full Scotland cap, against Wales and also represented the Scottish League side against their English counterparts.

In January 1909, he was to return to Manchester and join United, making his debut alongside former City team mates Burgess, Meredith and Sandy Turnbull, ironically against Manchester City, scoring twice in a 3-1 win.

He was disappointed at missing out on a place in the Cup Final line up, as he had played in the League fixtures prior to both the semi final and the Final. Two seasons later, he was again to miss out on United's trophy success, as he could only manage ten games in the Championship winning side of 1910-11.

Playing a fair percentage of his games in the United reserve side, he was appointed player-manager of the second string, a position that he was to hold until announcing his retirement during the First World War.

At the end of the hostilities, he once again returned north of the border, taking over the managerial role at his hometown club, Dumbarton, for a short period, before moving along the Clyde coast to take up a similar appointment with Clydebank.

In July 1920, he rejoined Glasgow Rangers as trainer and under his supervision, the team enjoyed League successes in 1920-1, 22-3, 23-4, 24-5 and 26-7. July 1928 saw him take up a similar role with Bradford City, where he remained until retiring from football altogether in May 1935.

As United struggled to maintain their dignity when it was clear that they were not going to retain their League Championship crown at the end of season 1908-09, the team was changed from game to game, as a winning formula was sought, although the team for the F.A.Cup run bore some form of stability.

One of the relatively unknowns who appeared in the side was **John Quinn**, born at Barrhead in Renfrewshire, but who was an adopted Mancunian, having lived in the area since he was twelve years old.

He began playing in local competitive Leagues with Manchester Xaverian College, Higher Broughton and Cheetham Hill, before being approached by Manchester City. Following a successful trial, he was duly signed.

Not finding life at City to his immediate liking, he refused to sign for a second season and accepted United's invitation to move across Manchester to join them at the end of season 1907-08.

With United, he was content to remain a part time player, with his teaching job clearly his main priority in life. Perhaps if he had taken the gamble and thrown his lot into a full time career, reverting back to his teaching in later years, he may have made the grade. As it was, his first team opportunities were to be clearly limited.

His League debut and one of only two first team appearances came on April 3rd 1909, at centre forward, in the 2-0 defeat at Sheffield Wednesday. He had then to wait until January 1st 1910 for his second, against Bradford City, when he replaced an injured Billy Meredith.

At the end of season 1909-10, he moved to Nelson, later playing for Chorley and Eccles Borough before eventually turning professional with Grimsby Town in May 1912.

At the end of the First World War, he returned to his native Scotland and joined Clyde, where he played for two years before ending his rather modest playing career at Ayr United. He retired at the end of season 1922-23.

The fine form of goalkeeper Harry Moger between March 1903 and January 1910, saw other custodians rarely given the opportunity to show what they were capable off. Injury, however, saw him omitted from the team in February 1911 and he was to make only fleeting appearances after this, before retiring in June 1912.

His immediate replacement between the posts in the United line up was **Hugh Edmonds**, the Bolton Wanderers reserve team goalkeeper, who had enjoyed a couple of years in Irish football with Belfast Distillery and Linfield.

Born in Chryston, Ayrshire, Edmonds had begun his career with Hamilton, before crossing the Irish Sea in the summer of 1907, returning to the mainland to join Bolton in October 1909. With the Wanderers, he made only a handful of first team appearances when he was signed by United in February 1911, as successor to Moger.

He made his debut in the 3-1 home victory over Bristol City on February 11th 1911 and kept his first clean sheet for the club seven days later in the 1-0 victory over Newcastle United at St James Park. Following this game, 'Jacques' of the Athletic News was quick to praise the new goalkeeper.

"The Manchester man was more heavily worked and performed admirably when called upon. I liked his clear fielding of the ball, though the Newcastle forwards did not provide him with the opportunity of showing how he could get down to a low shot. In the first half, he once showed excellent judgement in advancing to tackle Rutherford, when the home winger had left the backs behind and kicked the ball a little too far".

By the end of season 1910-11, he had kept a further five clean sheets in eleven more appearances and was the owner of a League Championship medal.

Such were his performances, it began to look as if he would enjoy a reign similar to that of his predecessor Moger. But after playing in 30 of the 38 League fixtures of the following season, he left the club and returned to Ireland and became player manager of Glenavon. An appointment which only lasted a year, as he returned to one of his former clubs, Belfast Distillery at the end of season 1912-13.

Season 1910-11, with everyone now firmly settled in their new Old Trafford surroundings, began favourably, with the signing of Enoch West bolstering the attack as a replacement for the departed Jimmy Turnbull.

On October 15th, a 2-0 victory over Newcastle United at home, gave United their seventh win in the opening eight fixtures of the League programme, taking them to the top of the table.

West had made an immediate impact, with four goals, but it was Sandy Turnbull who showed the way with five.

As the season progressed, any one of five clubs had the look of Champions and as winter moved into spring, there was still little to separate the leading pack. Two draws against the Sheffield clubs, 1-1 against United at home and 0-0 against Wednesday away, in mid-April, followed by a 4-2 reversal at Aston Villa on the penultimate day of the season ensured a nervous seven days for United player and supporter alike.

On that final Saturday of the season, it was a case of ifs and buts, with United having to defeat third place Sunderland away, while Liverpool had to defeat Aston Villa, who were going for their second consecutive title.

By the end of the afternoon, Manchester United were Champions, having beaten Sunderland 5-1 (with goals from Halse 2, Sandy Turnbull, West and an own goal), while Villa lost 3-1 to Liverpool.

One player who had enjoyed the involvement in the end of season drama was **James Hodge**. Signed back in May 1910 from Stenhousemuir, he had languished in the reserves until

the third last fixture of the season at Sheffield Wednesday, before making his debut at right half.

The nineteen year old had begun his career like numerous others, with his home town club and was not in the least bit phased by stepping up to a higher level of football and quickly "won the good opinion of the experienced judges at Old Trafford".

He was missing from the line up for the 4-2 defeat by Aston Villa the following week, but returned for the final match of the season against Sunderland, this time at left half. Here he was to give a favourable performance, especially as he was up against the seasoned and notable footballer Charlie Buchan. The following season, 1911-12, saw him back in the reserves until February when he re-appeared in the side, to enjoy a ten match run, appearing in both wing half positions.

He began to wonder, if this was an indication as to how his United career was going to fare, with no regular first team place guaranteed and whatever appearances he made would be in a number of different positions.

On December 28th 1912, his luck took a turn for the better, with selection at right back against Manchester City away. Following this fixture, he held on to this position for all but three of the remaining games of that season and continued there for most of 1913-14.

Much to his disappointment, however, he failed to make the starting line up for the opening fixture of season 1914-15 and only made four appearances throughout that campaign. One at centre half and the others at outside left!

On the resumption of organised League football following the Great War, he was a surprise inclusion in the side on the opening day of season 1919-20, against Derby County, playing at outside right. Such were his capabilities, that he enjoyed an eleven match run in this position, even managing to score his first of only two goals for United in a 3-3 draw against Manchester City.

Further appearances at inside left and inside right followed, but after being left out of the side once again, he asked for a transfer. A fee of £1,500 took him to Millwall Athletic, then in the Southern League, where he had a three year spell before moving to Norwich City and later Southend United.

James Hodge, was joined at United by his brother **John**, in the summer of 1913, having also been signed from Stenhousemuir.

Like his brother, John also made his League debut against Sheffield Wednesday, with his initial appearance coming on December 27th 1913 in the centre half position, taking over from Arthur Whalley.

Despite this being something of a problem position at the club, he was to make only three more appearances during this season, with one of those at right back.

At the start of season 1914-15, John Hodge took over the right back berth on a more regular basis, but like many others, was to find his footballing career curtailed by the outbreak of war. He was to subsequently disappear from the scene following his being made available for transfer at the pricey sum of £25!

With the influx of Scots into the United and Newton Heath sides over the years maintaining a steady flow, something of a drought occurred between 1910 and 1920, with only four arrivals taking the road to Manchester from north of the border.

The last of the quartet to follow the Hodge brothers and Hugh Edmonds south was **James Thomson**. Dumbarton born and signed from Renton in May 1913, following a spell with Clydebank. There were high hopes for the youngster making the grade with United, as he was eyed as an eventual successor for the veteran George Wall. The expectations, however, did not bear fruition and his United career was limited to a mere six outings, with a gap of fifteen games between his first appearance on December 13th 1913, against Bradford City and his second, against Sunderland on April 10th 1914.

In May 1914, he was one of the players made available for transfer, with a fee of £200 being mentioned. This, however, was later reduced by a quarter and due to the lack of interest was eventually discarded altogether.

He was to return home disillusioned, but still determined to make a career in the game. Following a spell with Dumbarton Harp, he eventually enjoyed some success with St Mirren in a ten year spell, between 1918 and 1928, winning a Scottish Victory Cup medal in 1919 and a Scottish Cup winners medal in 1926.

BETWEEN THE WARS

The First World War of 1914-18 brought many sporting careers to something of a standstill. On the resumption of the League competition on August 30th 1919, many players were now too old and past their best, to regain their place with their club's, while others, like Sandy Turnbull had been killed in action. The difference that the War had made to United was clearly obvious when looking at the team from the last day of season 1914-15 and the opening day of 1919-20. Against Aston Villa on April 26th 1915, it read – Beale, Allman John Hodge, Montgomery O'Connell Haywood, Meredith Woodcock Anderson West and Norton. While on August 30th 1919 against Derby County, it was – Mew, Moore Silcock, Montgomery Hilditch Whalley, James Hodge Woodcock Spence Potts and Hopkin. A new era had begun.

The first Scot to be signed in the aftermath of the Great War, was **George Bissett**, a twenty two year old, arriving at the club from Army football.

A native of Cowdenbeath , he had began playing in the junior ranks with Glencraig Thistle and prior to the war had been on the books of Third Lanark.

With the rigours of the hostilities having taken its toll, Bissett took some time to regain his fitness and settle into ordinary life again. Following his debut against Burnley, on November 15th 1919, a game that United lost 3-0, reports singled out the newcomer for some unwanted attention, with comments such as "The attack including Bissett, the ex Third Lanark player, who gave distinct promise" and also "All eyes were turned on Bissett and though it would be unfair to judge his merits owing to the conditions, yet he gave ample evidence of ability, even though facing such a master as Watson".

Following a run of three games, he was omitted from the side, returning for one solitary outing before the turn of the year against Newcastle on December 27th. On February 7th, against Sunderland, he returned to the first team picture, refreshed and eager to make a go of things. Despite United losing 3-0, he retained his place the following week, scoring the only goal in a 1-1 draw against Oldham Athletic and held onto his first team place for the remainder of the season, scoring a further five goals. His performances were noteworthy in the press, with the 0-0 draw against Bradford City on March 20th bringing "The forwards, with the exception of the right wing were poor and once again Bissett distinguished himself with fine footwork".

Season 1920-21saw him begin where he had left off, lining up at inside right for the opening fixture against Bolton Wanderers, with the prospects looking promising.

In the Athletic News pre-season summary on United's players and chances of success it was written…"If Bissett is kept at outside right, he will probably be one of the forwards of the season".

A 3-2 defeat, however, saw him missing from the team for the next fixture and he was to make only a further three appearances up until March 28th, when he returned to face Burnley. Despite a 3-0 defeat, he kept his place this time and five days later he scored both goals in the 2-0 win over Huddersfield Town, ensuring himself a place in the team for the remainder of the season.

The opening fixtures of 1921-22 again saw him in and out of the side, playing two games at inside right and four at outside right between August and mid-November. Due to his limited opportunities, he decided that the time was now right to move on, joining Wolverhampton Wanderers at the end of November. Further spells at Pontypridd and Southend United followed, before retiring in April 1926.

In September 1920, Manchester United made something of a controversial signing, when they secured **Tommy Miller**, a member of Liverpool's 1914 F. A. Cup winning side, for £20,000. The player had been one of the four Liverpool players involved in the notorious match against United, on April 2nd 1915, which was reportedly 'fixed'. However, because of his army service, he was, along with his team mates given the opportunity to apologise for their misendeavours and returned to the Liverpool ranks after the war, scoring some fifteen goals in his first twenty four games during that first season. His performances also earning him a Scottish international cap against England.

He had began in the junior ranks, with Larkhall Hearts, a side close to his Motherwell home and following a brief period with Gleniven, Lanark United and Third Lanark, before he joined Hamilton Academicals in 1910.

His ability as an inside forward was soon noted and mid-way through his second season with Hamilton, a club three other members of his family played for, he joined Liverpool for £400.

Fifty-two goals in 127 appearances on Merseyside were enough to earn the quality forward with a excellent turn of speed and shooting ability, a move to United, with Liverpool making a tidy profit on the transaction.

His debut for United, against Tottenham on September 25th passed almost un-noticed, with one report stating – "Miller, the United's new £2,000 centre-forward from Liverpool, forced Jacques to a particularly fine save early in the game, but little more was seen of him".

A goal against Oldham Athletic, in his third outing, did much to help him settle and a fortnight later he proudly lead out United as captain against Preston North End, marking the occasion by scoring the only goal of the game. "Miller, who was named centre for the Old Trafford side, played a cool and judicious game, scored the all important goal and is the best man United have had in this position so far" said one report.

Unfortunately, things took a downward turn and in the second half of the season, he found himself out of the side with the reports having changed to "Miller was slow" and "Miller's re-appearance did not improve the forward line". Despite being out of favour at Old Trafford, he was selected to play for Scotland against England and Northern Ireland in 1921. But despite the international recognition, he decided that his first team opportunities were now somewhat limited and he returned to Scotland, joining Heart of Midlothian in a player exchange deal which gave United £550 plus Arthur Lochhead.

His Tynecastle career was brief and he was clearly now past his best, with the following season finding him back in England with Torquay United, where again he was only to remain for one season before returning north again in 1923 to join Hamilton Academicals for a fee of £100. For the first time in a number of years, Miller had time to unpack his bags, remaining with the Lanarkshire side for three years

before joining what was to be his final League club Raith Rovers in December 1926, retiring the following year.

On April 2nd 1920, another of those nondescript individuals, who materialised out of the reserve side and into the first team spotlight, only to make the one solitary appearance had his ninety minutes of glory. His name was **John Prentice**.

Although Glasgow born, he had been brought up in Manchester and was a product of Manchester Amateur League football. His early life as a Manchester United footballer were passed as an amateur, before signing professional forms in November 1919.

Coming into the side against Bradford Park Avenue on April 2nd 1920, replacing the injured Hopkin at outside left, he made little impact during the 1-0 defeat. With Hopkin sufficiently recovered to face Bolton Wanderers the following day, it was back to the reserves for Prentice.

At the end of the season, he turned down the new terms offered to him by United and was subsequently transferred to Swansea Town. Failing to settle with the Welsh side, he quickly moved to Tranmere Rovers.

Although he managed to make a number of first team appearances with Tranmere, he found himself released at the end of season 1921-22 and made what was to be his final career move, returning to his adopted city of Manchester to join Hurst.

The performance of the team since the resumption of play after the war had been disappointing, finishing twelfth at the end of season 1919-20 and one place lower the following year. A transfusion of Scottish blood into the side had helped in previous years and perhaps the clubs management felt a similar influx could once again pay dividends and help matters, as the summer of 1921 saw the signings of Johm Scott, who according to the Athletic News "lacked speed, but his skill is too well known to need comment here" and Arthur Lochhead.

Twenty-two year old, Lanarkshire born **Arthur Lochhead**, as mentioned earlier, was brought to the club as part of the deal that took Tommy Miller to Hearts in 1920. He had joined the Edinburgh side from army football and such was

his performance in their pre season trial game of 1919-20, he was thrown straight into the first team instead of finding his feet, as expected, in the reserves.

Eighteen goals in his first twelve appearances in the Scottish League saw him mark in the professional game. He was later to score a controversial goal in the quarter final of the Scottish Cup against Celtic, kicking the ball out of the goalkeeper's hands to win the game. Following his transfer south, United were confident that they had come out best in the player/cash deal which was valued at £2,300.

Season 1921-22 could not have got of to a worse start, with a 5-0 defeat at Everton, where Lochhead played at centre forward and his compatriot, Scott, at left half. A 3-2 defeat at West Bromwich Albion followed, but with the return against Everton won 2-1, it was though that an improvement was about to be shown. However, only one more of the opening eleven games were won.

Following the 5-0 defeat against Everton, an immediate re-shuffle took place, with surprisingly, the forward line showing the most changes, Arthur Lochhead being one of them.

He returned to the side five games later, but made little difference in a 0-0 draw against Chelsea. He did, however, open his Old Trafford scoring account the following Saturday at Preston in a 3-2 defeat.

Goals were something that United were really desperate for, as they struggled throughout the season, with Lochhead's return of eight from thirty one appearances not helping matters very much at all.

A run of six games unbeaten during February and the beginning of March, were followed by six straight defeats and with a meagre twenty-eight points from their forty-two games, United found themselves relegated from the First Division.

In Division Two, Arthur Lochhead fared slightly better, finishing the 1922-23 season as joint top scorer with thirteen goals, improving that total by one, a year later and a further thirteen goals in the promotion winning season of 1924-25.

It was thought that Lochhead's goals would play a major

part in the club's consolidating their place in the top flight, but to everyone's surprise, he was transferred to Leicester City in October 1925 for a fee of £3,300.

The Manchester Football Chronicle reported that "The transfer of Lochhead is in the nature of a tragedy to thousands who have delighted in the skilled footwork, long stride and beautiful body swerve the young Scottish schoolmaster showed".

The move was perhaps a good decision by the player, as with Leicester, his career blossomed further, scoring 106 goals in 303 appearances, helping them to a Division One runners-up spot in 1928-29. In October 1934 he was appointed team manager, but was later to resign from the post in January 1936.

The other arrival from Scotland in the summer of 1921, John Scott, was born in Motherwell, but began his career with the team from the opposite side of the A74, Hamilton Academicals, before moving to Bradford Park Avenue in October 1910. With Bradford, he was a member of their promotion winning Division Two side of 1913-14.

A fee of £750 took Scott across the Pennines to Old Trafford, where he began season 1921-22 at left half, playing seventeen games, before playing a further five games at full back.

He returned to the left half berth on New Years Eve against Newcastle United, but the 3-0 defeat, not only marked the final game of that year, but also the final first team match of Scott's United career.

He was to languish in the reserve side until the end of the season and during the close season returned to Scotland and joined St Mirren.

United's relegation at the end of season 1921-22 had not been helped by the resignation of manager John Robson on October 31st, due to ill health. His place being taken by John Chapman. Robson had been the first person with either United or Newton Heath to hold the title of club manager, with his predecessors all answering to the title of club secretary. To his credit, he had always been able to maintain United's presence as a First Division club, but in the end he was unable to give the club his full commitment due to his failing health. He did, however, stay on as Chapman's assistant.

A former amateur outside right with Glasgow Rangers, **John Chapman** had cut his teeth as a manager with Airdrieonians, where he had received favourable praise for his fifteen years service. So much so, that the Athletic News of October 10th 1921 stated that "he had done so much to make Airdrieonians one of the foremost clubs in the Scottish League".

It was unfortunate that it was after he left the Lanarkshire club that all his good work began to show fruition, with Airdrie finishing runners-up in the Scottish First Division four seasons in succession, between 1922-23 and 1925-26, as well as lifting the Scottish Cup in 1924.

Managing Manchester United, however, was to prove a much different story.

Joining United on a five year contract, he was one of the highest paid managers in the Football League at that time. His managerial career at United did not get off to an ideal start, with a 5-3 defeat at home to Middlesbrough, and only five victories during the remainder of the season saw the name of Manchester United in the Second Division fixture list for the following season.

It was to take Chapman three seasons to lift the club out of the lower Division, as runners up, and ninth place in the First Division upon their return, was looked upon as being a good foothold for the future. Unbeknown, the future had a dark cloud looming on the horizon.

Little did Chapman realise when he signed his five year contract that his time in the role would be more or less exactly the five years. In October 1926, he was suspended by the Football Association for "improper conduct in his position as secretary/manager of Manchester United Football Club" and "Banned from taking part in football and football management during that season".

Further details of Chapman's irregularities were never made public and United dispensed of his services, with a new authorising signature immediately brought in to force to sign all club cheques. Chapman's position at the club was taken over by one of the senior members of the playing staff, Clarence Hilditch.

Upon his appointment, John Chapman could not have been aware of the difficult job that he had on his hands, as he inherited a team that certainly required considerably strengthening. Chapman was not averse to making signings, with one of his last transfer dealings with Airdrie was to 'steal' a young Hughie Gallagher from under the nose of Queen of the South as he lay in a Dumfries hospital bed. Almost immediately, upon sensing the team requirements, he returned to Scotland and to his previous club Airdrie. Unfortunately not to bring the talented Gallagher south, but to sign William Henderson and then to move quickly to Ayr United to pursue the signature of Neil McBain. Of the two individuals, Henderson took the longest to settle in Manchester, despite scoring United's goal in a 1-0 win over Aston Villa on his debut.

A former Edinburgh schoolboy star, **William Henderson** was associated with Edinburgh Waverley and St Bernards, before joining Airdrie in May 1920. The solidly built centre forward soon made a name for himself in the Scottish First Division, scoring 36 goals in 39 appearances, making him the countries leading goalscorer during season 1920-21. The following season, he scored a further three goals in eleven outings.

John Chapman had obviously kept up to date with the Scottish game and knew only too well of Henderson's capabilities and had no hesitation in paying out £1,750 to take him to Old Trafford in November 1921. Against Aston Villa on November 26th at Old Trafford, Henderson took over the centre forward role from Joe Spence, with the big crowd favourite moving to inside right and the newcomer's goal was enough to earn United both points in a 1-0 win.

Henderson's homesickness, or whatever it was, in those early days at United soon became apparent, as he only featured in a further nine games (three of which saw United fail to score), during that relegation haunted season of 1921-22. He was to score only one other goal, on December 10th in the 1-1 draw with Bradford City. The following season, 1922-23, appearances were once again limited, with the two at the end of September – beginning of October, his total for the season. During 1923-24, his name failed to appear in the first team line up at all.

An injury to Ernie Goldthorpe in the opening fixture of 1924-25 gave William Henderson a surprise break and he found himself back into the limelight as the replacement centre forward. His performances astonished many of the Old Trafford regulars as he scored fourteen goals in a run of twenty-two appearances, with a notable hat trick against Oldham Athletic on September 20th.

Preston North End, noting his return to form, made a move for the big front man in January 1925 and despite his recent successful run in the United side, Henderson decided to move to Deepdale.

Strangely, his half season goal tally at United was not beaten and he still finished top scorer!

Preston, however, turned out to be only a half season stop over, as he moved to Clapton Orient at the end of 1924-25. A year later, he returned to Edinburgh and joined Heart of Midlothian, spending one season there before moving to Morton in the close season of 1927.

The final two years of his playing career were to be spent on the south coast of England, with Torquay United and Exeter City.

While William Henderson struggled to settle with United, the exact opposite could be said about John Chapman's other early signing, **Neil McBain**, a skilful centre half, for whom United had to pay Ayr United £4,600 to secure his signature, quite a fee in the early days of the 1920's.

The Argyllshire born McBain's thirty-two year playing career began with his local side Campbelltown Academicals and it was from here that he joined Ayr United in the close season of 1914, following a trial with the more familiar Academicals from Hamilton. It was perhaps an outstanding performance in the Renfrewshire Junior Cup final replay between Hamilton and Neilston Victoria in May 1914 at Ayr, which inspired the host club to sign him.

Having made his debut in March 1915, his career with Ayr's 'Honest Men' came to an abrupt and premature end with the outbreak of war.

Despite the hostilities, he managed, unlike some, to pursue his footballing career, turning out for both Portsmouth and Southampton while stationed on the south coast.

When football returned to normality, McBain carried on where he had left off with Ayr United and was seen to make a name for himself as a stylish defender who preferred to use his skill rather than be content to simply clear his lines.

"The lure of the financial return would tug strongly at the sentimental bonds that bound the club and player" reported a newspaper correspondent covering what was to be one of his last games for Ayr.

Arriving at Old Trafford in November 1921 he made his debut, along with William Henderson, against Aston Villa and missed only a handful of games between then and the end of the season. One reporter of the period was to write, "The introduction of McBain at centre half, has had a wonderful effect. His defensive play is fine, but his judgement in working out attacks is even finer".

1922-23 saw him begin the campaign in his favoured position of centre half, but the arrival of Frank Barson, in September, saw him switched to left half. The signing of Barson, a no nonsense defender delighted the United support, but they were disappointed that McBain had to be moved to wing half, as he was considered one of the best central defenders at that particular time.

In contrast to Barson, who mastered the ball in the air, the four inches smaller McBain played a more skilful game, with the ball on the ground. A style, that saw him tour Canada and the United States of America with the Scottish international side in 1921and earn him the first of three full Scotland caps against England at Villa Park in April 1922. Eight appearances at inside left, during season 1922-23, producing two goals, followed half a dozen games at left half, having begun the campaign in his more familiar centre half role for United. An appearance at right half followed this, before he returned to the centre half spot at the end of December, for what were to be his final two games of that season.

To everyone's surprise, McBain requested a transfer in January 1923. His reasons for doing so were never made public, although many offered the opinion that it was mainly due to his selection in the unfamiliar and unwanted role at inside forward. When news of his impending transfer was announced, a vast number of United supporters held a protest meeting in a local hall, but it was to no avail.

There were obviously many teams interested in such a talented individual and after much deliberating he decided to join Everton, with United receiving a fee of £4,200.

At Goodison Park, he was to regain his place in the Scotland side, winning a further two caps against Northern Ireland in Belfast in 1923 and against Wales in Cardiff the following year.

After three seasons in the blue of Everton, he set of on something of a footballing adventure, beginning with a return to Scotland, joining St Johnstone in July 1926 for a fee of £1,000.

In March 1926, he was back on Merseyside, joining the red half of the city, but eight months and a dozen games later he was off again, this time southward to sign for Watford.

His first season with the Hertfordshire side was spent solely as a player, but he was then to take on the role of player manager for a further two, before retiring from the playing side in 1931, to concentrate on the managerial side of things until August 1937.

Season 1937-38 found Neil McBain back at his first senior club, Ayr United, as manager, but this appointment was to last only twelve months, as did his next managerial role at Luton Town.

In June 1946, he was appointed secretary/manager of New Brighton and when travelling difficulties prevented the regular goalkeeper Alex Corbett from reaching Hartlepool for a Third Division North fixture on March 15th 1947, McBain dug his boots out of the cupboard and forsook his retirement to play in goal. At the age of fifty-one years and four months, he became the Football League's oldest ever player.

It is reported that the stand-in goalkeeper played well, making some fine saves on what was a waterlogged pitch. His team, however, lost 3-0!

Leyton Orient were to be his next club on an ever increasing CV, employed at first as assistant manager in February 1948, taking over the role completely two months later.

August 1949 saw him on the move once again, making the long trip to South America, to take over a coaching post with Estudiantes De La Plata in Argentina.

A second managerial spell at Ayr United followed during 1955-56, as did a second spell at Watford between 1956 and 1959, a move that he was reluctant to make. But as Ayr would not match the wages Watford were willing to pay, he moved south.

This was followed by numerous scouting jobs, before taking up his final managerial appointment in 1963 back where it all began, at Ayr United. It was once again, something of a tempestuous relationship and after numerous disagreements at boardroom level, he decided to walk away from the club. Neil McBain's career was certainly a colourful one, but it was unfortunate that his style and commitment could not have helped Manchester United escape relegation back in season 1921-22 and secure promotion at the first attempt the following season.

Prior to the start of 1922-23 and a second season in Division Two, John Chapman brought another two Scotsmen onto the United pay role in the hope that the noted qualities of Scottish footballers could be beneficial to the club as it strove for the much wanted success.

In the seasonal prospects of Manchester United, the Athletic News was to write – "Certainly the right wing should be greatly strengthened by the appearance in the outside position of John Wood, the 5' 8", 11st attacker, secured from Dumbarton.

"There was a great deal of bargaining in June before the afternoon on which United manager, Mr John Chapman, reached Glasgow at half past three o'clock, and returned to Manchester the same day with the signature of the player.

"Wood played much as a centre forward and inside right with Dumbarton, but did impressive work at outside right – particularly in a cup-tie at Aberdeen. There is no doubt he is intended as the outside right at Old Trafford. Over £1,000 was paid for him and this is much the largest sum paid for a United recruit this summer".

Fife born **John Wood** (see Fig: vi pg 59) crossed the Firth of Forth and joined Hibernians in 1914, making his debut on the 29th of the month against Morton. He was quick to show his ability to the green half of the Edinburgh football supporting public, playing his part in helping Hibs to the Scottish Cup Final, which was lost to Celtic after a replay.

Fig: vi

MANCHESTER UNITED 1922/3

LOCHHEAD, RADFORD, MEW, SILCOCK, HILDITCH, BARSON,

WOOD, GRIMWOOD, SPENCE, McBAIN, PARTRIDGE, THOMAS

A tricky, hard working player, who always gave 100%, but was unfortunate that the First World War was to step in and play havoc with his career in the game.

As life attempted to get back to some sort of normality after the war, he did not return to Hibs, but instead headed for his native Fife to join Dunfermline, then a Scottish Central League side, for a fee of £300.

With Dunfermline for only a matter of months, he then once again surprisingly took a step downwards and joined Lochgelly United, but returned to the big time when he signed for Dumbarton in June 1921.

His spell in the backwater of Scottish football with Lochgelly had done him no harm whatsoever, as he ended season 1920-21 as the third highest goal scorer in Scotland, with 25 in 36 appearances.

With a clear shortage of goals at Old Trafford during the relegation season of 1921-22 – forty-one in forty two games, more firepower was certainly required and Wood was considered capable of increasing the goals for column, but at the cost of £1,750.

Two goals in the pre-season trial matches, followed by another on his debut against Crystal Palace on the opening day of season 1922-23, it certainly looked as if United had indeed signed a player of some goal scoring ability.

One reporter covering his debut match wrote – "Wood, the United's new player from Dumbarton, distinguished himself by scoring the opening goal midway through the second half". A goal described in another report as "a fine low shot". The rising early hopes were soon deflated, as he failed to score again, in his fifteen outings scattered through the first half of the season.

Following the 1-1 F. A. Cup first round draw at Bradford City, he was promptly dropped for the replay and was not to be seen in the first team line up again.

At the end of the season, he was placed on the transfer list and eventually returned to Scotland and to Lochgelly United. His goal scoring form was soon to return, with a move to St Mirren following shortly afterwards.

He was to spend two years with the Paisley side, before moving down the ranks to sign for East Stirlingshire where he saw out his career.

Signed around the same time as John Wood, was **David Bain**. The former Rutherglen Glencairn player was no stranger to his new Old Trafford surroundings, having previously had trials with the club on a couple of occasions,

but returning home unsigned and disappointed. John Chapman, however saw something that others had missed and felt that the junior internationalist could make a good addition to the squad and was hastily recruited.

His first team opportunities, however, were to be limited during his initial season, following his League debut at inside right, against Port Vale away, on October 14th. He was not to reappear in the first team until April 11th, against Southampton, this time as centre forward and played in the next two fixtures, scoring the only goal of the game against Leicester City on April 14th.

In his second season, 1923-24, he began where he had left off, in the reserves, but on October 13th, he was re-introduced into the side at centre-forward against Oldham Athletic and scored twice. Seven days later, he was on the mark again, scoring once in the 3-0 defeat of Stockport County.

Such form earned him an extended run in the side, making a total of eighteen appearances and adding a further five goals, including a hat trick against Port Vale three days before Christmas.

A further two goals at the beginning of January, against Coventry and Bradford City kept him in the firs team picture, but two blank score lines for both player and team at the beginning of the following month saw reserve team football beckon.

Out of the first team picture, David Bain became desperate to be involved at this level of football and eagerly accepted a move to Everton, who paid a four-figure sum for his signature. If the move itself came as something of a surprise for the player, he received an even bigger one when the Goodison Park management converted him to into a wing half. However, as it meant the first team football that he wanted, there was obviously no complaint.

Four years at Everton were followed by spells with Bristol City, Halifax Town and Rochdale before retiring.

On the opening day of season 1923-24, against Bristol City, the outside right position was filled by **David Ellis**, a player familiar to manager John Chapman, as the Athletic News was to explain to its readers.

"What was undoubtedly the weakest part in Manchester United's armour last season seems to have been strengthened by the signing of David Ellis, who last season was with Maidstone and who formerly made a reputation on the extreme right wing of Airdrieonians".

"As the present Manchester United manager, Mr J.A. Chapman, himself discovered Ellis for Ardrieonians, he should know all about the ability of the player, who is 23 years of age and has exceptional speed".

Kirkcaldy born Ellis, was playing with Glasgow Ashfield, when he was invited to Airdrie for a trial in a friendly match with Glentoran in Belfast. Such was his contribution to the game, John Chapman wasted no time in securing his signature on the return journey home, fearful that his performance had been seen by others who may make an attempt to procure the player upon his return home.

With the Lanarkshire side, where he played for three seasons, he made sixty-three appearances in the League, scoring four goals, with a further four appearances in the Cup. During season 1920-21, Ellis was selected as a reserve outside right, for the Scottish League versus the Irish League.

In May 1922, he joined non-League Maidstone United, who, because of their status, did not have to pay Airdrie any fee. However, when they folded, in April 1923, Airdrie still held the player's registration, allowing them to profit on any subsequent sale.

A fee of £1,250 was enough to persuade Airdrie to allow the player to join his former mentor at Manchester United, but after what can only be described as a disappointing season, despite playing in the opening eight fixtures, United cut their losses and allowed Ellis to leave mid way through the campaign, having added only a further three appearances to his total.

Disappointed and disillusioned, Ellis returned homeward and signed for St Johnstone for the greatly reduced fee of £500. Unhappy at his treatment at Old Trafford, he made a claim for half of the transfer fee. Not unexpectedly, but to David Ellis' annoyance, the claim was dismissed without the slightest consideration.

Eager to prove United wrong and prove to himself that he was capable of playing at the highest level in the Football League, he returned south and joined Bradford City. Here, he had to experience an even bigger nightmare than that at United, as he failed to make the Bradford first team. Realising that his dream of success was to remain unfulfilled, he once again took the road north and joined the popular junior ranks with Arthurlie.

During season 1923-24, one other Scot, **James Miller**, whose career was brief to say the least, featured in the United first team, making only four appearances and scoring once.

Born on the Firth of Clyde at Greenock, his first three clubs were all from the same geographic location – Port Glasgow Athletic, St Mirren and Morton.

After spending only eight months with the latter, he joined Grimsby Town prior to the start of season 1921-22, where he quickly made a name for himself, scoring thirty-two goals in ninety-eight appearances. Several clubs had noted his displays, but it was Manchester United who moved the quickest, securing his signature for a fee of £500 in March 1924.

He was immediately thrust into the first team at inside left to face Hull City at Old Trafford and performed well enough to retain his position the following week when his goal earned United a point in the return fixture at Hull. A draw and a defeat, both against Stoke City, in what were to be his last appearances for United followed and he was duly released at the end of the season.

He subsequently moved to York City, then a Midland League side, where he showed that his brief spell at United had done him little harm, as he finished season 1924-25 as their leading goal scorer.

By the late 1920's, he had also played non-League football for Boston United and Shirebrook.

The introduction of his fellow Scots failed to help John Chapman bring instant success to Manchester United, but the goals of Lochhead and Henderson, with thirteen and fourteen respectively played a major part in winning promotion as runners up at the end of 1924-25.

The defensive record of having only conceded twenty-three, also had a significant bearing on the final outcome of that particular season.

Going into the final Saturday of the season, United sat in second place, two points behind leaders Leicester City and two points in front of third place Derby County. By the end of the afternoon, both United and Derby had drawn, the latter 2-2 with Blackpool, while United had shared the points with Barnsley in a goal less encounter. This was only the tenth game in which United had failed to score, but it mattered little, as they were back in the First Division.

That promotion winning season of 1924-25 saw the debuts of two Scots, who managed only five games between them during this particular campaign, but whose careers, through the passage of time, took on entirely different paths.

The first to find his name on the team sheet for the first X1 was **James Bain**, younger brother of the aforementioned David, who was to make his United debut, and only appearance, against Clapton Orient, in the 4-2 win on February 7th.

Like David, he had begun playing with Rutherglen Glencairn, before moving to Glasgow Strathclyde, with whom he attracted United's attention, perhaps with the help of some prompting from his elder brother.

A Scottish junior internationalist, he had signed for Manchester United five months after David in October 1922, but had to be content with reserve team football until his debut against Clapton.

The game was obviously a memorable occasion for the debutant, but it was a game forever etched into the history books due to United's signing of Orient's Albert Pape shortly before kick off. Pape had travelled north with his Orient team mates, went from the away dressing room to the home one and duly scored against what was now his former club.

James Bain's career, however, never ventured anywhere near

making the headlines, as following his debut, he found himself immediately back in the reserve side, not re-appearing in the first team again until the opening day of 1925-26 against West Ham United. This was once again a one-off appearance and it was not until March 10th 1926, against Liverpool at home, that he made his second of that season.

Season 1926-27 was spent entirely in the reserves, with his fourth and final Manchester United appearance not being recorded until September 19th 1927, against Blackburn Rovers.

At the end of 1927-28 he joined Manchester Central for six months, later moving to Brentford in November 1928 for £250. Playing centre half for the Bees, he was soon made club captain and inspired them to promotion to the Third Division in 1932-33. He was to become assistant manager six years later, taking over the reigns completely for a brief spell between August 1952 and January 1953.

The other debutant of season 1924-25 was the notably named **Clatworthy Rennox**, known to one and all as Charlie.

Signed in March 1925 in an effort to make the final push for promotion more positive, Rennox made his debut against Portsmouth on March 14th, but was to only play in four of the remaining eleven fixtures.

Born in Shotts, Lanarkshire, Rennox had started his career with two comparatively unknown Scottish lesser League sides Dykehead and Wishaw. In June 1921 he abandoned the rural life of home and headed for the bright lights of London, having been signed by Clapton Orient, where he played for three years before his move to United.

The name of Rennox was missing from the first three line ups of the 1925-26 season, but on September 7th, he was re-introduced into the side, at inside left, for the match at Villa Park, scoring in the 2-2 draw. From then on, he only missed an odd game through injury, finishing the season as leading scorer, with seventeen goals from his thirty-four appearances, including a hat trick against Burnley on September 26th.

Season 1926-27 took on a similar look, first three fixtures

again missed (did he enjoyed an extended holiday?) and then almost a regular throughout, until April, when he failed to make a solitary appearance. This time, however, his goals return was a mere seven from his twenty-two games!

In the summer of 1927, Charlie Rennox left Old Trafford for Grimsby Town, but failed to make a first team appearance for them and drifted into non-League football.

Season 1925-26 saw the return to the big time with United consolidating their place in the top Division with ninth position in the final table. It was possibly the form away from home (5-0 defeats at both Liverpool and Huddersfield, 5-1 at West Bromwich Albion and 7-0 at Blackburn being good examples) that prevented it from being a more memorable step up from the Second Division. The F. A. Cup also created much excitement, but hopes of an appearance in the Final came to a halt at Bramall Lane Sheffield, with a 3-0 defeat at the hands of Manchester City.

Two newcomers to the side during the first season back in Division One for three years were William Inglis and James McCrae. Neither were to make much of an impact, either this season or throughout their careers with United, as they only managed a total of twenty three League appearances between them.

James McCrae was the first to make his debut at left half, on January 16th against Arsenal, at Highbury, in the 3-2 defeat.

Born into a footballing family in the Bridge of Weir, McCrae played with Clyde before joining West Ham United in 1919, at the end of the First World War. Half a century of League appearances later, a £750 fee took him to Bury, where he was to spend three years. From there he moved to Wigan Borough during September 1923, before becoming a Manchester United player in August 1925, joining them after spending a year with New Brighton.

Following his debut, he was only to play first team football on a further twelve occasions, all during 1925-26, (eight in the League and four during the F.A. Cup run).

Prior to the start of season 1926-27 he moved back to the London area and joined Watford.

William Inglis on the other hand, began his playing career in his native Fife, with Kirkcaldy United and Raith Rovers, where he was captain of a team which also included the legendary Scottish internationalist Alex James (who was later to make a name for himself at Arsenal).

With the Kirkcaldy side, whom he joined in August 1914,

he played a total of 204 League games, after making his debut during season 1914-15. He was also selected as a reserve for the Scottish League against the English League at Ibrox in March 1922.

Just over two years later, in June 1924, after having been on the transfer list, he was sold to Sheffield Wednesday for a fee of £250 and he took the road south to Yorkshire, hoping to earn fame and fortune.

His stay with Wednesday was to be brief and he joined United the following summer and as a full back, was considered "a sound, experienced and sturdy defender".

He had to wait until March 20th 1926 though, before making his debut against Everton in the 0-0 draw at Old Trafford and in a report of the match, which carried the headline – "United Newcomers Give A Good Display", the following was written. "Manchester's much changed side included Stewart (a misprint which should have been Steward) in goal and two reserve full backs, Inglis and Jones, who put up as good a show as anyone".

Missing the next four games, he returned to the first team for the last half dozen games of the season, scoring the only goal in the 1-0 win against Cardiff City and once again receiving favourable comments in the press.

He began the following season as first choice right back, but after only six games lost his place and was soon to find himself further down the pecking order following the signing of Charlie Moore.

In the reserve eleven, he became captain and seemed to be content to play at this level, as it was not until Boxing Day

1928 that he made what was to be his last appearance in the Manchester United first team, playing at right back against Sheffield United away. A game United lost 6-1.

Bill Inglis remained at Old Trafford until June 1930, when at the age of thirty six, when many players of that age were considering retirement, he joined Northampton Town. With the 'Cobblers' he played for a further two years, making sixty appearances.

Upon his eventual retirement, he took up the post of trainer with the Northampton side, gaining valuable experience, which was to stand him in good stead and enable him to return to his beloved United in August 1934 as assistant trainer to Tom Curry.

As reserve team trainer, the man who had at one time played sixty-five consecutive games in the United reserve and first team had a very big influence over the playing careers of many future stars.

A role that he filled enthusiastically until he eventually retired from the game for good in may 1961, ending a thirty-one year association with Manchester United.

The appointment of Lal Hilditch as United player manager in October 1926, following John Chapman's dismissal, did not bring much of an immediate change, results wise, in the team's fortune. However, in the latter half of his brief occupation of the manager's chair, the line up seemed to change from game to game, (between January and April, he was to use twenty six different players), something that is reflected in the results of that particular period.

One Saturday afternoon United were losing 6-0 at Sunderland, while seven days later defeating West Bromwich Albion 2-0 or going to the opposite extreme of beating Sheffield United 5-0 at Old Trafford, but losing their next home, game against Liverpool 1-0.

Hilditch's tenure at the helm came to an end in April 1927, when Herbert Bamlett replaced him. Bamlett had already had some brief involvement with United, albeit in controversial circumstances. The one time referee, had been the official in charge of the infamous F. A. Cup tie between Burnley and United when, with Burnley winning 1-0, he abandoned the match, amid a snowstorm, with some eighteen minutes still to play.

One of the players introduced by Hilditch during that Mid-season shuffle was **Albert Smith**, a centre forward, who had come to United in October 1925, from junior side Petershill in his native Glasgow.

Smith had managed to find consistent form in the reserve side, before making his debut against Leeds United on January 22nd 1927, as a replacement for John Hanson. After only two outings, he found himself back in the reserves, but a further injury to Hanson saw him brought back into the side at Bury on March 5th, when he scored United's only goal in a 2-1 defeat. Despite this, he was dropped once again, after playing against Birmingham City the following Saturday. Just over one month and one other first team outing later, he found himself on the transfer list.

In the summer of 1927 he made the relatively short journey across Lancashire and joined Preston North End. Unfortunately, there was to be only a slight change in fortune, as he found himself in and out of the side, making only forty appearances over four seasons.

Deciding on a complete change of scenery to re-charge his batteries, Smith crossed the Irish Sea and joined Dolphin F.C., who played in the Irish Free State League, where he played during season 1931-32.

The following season, 1932-33, was spent with Carlisle United, where he at last managed to command a regular first team place. It was, however, to be his last season in League football.

One of Herbert Bamlett's early signings for the club was **William Johnston**, a player of undoubted ability, who was soon to make a name for himself at Old Trafford. As a schoolboy, the Edinburgh born Johnston captained the city team before representing Scotland Schools against England at Wolverhampton and Wales at Hampden Park. Upon leaving school, he signed for Dalkeith Thistle, an Edinburgh Junior League side, where he was to play for eighteen months.

When he was little more than sixteen years of age, he lied about his age to enable him to enlist with the Royal Flying Corps and serve in the First World War. Whilst stationed near Montrose, he represented the RAF and upon a move to a station nearer to Edinburgh, he turned out a couple of times for Hearts.

Upon his demob, aged eighteen, he joined Yorkshire League side Selby Town, as a professional, having been stationed near there for some time.

He had only been a Selby player for three months, before Huddersfield Town agreed to pay their Yorkshire neighbours £250 for his signature. For their outlay, Huddersfield enjoyed his services over a five year period, although the majority of this was spent in the reserve team as an inside left.

He also spent some time out of action with a leg injury, which took some time to heal properly.

In December 1924, back at full fitness, Stockport County saw enough in William Johnston to offer Huddersfield £1,500 for the player and it proved to be money well spent, as he was soon became a firm favourite with the supporters during his three seasons at Edgely Park.

Having been watched by United manager Herbert Bamlett and captain Frank Barson, in a Stockport County reserve match against Tranmere Rovers, following recommendations by former Stockport team mate Frank Wilson, an approach was made to sign Johnston. It was to take two days of negotiations, before United paid double the fee that had taken him from Huddersfield to County.

He made his United debut the day after signing, against Cardiff City, at Old Trafford, on October 15th 1927 and was to miss only one other match all season. Scoring eight goals in his thirty-one appearances. Perhaps a disappointing scoring return for the number of games played, but the United programme of November 19th 1927, contained the following about the player – "It is not the number of goals he gets himself, but the way he creates openings for others. We at Old Trafford have appreciated what a great footballer he is".

Season 1928-29 saw him in and out of the side, mainly due once again to injury, playing in only twelve games (scoring five goals). During the close season, whilst negotiating a new contract, a difference of opinion arose between player and club, which led to Johnston being placed on the transfer list.

For an individual who was a superb creative player, it was somewhat strange that he was to drop into the Cheshire League with Macclesfield Town, captaining them on many occasions, upon leaving United.

The early 1930's saw United struggling once again and with Walter Crickmer now the man in charge of team affairs, Billy Johnson returned to Old Trafford, in May 1931, in a bid to help out.

Injury again played a big part in the number of games he managed to play in, although he was to score eleven goals in his twenty eight appearances.

In May 1932, he joined Oldham Athletic, who moved him from his familiar inside forward position to half back and during his three years at Boundary Park, he also turned his hand to coaching the clubs' youngsters. Leaving the 'Latics in June 1935, he joined Frickley Colliery, a Midland League club, as player manager, showing an eye for talent, signing numerous players who went on to play at a higher level.

Struggling at the wrong end of Division One in the early days of season 1927-28, with only two wins from the opening seven fixtures and again in the second half of the campaign, with only three wins between Christmas Eve and the beginning of April, manager Herbert Bamlett decided to install some new fire power up front, in what was a desparate attempt to avoid relegation. Following a 5-2 victory over Leicester City on February 11th, it took United a further eight games before they had scored five more goals.

Into the side came **George Nichol**, a relatively unknown reserve team player, who had scored a creditable nine goals in only four reserve fixtures since joining United from Saltcoats Victoria, his local side, at the beginning of 1928. Goals had always come easy for the well built centre forward, finding the net regularly for not only Saltcoats but also his other previous clubs Ardrossan Winton

Rovers and Kilwinning.

Nichol's introduction into League football could not have got off to such a good start, even if he had planned it himself, scoring twice in the previously mentioned 5-2 win over Leicester City. Failure to find the net in the cup tie against Birmingham City seven days later and in the following League fixture against Cardiff, he found himself back in the second string. Injuries presented him with a further two outings four games later, against Aston Villa and Bolton Wanderers.

Both failed to produce the hoped for goals.

Back in the reserves as season 1928-29 got under way, the goals once again came regularly, unlike his first team opportunities, as he had to wait until December before he got, what were to be, his final two United first team appearances.

Having asked for a transfer as the season came to a close, he was offered terms by Brighton and without hesitation joined the south coast club. Finishing the season as their leading marksman with nineteen goals in twenty-five appearances, it was something of a surprise that he left and signed for Irish League team Glenavon.

Twelve months later, he was back on the mainland, having signed for Gillingham, where after almost three years and numerous goals, he was to bring an end to his career.

The centre forward position was certainly proving to be something of a problem for Herbert Bamlett, with George Nichol failing to go even part of the way to solving it. The United manager had moved the outside right of the past few season's and supporter's favourite, Joe Spence to the centre forward role, with some degree of success and then, following Nichol's failure to grasp the opportunity of a regular first team slot introduced William Rawlings into the team.

The newcomer certainly did not let the opportunity pass him by, scoring ten goals in the final twelve goals of season 1927-28.

Rawlings began the following season as the first choice

number nine, playing in nineteen of the first two dozen games, but this time only managing to score six goals. Not prepared to wait on the player re-discovering his scoring form, the manager replaced him with **Thomas Reid**, whose thirty-one goals in fifty-one appearances for Liverpool, was a major factor in his transfer from one end of the East Lancs. Road to the other.

Motherwell born Reid, was yet another product of the Scottish junior game, a true hat bed for footballing talent, playing for Blantyre Victoria before signing for Clydebank in the close season of 1925, where he was not long in showing that he possessed a pair of shooting boots. Soon afterwards, he was a Liverpool player following a £1,000 transfer.

The robust leader of the attack made a big impression at Anfield, as his goalscoring record shows and it came as a surprise to many that Manchester United managed to prise him from the Merseysiders grasp in February 1929.

At Old Trafford, he made an immediate impact, scoring on his League debut against West Ham United on February 2nd which was followed two games later with a double against his former employers.

Described as a "bustling type of player who could barge his way through a defence and despite the buffeting that he inevitably received, he was usually able to finish with a strong shot.

"The opposition certainly knew when Reid was playing. He never left them alone and did a great job of keeping the weight off his inside men".

Tommy Reid finished his debut season with fourteen goals from seventeen games, seven of those coming in four of the final five fixtures and was obviously the first choice centre forward for the following First Division challenge.

However, he was to begin the season indifferently, making only five appearances in the opening twenty-five fixtures and ended the season with only five goals from fifteen games, which was disappointing following the most promising start.

The relegation season of 1930-31 found him once again filling the centre forward position on the opening day of the season, scoring against Aston Villa at Old Trafford. Despite missing a dozen games, he still managed to finish the season

as top scorer with seventeen goals, ten more than his nearest rival. He also managed to score a hat trick in his F. A. Cup debut that season, against Stoke City, a game that ended in a 3-3 draw.

Disappointed at scoring a hat trick and still not end up on the winning side was something that Tommy Reid would experience on one other occasion, as on September 13th 1930, he netted three, with Rowley adding a fourth only to see Old Trafford opponents Newcastle United score seven.

During the Second Division campaign, Reid hit two hat tricks, against Forest and Oldham and one newspaper correspondent wrote "Reid can be one of the most dangerous forwards in the Second Division if he is plied with the ball as he likes it. The through pass is the kind he desires and if he gets the ball running in front of him, then Reid is one of the most dangerous leaders in the division".

Despite his 67 goals in 101 appearances, United allowed him to join near neighbours Oldham Athletic on loan, in March 1933, later to become a permanent move, which due to the 'Latics financial difficulties, saw their supporters club paying the £400 transfer fee. It was to be money well spent, as the new signing was to score ten goals in the final thirteen games of that season.

Tommy Reid played two years with the Boundary Park side before moving on to Barrow and later Rhyl Athletic.

After joining Manchester United (or Newton Heath), many individuals have went on to write their names into the record books and to play their part in helping the club create some piece of footballing history. Few were involved in particular noteworthy moments prior to pulling on the famous red shirt or whatever colour the club played in at that particular time. One individual who could claim his place in football history prior to his arriving at Manchester United was **George McLachlan**. His name will be unknown to most of the present day Old Trafford regulars, but mention it around Cardiff and it will be recalled that McLachlan was a member of the Cardiff City team who defeated Arsenal 1-0 in the 1927 F. A. Cup Final, to take the famous trophy out of England for the one and only time.

George McLachlan was Glasgow born and his playing career blossomed with Crosshill Amateurs, Parkhead Juniors (where he only stayed for two weeks) before joining Queens Park Strollers. Again, his time here was only brief, before taking the short journey to Shawfield to join Clyde in 1924.

Two years later, he was to suffer something of a set back, when he broke his leg, an injury which came at a time when he was pushing for Scotland international honours. Fighting back to fitness, he managed to get back to his previous best and in November 1925, Cardiff City paid a fee of £2,000 to take him to Wales. Following the F. A. Cup success of 1927, McLachlan was once again unfortunate on the international front, failing to make the full Scotland side following his appearance in the Anglo's versus Home Scots trial in 1928.

Searching for players to bolster the Manchester United towards the end of 1929, club officials journeyed to Wales and the talented outside left caught their eye and was duly signed.

His debut came on December 21st 1929 against Leeds United at home, beginning a notable Old Trafford career, playing his part in the 3-1 win.

Midway through season 1930-31, a season that saw him play in all forty-two League games, he was to switch from his familiar outside left position to left half, a position from which he captained the United team during the latter half of season 1931-32.

During the following season, 1932-33, he missed several games and did, briefly, return to his outside left spot towards the end of April. By some quirk of fate, those four games in the position in which he made his name, were to be his last for the club, as he moved to Chester during the close season, taking up a player coach position.

Leaving Chester in 1934, he took up a managerial/coaching role with Le Harve and only left a year later as he had heard of a vacancy for a manager at Queen Of The South and upon applying was offered the position.

A notable professional, who during his twelve year career, played in over 400 League games and filled eight different positions.

Having consolidated their place in the First Division following promotion at the end of season 1924-25, the mid-table position soon altered to one of severe concern, with relegation creeping closer and closer with each passing campaign.

At the end of 1930-31, the inevitable eventually happened, with the name of Manchester United propping up the First Division table with a mere twenty-two points from their forty-two games. Their worst return since season 1893-94. What was equally disturbing was the goals against column, which showed one hundred and fifteen conceded. This included nineteen in a three game run in September (6-2 .v. Chelsea away, 6-0 .v. Huddersfield home and 7-4 .v. Newcastle home).

Following relegation, manager Bamlett resigned, with Walter Crickmer taking over on a temporary basis. United were, however, now a club in crisis.

By Christmas 1931, they were broke and even a public meeting, seeking financial assistance from the supporters failed to boost the diminishing coffers.

Having been rescued once, by Mr J. H. Davies, a similar benefactor was now sought. Mr J. W. Gibson, having already taken something of an interest in the running of the club and also having paid the players wages, agreed to become financially involved even further, as long as he was certain of the support from the terracing.

Attendances did increase, somewhat dramatically, with the 4,697 against Bristol City on December 19th 1931 becoming 33,123 eight days later against Wolverhampton Wanderers. It dropped to 6,056 for the following fixture, but as the second half of the season progressed, bringing something of an improvement on the pitch, it rose to around 17,000 to 20,000 mark.

During season 1931-32, Walter Crickmer called on the services of some 34 players, with the small Scottish contingent of McLachlan, Johnston and Reid strengthened by the arrival of **Dick Black** for the final few games of the season.

Signed from Morton, surprisingly after the transfer deadline day, United somehow managed to obtain permission to play him in their final three games .
His two goals in the latter two of those fixtures bode

well for the following season, but he was to face disappointment following the appointment of a new manager, Mr A. S. Duncan.

In the Manchester Evening Chronicle, prior to the start of the 1932-33 season, the merits of the two players vying for the centre forward spot – Black and Reid were debated. Following an "indifferent performance in the pre-season trial" by Reid, it was thought that Black would lead the line and the newspaper's United correspondent of the time wrote "Black's weakness appears to be in turning with the ball. He hesitates instead of getting away, but he is not the kind of leader to shirk a tackle and he is ready to avail himself of any weakness in the opposing defence.

"We must not forget, however, that he is now in English football".

Black did indeed claim the centre forward position for the opening match of 1932-33 against Stoke City, but failed to do so again that season. His next first team outing was not in fact until November 25th 1933, filling the outside left spot against Bradford City, in what was to be a four match run, scoring one goal, in the second of those against Port Vale.

Those were indeed to be his last games for the club, returning to Scotland in November of the following year, to join St Mirren.

It is somewhat strange that Black spent so long out of the United side without being giving an opportunity of an extended run in the team to show what he could do, as there were numerous occasions when his goalscoring ability would have been an advantage. In the reserves, he scored regularly, with thirty three goals during 1932-33, but there was obviously something in his style that the new manager did not care for. Surprising, as they were both Scots!

The signing of Dick Black after the transfer deadline in April 1932 was not the only one made by the club at that particular time, with fellow countryman **William McDonald** also taking the road south.

The Coatbridge born McDonald had played most of his early football in Scotland within the junior ranks, turning out for his hometown club, Broxburn United and Laws Scotia. He had, however, spent a few months with Dundee during season 1925-26, returning to the professional game

in May 1928 with Airdrieonians.

It was from Airdrie, where he played some 144 games, scoring 33 goals, that he joined United and like Dick Black, he was given permission to play in the last few games of season 1931-32, as they did not involve any Championship or relegation issues. He did in fact only play, at inside right, in two of the last three games.

Much was expected of the player during season 1932-33, following a good pre-season, but despite featuring in the opening half dozen games, he was to play n only twenty one of the fixtures, scoring four goals.

The following term, he featured in the first team on only four occasions and it came as no surprise that at the end of 1933-34 he left the club, joining Tranmere Rovers. Two years later, he moved to Coventry City for three seasons and in the summer of June 1939 he signed for Plymouth Argyle, but was to have his career brought to a premature end due the outbreak of the Second World War.

By the time season 1932-33 got underway, United were under the guidance of A. Scott Duncan, a manager with quite a notable career as a player and someone who was happy to enlist the help of Scottish born players to the United cause, in the hope that could turn around the club's fortune and take them back into the first Division.

Adam Scott Mathieson Duncan, to give him his full title, was the son of a Dumbarton butcher and upon leaving the local academy, began work in a solicitors' office.

In November 1905, the professional footballing side of his career got underway with Dumbarton, following an apprenticeship of sorts with the likes of Dumbarton Oakvale, Dumbarton Corinthians, Clydebank Juniors and Shettleston Juniors. Just over two years later, in March 1908, Newcastle United had taken the talented young outside right to the North-East of England, for a fee of £150.

Progress in the black and white striped shirts was quick and noteworthy, with a League Championship medal being won in 1909. His performances with the Magpies did not go unnoticed back home, and in 1913, Glasgow Rangers perhaps slightly aggrieved at missing out on the talented forward whilst playing practically on their doorstep, stepped in with a £500 offer that Newcastle accepted.

Six years at Ibrox came to a halt in 1919, with the outbreak of war and whilst stationed close to home, at the Royal Field Artillery barracks in Maryhill, Glasgow, he became one of a select band of footballers to play for both sides of the Glasgow 'Old Firm', turning out for Celtic in two war-time fixtures in January 1919.

This came as something of a surprise to many, as Rangers were only slightly ahead of their rivals in the League and victory in both the fixtures Scott Duncan played, saw them edge closer.

Upon the resumption of domestic football after World War One, following appearances with both Partick Thistle and Dumbarton, Duncan continued to turn out for the latter until Cowdenbeath secured his signature in 1920.

Having switched from the left wing to the right, he spent a couple of years with his latest club, before briefly returning once again to Dumbarton prior to taking up the post of secretary-manager with Hamilton Academicals in July 1923.

Success at this level was as instant as it had been as a player, with Hamilton reaching the semi-final of the Scottish Cup and a satisfactory position in the First Division.

In July 1925, he took up a similar post with Cowdenbeath, with the Fife side enjoying a prolonged stay in the top flight of the Scottish League during his seven years in charge.

His managerial ability was not passing unnoticed, with both Ayr United and Sunderland keen to employ him, but as it has been for many others, the lure of Old Trafford proved too strong and in the summer of 1932, he packed his bags and headed for Manchester.

A mid-table Second Division club when Scott Duncan took over, a jump of six places was made by the end of his initial term in charge. However, it was not to be a push for promotion twelve months later, as the team slumped badly and avoiding relegation by the skin of their teeth.

Season 1934-35 did see things improve, finishing the season in a more respectable fifth position, with the Second Division Championship being won twelve months later. Having begun their first season back in Division One for six years rather indifferently, improvement was hoped for. However, it came as something of a shock to supporters and board members alike, when Scott Duncan announced his resignation as manager.

The decision, had nothing whatsoever to do with football, but was made with the health of his wife in mind. Since moving to Manchester, Mrs Duncan had found the industrial atmosphere not to her liking and was eventually advised by her doctor that a change of environment would be for the best.

So, in November 1937, the Duncan's left Manchester for the fresh air of East Anglia, with Scott taking over the managers job at Ipswich Town, then in the Southern League.

At Ipswich, he was instrumental in their climb to Football League status, before stepping down in 1955, to become club secretary, laying the foundations for Alf Ramsey to take over and lead the club to the First Division Championship in the early sixties.

In 1958, aged almost 70 and having been awarded a long service medal by the Football League and a testimonial by Ipswich (in which United were due to play, but had to pull out of due to the Munich disaster), Scott Duncan finally retired from the game, returning home to Scotland and settling in Helensburgh.

No sooner had Scott Duncan unpacked his belongings and settled in Manchester in the summer of 1933, than he was heading back over Hadrians Wall in an effort to strengthen the United playing staff. As he only had a squad of some twenty seven full time professionals, not exactly spoiling him for choice, he felt that the quality of the team was rather poor and one or two of the positions required additional cover.

First to be recruited by Duncan was **James Brown**, whose transfer to Manchester United must rank as one of the most unusual in the club's history.

Brown was born in Kilmarnock and with the junior clubs in the Ayrshire area being ten a penny so to speak, it was no surprise that he should progress to this level from schools football. Firstly with the oddly named Loans Athletic and later Plainfield.

At the age of seventeen, in 1927, he decided to leave not just Kilmarnock, but Scotland and emigrate to America, to work as a blacksmith's striker.

With football being actively played in the States at this time, he was not long in finding a club with whom to pass away his leisure hours, joining the New Jersey based Boyonne Rovers. His performances were of a standard that did not go unnoticed and with a lack of real talent in the American game, his services as a footballer were eagerly sought by numerous American Soccer League sides. Newark Skeeters, New York Giants and Brooklyn Wanderers were all to benefit from the inclusion of James Brown in their line up.

1930 saw James Brown brought into the American squad, along with five other former Scottish professionals, for the World Cup competition in Montevideo. To everyone's surprise, the American's, mainly thanks to the outsiders within their ranks, made it through to the semi-final stage, defeating Belgium 3-0, with Brown at left half.

Paraguay were then defeated by a similar score line, before the American's were knocked out by Argentina. James Brown, playing at outside right, scoring the Americans only goal in their 6-1 defeat, two minutes from the end.

It is worth noting, that the score line did not necessary mean that the South Americans were a much better side than the U.S.A., who were in many quarters favourites to win the competition, it came about more because of the injuries suffered by the novice footballing nation.

After ten minutes, they lost their centre half with a broken leg, while at the end of the first forty-five minutes, their left half was seriously injured by a kick in the face. In addition to this, their goalkeeper played out the game barely able to stand, following an early collision with an opposing forward. In 1932, Brown decided to return home and news of his impending arrival soon spread swiftly amongst the football

world and set numerous club's on red alert. Partick Thistle and Heart of Midlothian were considered favourites in the race to obtain his signature.

In Manchester, Scott Duncan was also well aware of Brown's decision to return home and made discrete enquiries as to his route and time of expected arrival.

Obtaining the answers required, Duncan was soon to set off for Northern Ireland in what was indeed an undercover mission of extreme secrecy, akin to something from a spy novel.

Arriving in Londonderry, with Brown's liner, the S.S. Caledonia, still on the high seas, he somehow managed to make radio contact with the ship, eventually speaking to Brown himself and informing him of his intentions.

When the liner docked, Scott Duncan was waiting as Brown walked down the gangplank and the signing was finally agreed, with the player putting pen to paper a week later.

James Brown made his Manchester United debut on September 17th 1932, in the outside right position against Grimsby Town and added a few more lines to his rather amazing life story by scoring United's only goal in the 1-1 draw direct from a corner kick.

For the remainder of season 1932-33, the tall, lightly built forward drifted between the two wing positions, scoring ten goals in his twenty-five outings.

The following season, despite his early promise, saw him mainly employed in the reserves, with Jackie Cape securing the outside right berth for himself, in the second half of the season.

A move to Brentford in the close season of 1934 failed to bring the first team football Brown sought and following spells with Tottenham Hotspur, Guilford City and Clydebank between 1936 and 1940, he decided to return to America after the Second World War.

Back in the United States, he took up coaching appointments with various club's and schools, finally retiring in 1975.

Two weeks after his Manchester United debut, James Brown was joined at Old Trafford by two other Scots, Tommy Frame and William Stewart Chalmers as Scott Duncan, not content to rest on his laurels with his cheeky capture of Brown, decided to improve his United side with players who were already known to him.

Centre half **Tommy Frame** was signed from Cowdenbeath, whom he had joined in 1926 from his local side Burnbank Athletic.

As Cowdenbeath player, his attributes had not been entirely appreciated and it was only after he was loaned out to Lochgelly United, where he made a big impression, that he became a regular in the heart of their defence, playing some 161 games.

Such were his performances, that he was selected for Scottish international trial matches during 1930-31, only just failing to make the final eleven.

As an ex-miner, he had the physical strength to make an impression in the heart of the defence and it took a transfer fee of £1,000 to enable Scott Duncan to take him to Manchester United.

In his early days at United, he perhaps used the physical side of his play just that little bit too much, as he was sent off in only his fourth game, However, he was to miss only two fixtures during his first season in English football, contributing two goals.

The following season, 1933-34 saw him fill not only the centre half position but also right half, inside right and left back, as Scott Duncan's side struggled, despite having finished 1932-33 in sixth position.

With Frame's strength and determination a great benefit to United's relegation struggle, both club and player were dealt a severe blow when he received a broken leg during the 2-0 win against Blackpool at Old Trafford on March 31st.

The injury effectively brought an end to his United career, although it was the summer of 1936 before he was to leave Manchester, signing for Southport.

Despite playing in thirty-eight games during 1936-37, he called a halt to his professional career at the end of that season, moving into non-League football with Rhyl Athletic and later Bridgend Town between 1937 and 1939.

The other new signing, **W. S. Chalmers** had came from Heart of Midlothian and was a typical Scottish inside forward – small in stature, big in heart. He posessed exceptional ball control and the ability to trap and play the ball to a team mate in an instant, moving into space for the return pass.

Born in the Mount Florida district of Glasgow, Chalmers was a Schoolboy internationalist and not unexpectedly joined Queens Park, whose Hampden headquarters were within easy walking distance of his home.

Whilst with the famous old club, he won two amateur international caps and in June 1929, whilst still an amateur, was selected at inside right for the full Scotland side to face Northern Ireland in Belfast. In this match, which scotland won 7-3, he was something of the odd man out in a star studded forward line, which consisted of Alec Jackson, Hughie Gallacher, Alex James and Alan Morton

The summer of 1929 saw him join the professional ranks, signing for Heart of Midlothian, where on occasions he was left out of the team if the game was considered to be one which might have a physical edge to it, as he was more adapted to the finer side of the game.

A three year spell at Tynecastle, where he made fifty-eight appearances and scored thirteen goals, came to an end with his move to Manchester on September 26th 1932 for a fee of £2,500.

Stewart Chalmers, a qualified Chartered Accountant, who had sometimes found it difficult to get all the time off work that he required for games, made his United debut on the same afternoon as Tommy Frame. But, he failed to make the same impression south of the border as he had in Scotland and he was to see another of Scott Duncan's new signings, Ernie Hine, taking over his inside right position.

During 1933-34, he was in and out of the team, making only a dozen appearances out of the possible forty-two. His opportunities were now, obviously limited and it came as no surprise when he decided that he had had enough of life in Manchester and returned to Scotland to join Dunfermline Athletic. This was in September 1934 and he was to remain here until his retiral from the game in 1938.

Scott Duncan's expenses sheet during his first season in charge of Manchester United must have raised a few eyebrows and also the petty cash expenditure, with numerous trips around the countryside in search of new players. Scotland was as likely a destination as anywhere, returning to sign players who had attracted his attention during his time up there.

Another such signing was **William Stewart**, who made his United debut on November 19th 1932 against Fulham at Old Trafford. Glasgow born Stewart was already familiar to Scott Duncan through his performances with Cowdenbeath, a team he had joined at the start of the previous season from Shettleton Juniors.

The diminutive, 5'5" outside left became a big favourite with the Cowdenbeath support, scoring eleven goals in fifty-three games, thrilling them on many occasions with his wide array of talents.

Scott Duncan's return to his old club for his former player was to cost United £2,350, but despite this, he was to make only forty-nine appearances over two seasons, scoring a meagre seven goals. He also scored twice in United's 10-1 victory over Cowdenbeath in a friendly at Old Trafford.

With United involved in a fight at the foot of the table in the latter half of 1933-34, money was urgently required to invest in a player, or players, who could score goals. Stewart was considered a player who could bring in some of the much needed cash and along with Charles McGillivray, he was sold to Motherwell.

Back in Scotland, he helped his new club to the runners-up spot in the Scottish League First Division, arriving just in time to play in the last handful of games.

The Lanarkshire side was, however, to be Stewart's last League club, staying with them until 1937.

With an overdraft of around £15,286 at the bank, quite a sum in those days, it would be thought that the manager's spending would have been severely curtailed. He must, however, have had a very persuasive personality, as no sooner had he bought Stewart, Frame and Chalmers, than he was out spending a further £10,000 on Ernie Hine and yet

another Scot, Neil Dewar. Scott Duncan perhaps thought of the latter as being the final piece of his jigsaw, as Dewar was indeed a class act.

Neil Dewar was born in the Scottish Highlands, in Lochgilphead, Argylshire and played his early football with his school side and the local Lochgilphead United. Word of mouth soon brought his unquestionable talents to the attention of many outwith the heather strewn Highland hills, but the young Neil Dewar was content to remain in his local friendly community.

Persistence by Third Lanark eventually paid off and Dewar journeyed south for a few outings with their reserve side. It took little time for the Glasgow side to see that here was a player who could play a big part in the club's future and he was quickly signed, before any of their rivals could move in with a better financial inducement.

So, in October 1929, Neil Dewar became a Third Lanark player, leaving behind his beloved Highlands and his work as a trawler fisherman, for the hustle and bustle of big city life.

Dewar quickly adapted to life in Glasgow and to the rigours of Scottish League football, gaining new admirers with almost every ninety minutes that he played.

Almost six foot in height and weighing thirteen stone, he was certainly an imposing figure, with both attributes assisting him greatly in his quest for goals – 124 in four seasons with the now defunct Glasgow side.

Season 1931-32 saw Dewar, a well known public speaker in Scotland, at perhaps the pinnacle of his career Having scored thirty five goals in thirty six games with Third Lanark, the twenty-three-year old was selected to represent Scotland against England at Wembley.

His performance beneath the twin towers saw his talents noted by an even wider field, despite Scotland losing 3-0 and a thirty yard goal at Maine Road on November 9th 1932 for the Scottish League against their English counterparts confirmed and strengthened the opinion that many already had of him.

Further full caps had been won against France in 1931-32, when he scored a hat trick in a devastating display and Wales the following season, when he again scored. Further League representative honours had also followed by the time that Scott Duncan decided that he wanted Neil Dewar at Old Trafford.

His goal scoring form in the early months of 1932-33 had been on a similar level to that of previous seasons, with a total of twenty-three from twenty-eight games for the Hi Hi. So it was not surprising that the United manager had to pay out £5,000 to obtain his signature in February 1933. True to form, Dewar scored on his Manchester United debut, against Preston North End on February 11th, helping his new team mates to a 3-3 draw. In his fifteen games, playing at centre forward, in the latter half of that season, he scored a total of six goals. He had found the adjustment between the different League's a slight problem and went home to Scotland for the summer "in badly need of a rest".

There was definitely high hopes for the player whose clever footwork was a delight to watch, but perhaps the Manchester Evening Chronicle's United correspondent had been slightly more observant than most during the early days of the Scotsman's United career.

In his early season assessment for season 1933-34, he was to write – "In Scotland, Dewar was a great leader because the style of football there is different to that played here. A centre forward in English Second Division football has to takes knocks, and is usually carefully watched, especially when he has the reputation of Dewar.

"He has shown that he is a skilful player. He can manoeuvre the ball within a small area, but he has been overdoing his cleverness and has tried to walk the ball past the goalkeeper. "My advice to Dewar is to shoot hard and often whenever he is inside the penalty area. He must rid himself of the tendency to take the ball closer to goal, and believe that if he adopts this style he will be a big success".

Neil Dewar began season 1933-34 at centre forward and following a goal less opening six games, blasted his critics with four goals in the 5-2 win at Burnley. To the surprise of many, only a further four goals were to follow, as the player was never able to fulfil the reputation that he had developed and brought with him across the border.

In December 1933, United and Neil Dewar, (who was known by the strange nickname of 'Silversleeves' due to his habit of wiping his nose on the sleeve of his shirt during games) parted company, with the player crossing the Pennines to join Sheffield Wednesday in a player exchange for Jack Ball.

Sixth position in Division Two at the end of season 1932-33, a jump of six places from the previous season, was considered highly satisfactory in what could have been considered something of a transitional period as it was Scott Duncan's first season in charge. Many hoped that the foundations had been laid for a successful period ahead. The close season of 1933 brought a flurry of comings and goings, with a total of eleven departures and six signings, as having had time to assess his playing staff, the manager begun to build his own team.

Surprisingly though, only one of the new arrivals, **Charles McGillivary**, was Scottish!

The former Scottish Schoolboy internationalist was born in West Lothian and progressed into the junior game with Deghorn Juniors.

At the age of eighteen, he joined Ayr United and in two seasons with the Somerset Park club, he scored nineteen goals in forty-four outings. Such form, and excellent goal return for a winger, did not go unobserved and at the end of season 1931-32, Glasgow Celtic, following a successful trial against St Mirren, when he scored twice, snapped him up.

With the Parkhead club, he found it difficult to break into the first team, but continued to perform to a high standard in the second eleven. The lack of opportunities was a big disappointment for the twenty-one year old and his frustrations were brought to the attention of Scott Duncan. An approach was made to the club and player, and prior to the start of the 1933-34 season the United manager travelled to Glasgow to sign him, in the rather

peculiar surroundings of an ice cream parlour close to Glasgow's Central Station.

At the time, many associated with Celtic thought that the club had made a mistake in allowing him to leave.

"McGillivray, the former Glasgow Celtic outside right, is a great capture" commented the astute Evening Chronicle reporter. "He is a two footed player who knows the way to goal".

McGillivray began season 1933-34 as first choice outside right, but due to several poor overall team performances, including a 5-1 home defeat by bolton Wanderers, he found himself in the reserves after only five games.

Despite the poor team displays throughout the season, Charles McGillivray was only to find his name written on the first team sheet on two more occasions and in the summer took the road north, along with Willie Stewart to sign for Motherwell.

At Fir Park, his career continued along the same path that it had whilst with United and Celtic, finding himself more than often in the reserves throughout his four years there. Upon his departure from Motherwell in October 1938, he began a whirlwind tour of Scottish clubs, turning out for Dundee, Hearts, Albion Rovers, Morton, Dunfermline Athletic, Dundee United, Hibs and Dundee United again. All in a six year spell.

In January 1944, he was appointed player manager of the last mentioned club, Dundee United, holding the position for only one year, before joining Stirling Albion as a player. He was later to play for Arbroath and in local Dundee football before emigrating to America in 1949.

Emigration, was something that might have crossed the minds of many United supporters during the 1933-34 season, taking them far away from the disappointments of Old Trafford.

The campaign got off to a far from ideal start with a 4-0 defeat against Plymouth Argyle and with the opening five fixtures failing to produce a win, with only three goals scored and twelve conceded, it was obvious that it would be a long, testing season.

A 4-3 victory at Brentford on September 16th, was the first of the season and was followed by a 5-2 victory over Burnley, with Neil Dewar scoring four. The change in

fortune, however, was only temporary, as it was another month before the next two points were won with a 4-1 win over Hull City.

The 2-1 defeat at home to Notts County on December 9th was the beginning of a downward slide that would plunge the club into severe trouble. Had the final outcome been different, then it was more than a possibility that the Manchester United of today, would be a far cry from the club that we are familiar with.

Following that 2-1 defeat at the home of Notts County, United took only three points from the next twelve games, conceding thirty-eight goals. With only nine fixtures remaining, time was now slowly running out for Scott Duncan's beleaguered side.

With the transfer deadline looming on the horizon, the manager plunged headlong into the transfer market, with a frenzy of activity, in the hope that some new blood would help the club out of its present predicament. Onto the Manchester United pay role came goalkeeper Jack Hacking, right back Jack Griffiths and half backs William Robertson and William McKay. There had to be some Scottish blood in the transfusion, with the latter two fitting into that category, both being signed on March 15th.

William McKay, hailed from West Benhar, amid the Lanarkshire coal fields and was an unusually versatile player who could quickly settle in any position. He was also renowned for turning up on match day's besplendid in his immaculate three-piece suit and black bowler hat.

In 1925 he joined East Stirlingshire from Shotts Battlefield F. C., spending two years with them before Hamilton Accademicals managed to prise him away.

With Hamilton, where he played inside right, scoring twenty goals in seventy-eight appearances, over a two year period, was a satisfactory return and enough to earn him a move south to Bolton Wanderers in 1932. Strangely, his Bolton debut was a 1-1 draw against United at Old Trafford in December 1929 and he went on to play over 100 games for the Wanderers, scoring seventeen goals.

In the need to bolster his defence, as well as find someone

who could be a creator of goal scoring opportunities, Scott Duncan brought McKay, "a soccer tactician, who made full use of every ball", the short distance to Manchester.

After playing his part in the last gasp rescue mission, he contributed to the club's eventual climb from the verge of obscurity, serving United well up until the outbreak of the Second World War.

During the hostilities, he played with Stockport County and Port Vale, before joining Stalybridge Celtic in 1946.

McKay's fellow countryman **William Robertson** was one of the few Scots who did not come direct from a Scottish League club, moving to Old Trafford from Stoke City, having previously been with Third Lanark, and Ayr United, moving to the Potteries in October 1929.

His performances during Ayr's Scottish 'B' League Championship win of 1927-28 had brought him to the attention of other club's, but it was not until just over a year later that he was to move away.

With Stoke City, the Falkirk born wing half added to his collection of honours, with a Second Division Championship medal in 1932-33, playing in all but three of their fixtures. Like McKay, his solid tackling and prompting, played a big part in the nail biting final few games of United's 1933-34 season and he retained his place in the line up the following season, missing only the odd game through injury.

Season 1935-36 saw him dropped to the reserves, as James Brown took over the right half berth and with only one appearance by December, he decided his best option was a move to another club, eventually joining Reading in the Southern Section of the Third Division.

With one fixture of season 1933-34 remaining, against fellow strugglers Millwall away, United were second from bottom, seven points in front of the already relegated Lincoln City and one behind Millwall, with a much inferior goal difference. Nothing short of a victory was enough to keep United from the jaws of the Third Division.

Early in the game, Hine was injured and had to move to the wing, Manley moving inside. It was a move that soon turned out to be more a blessing than a hindrance, with the latter opening the scoring for United.

As the first half wore on, the home side pressed forward, but failed to capitalise on numerous scoring opportunities. Changing ends with a one goal lead, the United players felt slightly more confident than they had been at the start

A second goal by Jackie Cape was enough to give United the victory they needed to remain a Second Division club for at least another twelve months.

The contribution of McKay and Robertson to the afternoon's success could not be ignored, with both men playing their part in preventing the demise to the Third Division and possible obscurity.

Having survived by the skin of their teeth, with some thirty eight players called upon for first team duty throughout the season, season 1934-35 arrived like a breath of fresh air, allowing the team to play in a more relaxed style, away from the harrowing pressures of relegation.

Despite four defeats in the opening six fixtures, the team soon found its feet, winning the next eight on the trot, scoring twenty-three goals, conceding only four. Things were beginning look up.

One player who had made a distinct difference to the side was inside right George Mutch, who had scored ten of those goals (including a hat trick against Barnsley) in the opening fourteen games.

Aberdonian **George Mutch**, who, like his fellow countryman George McLachlan, etched his name into the football history books, through his involvement in the F. A. Cup, but this was to be after his days as a Manchester United player. Such thoughts, however, were far from the mind of the former Schoolboy internationalist, whilst playing his early football with the likes of Avondale and Banks o' Dee on the Scottish non-League circuit. Joining Arbroath, Mutch began to blossom into a player of distinct promise and one or two of the bigger Scottish club's were beginning to sit up and take notice of his performances with the Second Division outfit. South of the border though, he was something of an unknown, but Scott Duncan, with his astute knowledge of the

T / R

Scottish game, knew only too well that the £800 it cost to bring Mutch from the East of Scotland to Manchester, in the close season of 1934, was money well spent. Through time, the player was considered an excellent acquisition.

Mutch, however, was quick to play down his arrival in Manchester. Being somewhat rather nervous of his new surroundings, he was to tell a Manchester Evening Chronicle reporter – "It is a big place and I am afraid of going out in case I get lost. And what a lovely ground Old Trafford is. "I have never played before a bigger crowd than 10,000 and that was in a Scottish Schoolboy international match, so I may feel a little strange at first. But I have come to Old Trafford to do my best to help United to get back into the First Division".

And help them he certainly did. His eighteen goals in forty appearances during 1934-35 had seen United finish fifth and with the ghosts of the previous season now exorcised, the future looked bright.

Season 1935-36 opened with a defeat, 3-1 at Plymouth, and stuttered along until the turn of the year. A 1-0 defeat at Bradford City on January 4th, the first in five games, was actually the last reversal of the season and the unbeaten run of nineteen games took United to the Second Division Championship.

George Mutch's season had run a similar course to that of the team. Only four goals up until the end of November, then a burst of six in five games up until the defeat at Bradford. After that, they flowed with much regularity, ending the season once again as the club's top scorer, this time with twenty-one from his forty-two appearances. Again, like the team, his form during 1936-37 was rather indifferent compared to the previous two campaigns, appearing in only twenty-eight of the fixtures, scoring seven goals, as United slipped back into Division Two.

Despite this, and only making the United first team twice in the opening seven fixtures of 1937-38, Preston North End made a completely unexpected move for him. A fee of £5,000 eventually changing hands as George Mutch moved across Lancashire.

The intelligent inside forward felt immediately at home, with the Scottish accent predominant in the Deepdale corridors, with the likes of Andy and Bob Beattie, Tom

Smith, Bud Maxwell, Hugh O'Donnell and a certain Bill Shankly on the Preston North End pay role.

From the uncertaincy of whether or not he would be playing first team football at Old Trafford in the Second Division, to a regular place in the Preston side paid dividends for both club and player, with an end of season third place in Division One achieved, with his sixteen goals helping achieve this.

That, however, was not the only reward for their endeavours, as Preston swept away all before them and reached the Final of the F. A. Cup, where they were to face Huddersfield Town at Wembley. A venue where Mutch had made his first appearance at a few weeks previously, as a member of the Scottish team that faced England.

As George Mutch and his Preston team mates, six of whom were Scots, walked up the Wembley tunnel that afternoon, little did he know that by the end of the day his name would be one that claimed the headlines.

As Cup Finals go, the match was not a memorable one and it was not until the last minute of extra time that the destination of the trophy was determined.

With the game goal less and the seconds ticking away, Preston mounted what could well have been their last assault on the Huddersfield goal. The ball was threaded through to Mutch and as he moved forward, was heavily brought down by Huddersfield's Alf Young on the edge of the penalty area.

Such was the force of the tackle that Mutch was stunned by the impact and unaware that the referee had awarded a penalty kick, much to the disgust of young and his team mates.

Following treatment and still in something of a dazed state, Mutch was surprised to discover that he was to be entrusted with taking the spot kick. "I did not even understand that we had been awarded a penalty" Mutch was to say later. "They handed me the ball. I placed it automatically, thinking it was funny they had given it to me, an injured man."

"As I took my run I wondered what I was doing, and why. I don't remember aiming at goal".

The kick thumped against the underside of the bar, with the goalkeeper diving to his right, and bounced just over the line. George Mutch had scored with the first penalty kick ever awarded in a Wembley Cup Final and the F. A. Cup was Preston bound.

In the last pre-war season, he was an ever present in the Preston side, scoring another ten goals, but his career was to be one of hundreds that was interrupted by the Second World War, at time when he had the best years of his career ahead of him.

He continued with Preston during the War and also for the first few games of 1946-47, before joining Bury in October 1946. With the Gigg Lane side, he scored eight goals in twenty-one Second Division appearances.

A year later, he accepted the position of player/coach with Southport and eventually resumed his playing carer with the Lancashire side, before finally retiring at the end of season 1949-50, returning home to Aberdeen, where he set up in business and coached his former club Banks o' Dee in his spare time.

From the brink of disaster to fifth place in the Second Division was quite an achievement and the optimistic view of the club from the start of season 1934-35 certainly helped towards the consolidation of their place in Division Two. In the second half of this season, on February 9th, manager Scott Duncan introduced what he hoped would be some additional fire power to the attack with the signing of William Boyd, from Sheffield United.

The well built forward certainly had a commendable scoring record with his previous clubs and it was easy to see why Duncan had been tempted to add him to the Old Trafford playing staff.

Born in Cambuslang, twenty nine year old **William Boyd** had set off on his goalscoring trail with Regent Star, a Rutherglen side, moving to Larkhall Thistle, where he terrorised defences in the Junior Leagues, with over two hundred goals In three seasons.

Clyde were first to make a move for him and introduce him into Scottish League football, being rewarded with ninety-one goals in just over one hundred games, between 1930-31 and 1933-34, scoring five on one occasion for Clyde in the Scottish Cup against Leith Athletic in January 1931. Such form also won him three Scottish League caps and two full

Scotland caps, playing centre forward against Italy and Switzerland in May 1931, scoring once against the latter. In December 1933, Sheffield United paid the Glasgow side £2,250 for Boyd and the goals continued to flow – fourteen in eighteen matches, but they were not enough to save the Sheffield side from the drop from the First to the Second Division, or gain him further Scottish international honours.

His move to Manchester United in early 1935, however, did not have the desired effect of bringing more success, as it took him four games to open his United account, with a goal against Burnley on March 27th, following his debut at Swansea on February 9th. Breaking the duck, did come as a big relief and was followed three days later with a hat trick against Hull City.

This actually turned out to be his last game for United at first team level and in September 1935, he was transferred to Workington, moving to Luton Town three months later. This move also failed to work out and he joined Southampton in July 1936, before ending his career with Weymouth, whom he joined in August 1937.

Not the most noteworthy of careers, for a player recalled mainly for his goalscoring ability one hundred and forty-two in one hundred and eighty nine games, but not everyone can say that they scored a hat trick in their club's 3-0 win and was dropped, never to play again!

"Anything you can do, I can do better", go the words of a popular song and it was one that could quite easy have been sung, had it been around at the time, by David Robbie to William Boyd. As his United career could certainly equal, if not better that of the previously mentioned centre forward.

David Robbie had arrived at Old Trafford for a one month trial in September 1935, having previously played for Bathgate and Bury. It is something of a mystery how the player ever managed to obtain such a trial, as he had been rejected by Plymouth Argyle two months previously following a similar trial with the south coast club.

Was he on his way home and decided to pop into Manchester in the passing?

With Bury, whom he had joined at the end of season 1920-21, the career of the Motherwell born player had taken off. Over a lengthy fourteen season stay with the Shakers, he had played over 400 odd games, scoring over 100 League and Cup goals.

An injury to Bryant, gave him his opening in the League side at Old Trafford, but the 2-1 defeat at Southampton on September 28th, brought an end to his hopes of a permanent contract with United, as he failed to feature in the first team again.

One month later, he was back in the south of England where he had a four month spell with Margate, before moving to Luton Town for a further four months.

In July 1936, he returned to Plymouth Argyle despite his earlier rejection, to take up a coaching position and two years later, he joined yet another of his former employers, Bury, to fill a similar post.

One of the positions strengthened prior to the start of season 1935-36 was that of right half, with **James Brown** moving from Burnley to fill the position occupied during the previous campaign by William Robertson.

Former Scottish Schoolboy internationalist, Brown had enjoyed life in the lower regions with Belhavenrock, Maryhill Juniors and Wishaw YMCA, before signing for East Fife during season 1926-27, where he was to win a Scottish Cup runners up medal at the end of that first season.

In the summer of 1927, he moved south to join Burnley, where he accumulated 228 appearances during his eight seasons at Turf Moor, captaining the side for the last three of these.

To prise him away from their Lancashire neighbours, United had to pay £1,000, but his sterling displays, as captain throughout 1935-36, soon indicated that it had been money well spent.

Fifty-nine appearances over the following two seasons added to this opinion, but only three in the first month of season 1937-38 signalled that his days at Old Trafford were numbered.

In February 1939, he moved to Bradford City, but the Second World War intervened and with his future uncertain, he decided to hang up his boots shortly afterwards.

One other Scottish born player to make his debut during 1935-36 was **Tommy Lang**, who played in four of the final six fixtures, scoring once. Thirty-year old Lang, a junior with his home town club Larkhall Thistle, was signed by Newcastle United in October 1926, making his League debut a year later.

Eight years with the north-east side saw him register 215 League appearances, scoring 53 goals, but it was to be his F.A. Cup appearances that were to prove much more memorable.

In the Newcastle Cup run of 1932, he scored the winning goal in the semi-final victory over Chelsea and in the Final, he scored the highly disputed goal, which won the Cup. Arsenal defenders claimed that the cross from which Lang scored, had crossed the bye line before being centred.

December 1934 saw him move to Huddersfield Town, but it was to be a rather brief stay, packing his bags a year later and moving to Manchester. With United, he made his debut in the 4-0 win over Bradford on April 11th, scoring three games later, in what was to be his last match of the season, against Bury.

Lang was not to re-appear in the United first team line up until December 28th 1936, making another four appearances, before missing a couple. He returned to the side on February 6th, against Arsenal, making what was to be his last appearance in the red shirt of United against Brentford.

His stay with United turned out to be just as brief as it had been with Huddersfield, lasting only sixteen months and spanning only thirteen games. before joining Swansea Town in April 1937.

Despite playing every game for Swansea during 1937-38, he was placed on their transfer list and on August 7th 1938, the twenty-nine year old former Anglo-Scottish trialist returned to Scotland, joining Queen Of The South.

Unlike many professionals, war did not bring an end to

Lang's playing career, as he signed for Ipswich Town in October 1946, playing his final League match with the East Anglian club in April 1947.

The re-appearance amongst the country's elite football clubs during 1936-37 began favourably, with only two defeats in the opening six fixtures.
A 2-0 win against Arsenal on the first Saturday in October rekindled the optimism, but none of the following eleven outings produced a win, with a 6-2 and 5-2 defeats on subsequent Saturdays at Grimsby and at home to Liverpool showed the inadequacies of the team.
With the club in turmoil, manager Scott Duncan approached the board and asked for his release due to the health of his wife. Left without much of a choice, the board granted his wish and he left with immediate effect.
Into the breach once more stepped Walter Crickmer, with the directors left to plan ahead, re-building the beleaguered team a major priority, as was reducing the large overdraft incurred by Scott Duncan's frequent dealings in the transfer market.
One of Duncan's last signings, James McClelland, probably realised that he had made a mistake in joining Manchester United in the early days of season 1936-37 as the results went against them and the manager who had signed him left.

Brought into the side for the second fixture of 1936-37 against Huddersfield Town at inside right, Dysart born **James McClelland** was back in the reserves seven days later and did not future in the League again until March 6th, when he scored United's winner against Stoke City. The goal did little to extend his run in the team, as he was omitted once again the following week. Given a run in the team, the experienced McClelland could have been an asset during such a disappointing season.

The Manchester Evening Chronicle correspondent had written of McClelland prior to the start of the season - "Although not the be as fast as of yore, he will, I am sure, challenge strongly for a place in the senior team.
"Apart from possessing a good shot, he showed a commendable aptitude for getting the ball

away to the opposite wings and thus opening out the game".
A centre half in his schoolboy days, he played local League football in Fife with Rosslyn, before signing for his nearest Scottish League side Raith Rovers in October 1922.
The following season, he was with Southend United, but it was not until he joined Middlesbrough in March 1925 that he began to make a name for himself.
During his first full season in the north-east, he scored thirty-eight league and Cup goals in only forty games, playing his part in 'Boro's Second Division Championship triumph of 1926-27. In that same season, he scored all of his teams goals in the 5-1, 3rd round, F. A. Cup victory over Leeds United.
March 1928 saw his career with Middlesbrough come to an end, when Bolton took him to Lancashire, where he was to play a part in the F. A. Cup success of 1929, when Bolton beat Portsmouth 2-0 in the Final.
A few months after his Wembley appearance, he was on the move again, signing for Preston, moving along the Lancashire coast to Blackpool sixteen months later. In June 1933, another move took him to Bradford.
By the time he signed for United in June 1936, he was thirty-four years old and clearly had the best of his playing days behind him. Three games at inside left in the final fortnight of 1936-37 brought his United appearance total to its final figure of five and despite being retained for the following term, his playing days were effectively over.

Relegation at the end of season 1936-37 had obviously been a blow to the club. Few would have been surprised, or even disappointed, if United had spent a couple of seasons or so finding their feet again in the lower Division, before making a push for promotion and gaining re-entry into the top flight.
As it turned out, Walter Crickmer welded together a team who, with little to lose, could adopt a devil may care attitude and they sprang back to the First Division as runners-up, at first time of asking, scoring some eighty-two goals. This was almost thirty more than in the previous season.
The stand in manager's team for the opening match of the season differed only slightly to the one that had seen out 1936-37. Breen continued in goal, with Griffiths and

T / R

Roughton as his full backs. The half back line of Gladwin, Vose and Mackay was also the same. It was up front where the changes could be found, with the only difference to Crickmer's front line of Bryant, Murray, Bamford, Baird and Manley being the introduction of Robert Murray at inside right.

"Casual" of the Manchester Evening Chronicle wrote prior to the opening fixture against Newcastle United – "Interest in Manchester United's first match today centred chiefly in the appearance of Murray, the new forward from Hearts, whose selection to fill the inside right position apparently surprised a number of supporters.

"In the public practice game a week ago, Murray appeared first at outside right and later at inside left and did well, but I believe he has shown good form at inside right in private trials and that is why he was chosen to play there today.

His selection was certainly justified, as he had a hand in two of United's three goals as they opened the campaign in style with a 3-0 win.

Newhaven born **Robert Murray** came to the attention of Heart of Midlothian, whilst playing with Newton Grange Star in 1934, having previously served Leith Ivanhoe and Newhaven Victoria.

Going under the nickname of 'Fish', due to his fishing port birthplace, Robert Murray broke into the Hearts first team during season 1935-36, as an outside right, scoring four goals. The following season he had to be content with only nine appearances, with his infrequent outings being strung across the forward line.

Despite not being a regular in the Hearts first team, his transfer to United in June 1937 was no straightforward affair. An initial United bid of £750 was politely turned down, as was the increased offer of £1,250. Eventually, after much deliberating, United agreed to pay £1,500, which Hearts accepted.

Following his creditable debut, United lost their next two games 1-0 and Murray found himself relegated to the reserves in favour of Wassall, who in turn was replaced by Harry Baird.

He returned to the first team line up against Sheffield Wednesday on October 23rd, but again, despite the 1-0 victory, he was omitted the following Saturday and never saw first team action again.

At the end of the season, he was placed on the transfer list and eventually joined non-League Bath City, where he spent one season, before moving to Colchester United.

An injury, received whilst playing for Colchester forced him to retire from the game and he returned Scotland to live in the mining town of Loanhead in Midlothian.

Back in the First Division, the United staff and players worked hard, in order to achieve some stability and with more attention being paid to developing their own players instead of constantly delving into the transfer market, the club at last seemed to have something of a solid base to build on.

One player who did cost the club a transfer fee (£4,000 along with Bill Hullett) was **Tommy Dougan**.

Despite being born in Holytown, Lanarkshire, Dougan had played all his football south of the border, beginning with Turnbridge Wells Rangers before joining Plymouth Argyle in December 1936.

His career blossomed on the south coast and his performances had obviously been noted during their season alongside Plymouth in the Second Division during 1938. Upon arriving at Old Trafford in March 1939, he went straight into the first team, but played in only four games before losing his place to Bryant. Prior to the start of season 1939-40, it was thought that he would be pushing for a regular first team place, but with normal League football abandoned during the Second World War, his hopes of a career with United were dealt a severe blow.

In September 1940, he returned to Scotland and joined Hearts and towards the end of the War had a short spell with Kilmarnock, as well as making a handful of return appearances with United in the War League North, before joining Dunfermline in April 1946.

THE BUSBY YEARS

Finishing season 1938-39 in fourteenth position was most acceptable, with further improvement hoped for during the next season. Such hopes, however, were severely dented with the outbreak of war, the new season only a mere three games old.

By the time peace had been declared and League football resumed on its usual basis in August 1946, the Manchester United line up had changed beyond all recognition and there was a new man at the helm – Matthew Busby.

The Scots so far documented within the pages of this book, have all played a part of varying proportions in the history of Manchester United Football Club. None of their contributions, however, could come anywhere near that of Matt Busby. Little did club chairman Mr James Gibson realise at the time, what his persuading Busby to join the club as manager in February 1945 would create. This one brief meeting was to change the face of Manchester United for good.

Matt Busby was born in the mining village of Orbiston, near Bellshill, just south of Glasgow, on May 26th 1909. At school, he had the academic ability to do well, but with his widowed mother decided upon emigrating to America, such a future was put to the back of his mind. In something of a short term career stop gap, he took the only other employment avenue open to him and went down the mines, playing football for Orbiston "Canibals", the local village side, in his spare time.

From there, he graduated to Alpine Villa, a youth team, with whom he helped win the Scottish under 18 cup, before signing for junior side Denny Hibernian. Half a dozen games later, and the visa for new life in America sitting on the living room mantle piece, he was offered a trial with Manchester City. The great adventure was on hold.

Following a favourable display in a Central League match against Burnley, he was offered a professional contract and the American visa was discarded.

In his new surroundings, he found it difficult to adjust to the pace of the English game in his inside forward position, spending most of his early days at Maine Road, struggling in the reserves. More than once, he contemplated returning to the mines of Lanarkshire, especially when he found himself omitted from both City's first team and reserves.

Little did he know that one dark Manchester evening, as he contemplated what to do in order to pass the time, his life was about to change dramatically.

With nothing else in mind, he decided to stroll along to Maine Road and watch a Northern mid-week fixture in which the City 'A' team were involved. As kick off approached, it turned out that City were a player short and having been spotted by trainer Alec Bell (the former United star), Busby was summoned, told to get changed and pushed, unprepared, into the unfamiliar position of right half.

Such was his performance, he was selected to fill a similar role in the Central League side a few days later and from then on, never really looked back.

He eventually made his Football League debut for Manchester City during 1928-29, against Midlesbrough at Maine Road, but it was not until after playing at Huddersfield in November 1930, that he became an established first team player.

City reached the semi final stage of the F. A. Cup three seasons in a row, 1932, 1933 and 1934, going one step further in the latter two years. In the final of 1933, Busby found himself a Wembley loser, as Everton took the Cup to Merseyside, winning 3-0. Consolation came in the form of an international call up for Scotland to face Wales, in what was to be his only peace time cap.

Twelve months later he was back beneath the Wembley twin towers playing his part in City's 2-1 triumph over Portsmouth.

In March 1936, his time at Maine Road, where he had played just over two hundred League games, scoring eleven goals, came to an end, with a transfer to Liverpool for a fee of £8,000. This was a clear indication of how far Matt Busby had come in a relatively short time, as a few years earlier he had been offered to Manchester United for £150. Money that United at that time did not have, so the offer of the player had to be turned down.

At Liverpool, he continued to receive favourable reports, playing 115 League games for them, scoring three goals, up to the outbreak of the Second World War.

Joining the army, a posting to Kelso in the Scottish borders brought an approach to Celtic, offering his services, but this was declined, so it was in the green and white of Hibernian that he was to grace the Scottish wartime game. South of the border, he guested for both Reading and Middlesbrough.

He also came close to making an appearance for United at Old Trafford on the final afternoon of season 1939-40, against Everton on June 1st. Listed in the Manchester United programme as 'A.N.OTHER', in was mentioned elsewhere that it was hoped that Matt Busby would be free to play that afternoon. Unfortunately, it was not to be.

As a matter of note, if Busby had played that afternoon, he would have lined up in a real star studded United side, as they had the likes of Stanley Matthews, Alec Herd, Peter Doherty and Raich Carter in their forward line.

Like many professional footballers in the forces, he was given the position of a P.T. instructor and between making guest appearances at home and representing Scotland in un-official internationals, he became the player manager of the army side which toured numerous base's overseas and stadiums in this country, playing exhibition games with a line up which would include players such as Swift, Lawton, Matthews, Mercer and Carter.

In 1932, a conversation between the Manchester United chairman Mr James Gibson and a sports officer for the Southern Command, a Captain Williams, led to the former asking the captain if he knew of anyone whom he could recommend as being suitable to become manager of United. The name of Matt Busby was suggested.

It was therefore arranged that Busby would be asked to play a couple of games for Bournemouth, where Gibson had a house, so United man could see for himself what type of player and person he was considering for employment. Liking what he saw, it was decided that Busby was the man for the job.

Things, however, were not just quite so straight forward, as Liverpool, Reading and Ayr United were also keen on Busby as a manager or coach and of course, Liverpool still held his registration as a player.

An approach was made to Busby by Louis Rocca on behalf of United and having enjoyed his spell in Manchester with City and being keen to get into management decided that the United job was what he was looking for.

This was in February 1945, but it was not until October of that year that he officially took over at Old Trafford (or what

was left of it after the visits of German bombers) upon his demob from the army.

From the offset, he set his stall out how he wanted it, asking for a five year contract instead of the three he had been offered and he quickly installed an old army friend, Jimmy Murphy as his assistant.

As manager of Manchester United, his first fixture was in the War League North, against Bolton Wanderers at Maine Road, United's home ground for the first few post war seasons. At that time, United were in sixteenth position in the table, but by the end of the season, they sat in fourth.

Despite an overdraft at the bank of around £15,000 and having no ground to call their own, Busby soon realised that he had inherited some quality players in the likes of Carey, Pearson, Rowley, Chilton and Crompton and was confident that he had the foundations of team at his disposal.

His signing of Jimmy Delaney put the finishing touches to his favoured team and at the end of that first post war season, Manchester United finished runners up, their highest First Division placing for twenty five years.

The following two seasons also ended in second place, but 1947-48 also saw Busby's side reach the Final of the F. A. Cup, defeating Blackpool 4-2 in one of the best Finals seen at the stadium for some time.

Despite being something of a novice in the managerial stakes, Matt Busby was appointed manager of the Great Britain Olympic football team for the 1948 games, which were to be held in London. Sadly there was no gold medals, or indeed any medals to be won, as the British side lost to Yugoslavia in the semi finals, after beating Holland and France. A 5-3 defeat by Denmark deprived them of third place in the competition.

League runners up again in 1950-51, it began to look as though the Championship crown was out with their reach, but at the end of 1951-52 Manchester United were eventually crowned First Division Champions.

By now the ever-astute Busby had noticed the cracks beginning to appear in his talented side and had already introduced the likes of Roger Byrne and Johnny Berry in the team. Having put more emphasis on the already in place youth policy at the club, Busby decided to see what its products were like, slowly introducing many of the talented up and coming youngsters, such as Viollet, Jones, Blanchflower and Edwards into the side.

It was those players, plus rare signings such as Tommy Taylor in which Busby placed his faith, a faith which was rewarded as his team began to develop a style admired by many and made a challenge for the games top honours.

The League Championship was won again in 1955-56 and brought with it the invitation that was to change not only Manchester United, but also British football itself.

The European Cup had been instigated the previous year, Chelsea the Football League Champions refused permission to take part by the Football League. Busby heeded not their advice and with the backing of his directors and the Football Association informed the organisers that Manchester United would certainly participate in the 1956-7 competition.

Busby was certain that much could be learned from playing overseas opposition, but in the opening rounds it was the continentals who were the learners and United the teachers as Anderlecht, Borussia Dortmund and Athletico Bilbao were all defeated. It was only the experience of Real Madrid who prevented Busby's "Babes" from reaching the Final.

If foreign teams could not stop United, there was little hope of the more ordinary British sides doing so and United lifted the Championship again in 1956-7, just failing to also add the F.A.Cup, mainly due to an injury to goalkeeper Ray Wood.

Back in Europe the following season, United were once again enhancing their reputation as they strode to the semi finals for the second consecutive season.

The opportunity, however, to go one better than in the previous campaign came to a sudden, abrupt halt at Munich airport as the team returned from their quarter final victory over Red Star Belgrade.

Crashing as their plane attempted to take off, eight members of the team were killed and two others had later to retire through injury. Busby himself came close to death, but miraculously pulled through, returning to Britain in time to see a quickly rebuilt Manchester United loose to Bolton in the F.A.Cup Final.

Munich also deprived Matt Busby of the opportunity to manage the Scottish national side in the 1958 World Cup tournament. He had intended travelling to the Finals, but was prevented in doing so on the advice of his doctors.

Slowly, Busby recovered from his injuries and was soon
planing again for the future, buying players such as Herd,
Quixall, Setters, Cantwell, Crerand and Law.
A disastrous League season in 1962-63 was almost
immediately forgotten, as Busby lead his team, at last, to
Cup Final success over Leicester and from then on, the team
progressed rapidly.
The Championship was again won in 1964-64 and 1966-
7, but it was the European Cup that Busby yearned for,
feeling that he owed it to the players who had died
almost a decade before.
In 1967-68, United again reached the semi final stage and
again it looked as though Real Madrid were to be the
stumbling block in the attempt to reach the Final itself.
This time, however, they were overcome, Busby had taken
his team to the Final of the European Cup and was ninety
minutes from fulfilling his dream.
It took thirty minutes of extra time before a jubilant Matt
Busby could lift the European Cup high above his head,
having watched United destroy Benfica 4-1. His dream had
finally came true.
Soon after this victory, Matt Busby was awarded a
knighthood for his services to football, something to add to
his CBE, awarded in 1958 and the Freedom of Manchester
that he was given in 1967.
So, having achieved his goal, with no mountains left to
climb, thoughts of retirement began to surface and in 1969
he decided that the time was now right for such a decision
and he moved into the role of general manager, with Wilf
McGuinness taking over as team manager.
The appointment of the untried McGuinness was soon to be
seen as a failure and in December 1970, Busby once again
occupied the managers office at Old Trafford with the
former United wing half, McGuinness sacked.
In June 1971, he finally closed the door of the managers
office for the last time and was later appointed a director
and in 1980 upon stepping down from the board, was
appointed club president
Awarded a testimonial in August 1991, it was seen by many
as a scant reward for everything that he had done for the
club and upon his death on January 20th 1994, the public
tributes showed just how much he meant to the supporters
of Manchester United.

Matt Busby, the novice manager, surprised many with his
first signing for Manchester United in February !946,
bringing to the club thirty-four year old right winger
Jimmy Delaney. A player considered by many to be long
past his best.

Upon leaving Cleland St Mary's school,
Jimmy Delaney began working down the
mines, the only career open to many,
playing football for Stoneyburn Juniors in
his spare time, following an unproductive
trial with Wishaw Juniors.
By the time of his twentieth birthday, he
had signed for Celtic, beginning a notable
career and lifelong love affair with the
club from the east-end of Glasgow.
Success for Celtic and Delaney ran on a
parallel and the deft touches and the
ability to move inside defenders for
attempts at goal soon endeared him to the
Parkhead faithful.
On the domestic front, he won League Championship
medals in 1936 and 1938, along with a Scottish Cup
Winners medal in 1937 (a match in which he made the
winning goal with only ten minutes remaining). He could
also boast that he played in front of over 300,000 spectators
on successive Saturday's, with Celtic and Scotland.
International recognition duly followed, sandwiching nine
Scotland caps in between his seventy-nine goals from one
hundred and seventy eight appearances with Celtic.
A badly broken arm, sustained when stamped upon by an
Arbroath defender in 1939, required a bone graft, after a
surgeon wanted to amputate and it was to keep him on the
sidelines for some two and a half years. It also lead to a
minor dispute with Celtic, who were by now wary about
playing a player who was now considered injury prone,
resulting in problems obtaining insurance cover.
The SFA were also wary about selecting him for the
Scotland side, because of the insurance problem and on one
occasion, with a international side due to be named, a crowd
gathered outside the SFA offices in April 1944, shouting
"We want Delaney".
Whether worried about their future well being or what,

Delaney was selected to face England ten days later. After turning in a superb performance at Hampden, Delaney returned home later that evening, to find his infant son close to death. The hero of a few hours earlier could do little, as his son passed away.

Due to the ongoing problems relating to his fitness, he soon became unsettled at Celtic and when his request for a £2 per week rise in wages in May 1945 was turned down, with his name placed on the transfer list, he knew that his career in the green and white hoops was coming to an end. The supporters, however, made their feelings known about what they thought was poor treatment of one of their favourites. The necessary insurance cover was eventually found for Delaney, but it was south of the border, with Manchester United. Other clubs had contemplated over signing him, but it was his former international team mate Matt Busby who paid out £4,000 for his services, travelling north to Motherwell to conclude the deal.

Delaney's debut for United was on February 9th 1946 against Liverpool, a fortnight after staring for Scotland at centre forward against Belgium at Hampden Park, scoring twice.

He was soon to prove an asset to the United side, convincing the doubters that Busby had certainly not gambled in signing him and becoming an integral part in the club's immediate post war success. A further four Scottish caps were to follow.

Shortly after the start of season 1950-51, he lost his place in the Manchester United side and following a friendly against Aberdeen in September, the Scottish club enquired as to his availability.

Busby felt that there was still some mileage in the thirty-six year-old and wanted the player to stay in Manchester, but Delaney himself considered his opportunities at Old Trafford were now somewhat limited and that a move was probably to his advantage. Reluctantly, Busby relented and a £3,500 fee exchanged hands.

His first match 'back home' resulted in a 5-1 win for his new club, with their new captive playing a prominent part. After a few weeks, he was being hailed as the club's best ever signing.

In December 1951, thirteen months later, he was on the move again, joining Falkirk for a similar fee to that

Aberdeen had paid United.

His wanderings continued in January 1954, when he crossed the Irish Sea to join Derry City for an Irish record fee of £1,500. During his spell with the Irish side, he completed a hat trick of Cup Winners medals in 1954.

The feet that had tormented numerous defences over the years became itchy once again during season 1955-56 and he crossed the Irish border, heading into the Republic to become player manager of Cork Athletic. An appearance in the F.A. of Ireland Cup Final at the end of this season almost brought him a fourth Cup winners medal, as Cork were leading Shamrock Rovers 2-0 with only thirteen minutes to play, only to lose 3-2. The chance of an unique achievement was gone.

Jimmy Delaney's love for the game and overall fitness enabled him to continue playing until he was forty-three, ending his career back in Scotland, with Highland League club Elgin City, before retiring to his native Cleland. During his retirement, he was a regular visitor to Celtic Park and would also often journey down to Manchester, being made more than welcome at both venues. In later years, arthritis restricted his travels, but he never lost his love for his first club, admitting his desire that when he died that he wanted to be buried with a Celtic shirt in his coffin.

Described by former Glasgow Rangers full back Jock Shaw as "the cleanest player I ever played against" and by Matt Busby as " just about the best signing any football manager could desire", Jimmy Delaney was something of a rare breed in footballers. Hopefully, he got his final wish.

Despite Busby's inexperience on the managerial front, the first three post war seasons, playing at neighbouring Maine Road due to the bomb damage at Old Trafford, saw the team scale heights that could only have been dreamt about over the past thirty odd years. Adding to that, the F.A.Cup triumph against Blackpool, United were indeed on a firm footing and heading in the right direction.

Unlike his predecesor, Scott Duncan and to a lesser extent John Chapman, Matt Busby did not make any hasty journey's up the A6 to Scotland in order to boost the United playing squad with fellow Scots. If anything he was rather the opposite.

One youngster who did come to the club in those immediate post war years was Glasgow born **Tommy Lowrie**.

Lowrie's early football had been played in the Perth and Glasgow area, before moving down the west coast to join Troon Juniors.

Whilst holidaying in Ireland, he managed to become involved in a charity match, where one of the interested spectators was Jimmy Delaney. The performance of Tommy Lowrie was noted by the impressed United winger and upon his return to Manchester immediately spoke to Busby about the youngster. Following a further look at the player, he was signed in August 1947.

The nineteen year old half back showed promise in the reserves and three months after his twentieth birthday, on April 7th 1948, he stepped into the limelight as a replacement for Henry Cockburn against Manchester City, playing his part in the 1-1 draw.

A second appearance the following Saturday was to be his last until almost exactly a year later, when another injury, this time to John Anderson, allowed him to return to the first team at Bolton. His first team run this time was for a more extended run of eight games.

In the opening couple of months of season 1949-50, he replaced Jack Warner on three occasions, but they were to be his last first team outings for United. Unlike his more illustrious namesake, (although with a different spelling), the streets of Salford were certainly not going to make him a fortune or gain him world wide recognition.

With such a strong playing staff, a permanent first team place, or indeed an extended first team run, was always going to be difficult and in March 1951, he returned to Scotland, signing for Aberdeen.

At the start of season 1952-53, Lowrie was back in Lancashire, having signed for Oldham Athletic, where he won a Third Division North Championship medal at the end of his first season. Following a successful three years at Boundary Park, he retired from the game.

One month before Tommy Lowrie made his initial appearance in the first team, another Scot had made his Manchester United debut, but unlike Lowrie, he had stepped straight into the first team following his signing.

Johnny Downie had been spotted by Bradford Park Avenue whilst playing for Lanarkshire A.T.C. at centre forward and was signed as on amateur forms in 1942. By the time he signed professional, at the age of nineteen, just over two years later, he had already made a few first team appearances, mostly as an inside left.

He was to spend almost five years with the Yorkshire side and was their top scorer during season 1947-48.

In March 1949, Downie was signed by United as a replacement for Johnny Morris, (who had left to join Derby County), costing a then record fee of £18,000. His performances against United in the F.A.Cup epic three match confrontation a few weeks earlier, played a major part in his transfer.

Johnny Downie had a good footballing brain and was a creator as well as a taker of chances. A fact clearly illustrated on his United debut against Charlton Athletic on March 5th, when he scored and played a big part in the 3-2 win. He was again on the mark the following Saturday in the 3-0 win against Stoke City.

He played in most of the remaining fixtures of that season, but during United's summer tour of Eire, he injured his ankle, which was to trouble him for some time, affecting his form and bringing a prolonged spell in the reserves.

Season 1949-50 had been a major disappointment, with only eighteen first team appearances and only six goals, but the following year saw a vast improvement in both sets of figures, playing in twenty nine games and scoring ten goals, as United finished runners up in the League. 1950-51 also saw him widely tipped for Scottish international honours and also a transfer to Burnley, neither of which materialised. He began season 1951-52 as first choice inside left and totalled up thirty-one appearances, with his ten goals helping United to the League Championship for the first time since 1910-11.

Despite playing twenty times the following season, he

became unsettled, with his unsuccessful request to Matt Busby for a switch to wing half being turned down, playing a big part in this. Numerous clubs had shown an interest in him on previous occasions, but had been turned down. However, in August 1953, at the age of twenty eight, he joined Luton Town for a fee of £10,000.

He found it difficult to settle in the south and a year later joined Hull City. After a two year spell at Boothferry park, he moved out of League football and joined Kings Lynn, this was followed by a brief stay with Wisbech Town, before returning to the Football League with Third Division Mansfield Town in October 1958.

Spells at Darlington, Hyde, Mossley, Stalybridge Celtic and Halifax were to follow. In fact, during 1962-63, the latter were keen to have the now thirty seven year old in their League side, but having already taken his Football League retirement pension, he could not be re-signed to play at this level.

In August 1949, Busby increased his Scottish contingent by one, with the signing of Tommy Bogan from Preston North End.

Glasgow born Bogan had already written himself into the history books, prior to his arrival at Manchester United, with the briefest International appearance on record, on April 14th 1945, whilst with Hibs.

Playing against England at Hampden Park, in a Scottish side that also included Matt Busby, he collided with the England goalkeeper Frank Swift and was carried off with a broken arm in only the first minute of the game.

Strathclyde had been the starting point of **Tommy Bogan's** career in 1937, joining Blantyre Celtic two years later and then moving on to Renfrew Juniors early in 1943, before being signed by William McCartney (son of former Newton Heath player John McCartney) for Hibs in September of that same year.

With the Easter Road side, he gained a reputation of being a quick and skilful winger, before joining Glasgow Celtic on February 1st 1946.

With Celtic, he won Scottish League representative honours, but also suffered a career set back with a broken leg in October 1946 and although a firm favourite with the Celtic

support, he never really felt entirely happy there, making only forty-seven appearances and scoring eight goals.

In July 1948, Preston North End wanted to sign him, but Bogan turned the move down, only to agree to a similar transfer two months later. A move that was to cost Preston £3,500.

He adapted well at Deepdale, soon proving himself to be a useful and versatile individual. Having noted his progress, Matt Busby, with an eye for the future, brought him to Manchester in August 1949 and installed him in the first team at inside right, against Charlton Athletic at Old Trafford, where a run of eighteen games brought him four goals, before losing his place to Johnny Downie.

His appearances during season 1950-51 were few and far between, eleven, scoring three goals, and in March of that season he was transferred to Aberdeen, along with Tommy Lowrie.

His stay in the north-east of Scotland was brief, lasting only nine months, before joining Southampton. Later moves saw him join Blackburn Rovers in August 1953 (Johnny Carey's first signing as a manager) and Macclesfield Town the following year, before deciding to hang up his boots.

United's summer tour of the United States of America in 1950 found Matt Busby's attention grasped by the performance of Scottish born emigrant Eddie McIlvenny, during a match against Philadelphia Nationals. An offer was made to the player there and then, which was accepted and the return journey across the Atlantic was made.

Eddie McIlvenny had been born in Greenock and had joined his local League club Morton, before becoming a Wrexham player in March 1947, where he was to play eight Football League games, before being released on a free transfer in May 1948.

Deciding to emigrate to America, with his football boots carefully packed away amongst his belongings, it was soon obvious that he had made the correct decision. His Stateside adventure not only took in the Philadelphia club, but also Fairhill Club Inc. and the surprise selection for the

American National side.

Like James Brown some twenty years before him, McIlvenny found himself involved in the World Cup with his adopted country and there was not a prouder man in all of America when he led his makeshift team, as captain, to a 1-0 victory over England at Belo Horizonte.

Following his arrival at Old Trafford, he was included in the United side for the opening two fixtures of season 1950-51, but he was not to enjoy any of the success that he had in America, as those were to be his only two outings in the first team. Despite this, he remained with United until the end of season 1952-53, when he was given a free transfer, moving to League of Ireland side Waterford, where he was to eventually to become player manager.

There was to be one other debutant from north of the border in the early days of season 1950-51, he was **Harry McShane**. Born in the same mining village as Matt Busby, he was to begin his playing career with Bellshill Athletic, before being snapped up by Blackburn Rovers in January 1937, on amateur forms.

Signing as a professional that same year, he made only two League appearances before the outbreak of World War Two interrupted his career. He subsequently joined the RAF and for a while was stationed back over the border in Dumfries.

Due to the hostilities, a large part of what could have been a promising career past him by and it was not until September 1946, having now signed for Huddersfield Town, that he re-appeared in a Football League fixture.

His stay in Yorkshire lasted less than a year, as he returned to Lancashire in the summer of 1947, joining Bolton Wanderers.

McShane had the ability to perform well in either of the wing positions, but prefered outside left and it was his reluctance to perform on the right side of the forward line that led to his departure from Burnden Park, in September 1950, as part of an exchange deal which saw United's John Ball, along with £4,500, going in the opposite direction.

He began his Manchester United career against Aston Villa on September 4th 1950 in his favoured outside left spot, but was to find himself switched to outside right in the latter half of the season, to surprisingly no complaints.

At 5'8", he did not exactly tower above many players, but he made up for his lack of height by possessing a good touch on the ball and having a strong shot, scoring seven goals during his first season.

He began season 1951-52 as first choice outside right, later switching back to outside left, but the need for a cartilage operation in November, ruled him out for the rest of the season, forcing him to sit and watch as his United team mates strode towards the League Championship.

He returned to first team duty on November 1st 1952, almost a year after his last outing, but made only five appearances due to the emergence of David Pegg. Although his first team opportunities were now limited, he contentedly played in the reserves until February 1954, when at the age of thirty-four, he joined Oldham Athletic for a fee of £750.

With the 'Latics, he made forty one appearances, scoring ten goals, before stepping down to non-League football with Chorley, where he was to become player coach, Wellington Town, Droyslden and Stalybridge Celtic, again as coach.

In the 1960's Harry McShane returned to Old Trafford, becoming the match day p.a. announcer and in later years was a founding member of the Association of Former Manchester United Players.

The League Championship of 1951-52 was won in style, with Busby installing free flowing attacking football into his team. Something that was clearly outlined in the final five games of the campaign, when twenty-one goals were scored.

Unlike the last First Division Championship success in 1910-11, when some six Scotsmen were involved, there was only Johnny Downie and the manager himself, this time around.

Busby continued his team building despite the Championship success, as a number of his players had by now enjoyed the best days of their careers, with age beginning to catch up with them.

Over the next three seasons, a steady influx of youngsters were introduced into the team, as what were to become the legendary "Busby Babes" began to take shape. There was, however, a lack Scottish accents to be found in this productive nursery!

League Championship success was again achieved in 1955-56 with a third post war title a year later. The illusive League and F.A.Cup double was taken from United's grasp in controversial circumstances at Wembley in 1957. Injury to goalkeeper Ray Wood reducing United to practically ten men for most of the game in their 2-1 defeat by Aston Villa. With a third successive title looking extremely possible and with the multi- talented United side on the threshold of domestic and European success, disaster struck.

The events of Munich would have finished many clubs, unable to fulfil their obligations and devastated by their losses. United, after their initial period of mourning, did as they had done so often in the past, simply got on with the job in hand.

Jimmy Murphy, Busby's right hand man, took over the running of the club and faced with a F.A.Cup fifth round tie against Sheffield Wednesday at Old Trafford had to scrape together a team. This was eventually made up of Munich survivors Foulkes and Gregg, new signings Crowther and Taylor and a sprinkling of reserve and junior players with little or no experience of top class football.

One of those thrown in at the deep end amid the turmoil surrounding the aftermath of Munich, was **Alex Dawson**. Although born in Aberdeen, the Dawson family moved south to Hull, when Alex was only eleven, due to his father's occupation as a trawlerman.

His footballing ability quickly helped him settle in at school and during season 1954-55, he was chosen to represent England Schoolboys on no fewer than six occasions, also representing Hull Schoolboys.

Such were his performances at this level, many clubs took an interest in the dark haired youngster. But it was Manchester United who were to add him to their pay role, while at the same time move him from the outside right position in which he had been playing to the one where he was to make

his name - centre forward.

With the 1957 League Championship won and with one or two fixtures still to play, Alex Dawson was given his first team debut against Burnley on April 22nd, having shown promise in the Central League side. In what was a rather bruising affair, but which suited Dawson's somewhat robust style, the youngster celebrated his first team call up with a goal in United's 2-0 win. He retained his place in the side for the remaining two fixtures of the season, against Cardiff City and West Bromwich Albion, in what were rather unfamiliar Manchester United line ups and scored on both occasions.

It was back into the reserves at the start of the following season, as United set out to retain their Championship crown and make a renewed challenge on Europe. Prior to the events in Germany on a cold February afternoon, there was only to be one appearance, against Portsmouth in a 3-0 defeat at Old Trafford, before being thrust into the limelight and under the nations microscope, leading the attack and scoring one of the goals in the 3-0 F.A.Cup 5th round tie against Sheffield Wednesday on February 19th, thirteen days after that fateful Thursday.

He was to score again, the only goal of the match, in United's first League fixture following the crash, against Nottingham Forest and acting manager Jimmy Murphy's description of the effort emphasise the youngster style. "You could see when the corner came across", said the genial Welshman, "that Alex Dawson had made up his mind that this was it.

"In he went. I saw two Forest players go down and the ball was in the net."

It was in the F.A.Cup campaign that Dawson continued to show his ability. Scoring United's second in the 2-2 6th round draw against West Bromwich Albion –

"...there was dreadnought Dawson scoring with an eagle splendour to head in two minutes before half time".

Then notching a hat trick in the 5-3 semi-final replay against Fulham at Highbury.

"Dixie Dawson Flattens Fulham" shouted the headlines, as he wrote his name into the record books as the youngest post war player to score three in one game, at the age of eighteen years and thirty three days. Unfortunately, he failed to conjure up a goal in the Final itself, when United's luck finally ran out.

In January 1961, Dawson proved himself not only as a goalscorer but also a goal stopper, taking over from the injured Harry Gregg against Tottenham Hotspur at Old Trafford. A game United won 2-0.

With the arrival of David Herd from Arsenal during 1961, his first team appearances were therefore limited and a £18,000 offer took him to Preston North End in October of that same year.

His direct, physical approach to the game did not endear himself to everyone, but it did produce the goals, fifty-four in ninety three games for United and they continued to flow at the lower level with Preston.

In his 197 outings with the Deepdale side, he found the net on 114 occasions. He was also to suffer a second Wembley disappointment.

Playing alongside former United team mate Nobby Lawton, Preston fought there way through to the Cup Final of 1964 and surprised the more illustrious West Ham by taking a 2-1 lead, though a goal scored by Alex Dawson, before the Londoners fought back to win 3-2.

In March 1967, he crossed Lancashire for Bury, in a record £20,000 deal, where it was hoped that his experience could help the club avoid relegation. Despite scoring four goals in eleven games, Bury went down. However, his goals during the following season, 1967-68, played a major part in the Shakers winning promotion at their first attempt.

After scoring twenty one times in fifty league games for Bury, Alex Dawson then moved to the south coast, joining Brighton in December 1968 for £8,888, (managed at the time by another of his former teammates, Freddie Goodwin), a move which was punctuated with a loan spell at Brentford.

The final two years of this career were to be seen out at non-League Corby, having enjoyed a League career of some 407 games and scoring 221 goals.

Upon retiring, he did consider a career in coaching, but eventually decided against this and sought for employment out with the game.

The aftermath of the Munich Air Disaster taxed United's playing staff severely, with players such as Alex Dawson having to develop into first team footballers quicker than was expected, with other young players taken from the obscurity of the juniors and pushed into the reserves in what was something of a domino effect.

The likes of Shay Brennan became a star overnight with his two goals against Sheffield Wednesday in the F.A.Cup, while others like Mark Pearson, Bob Harrop and Ronnie Cope also established themselves as first team regulars.

The door of opportunity also opened for a young Ayrshire lad called **Tommy Heron**.

He had begun his playing career as an amateur outside left, with Queens Park upon leaving school and finishing his two years national service, but was never to gain a regular place with the Hampden Park club.

A short spell with Kilmarnock followed, before he ventured across the Irish Sea to join Portadown for a career which was to last a mere two and a half months. However, it wasn't an entirely unsuccessful period, as after only seven games, he was selected for the Irish League side. Much to his disappointment though, he was forced to withdraw through injury and missed out on the opportunity of playing alongside Jackie Milburn, who was playing for Linfield at that time.

His display's in the Irish League caught the attention of Manchester United's chief scout Joe Armstrong and despite the Portadown supporters raising a petition to keep him at the club, Tommy Heron moved to Old Trafford for a fee of £8,000, in March 1958.

He quickly found himself thrust into the first team, making his debut on April 5th, against Preston North End, at outside left, but it proved to be just a one off and he was pushed back into the reserves the following week.

The name of Tommy Heron was not to appear in the first team again until March 30th 1960 and by then, he had been switched to full back. "Matt Busby saw something in me as a defender" he was later to say, "and that was alright by me.

I was simply happy to play anywhere".

In a match report for his second first team match against Sheffield Wednesday, Len Shackleton, writing in the Daily Express, wrote of United's 4-2 defeat - " It was a pity that only Viollet and left back Heron (what a great player he'll make) copied the Charlton game – pure football all the way".

Despite having played only one game that season and two in two years at first team level, he was included in the United party to tour the United States of America in the summer of 1960. Although enjoyable, it did little to help his first team opportunities, with the full back positions being shared between Shay Brennan and Bill Foulkes. After making his third first team appearance at the end of October 1960, he found his opportunities dealt a further blow with the signing of Noel Cantwell.

He was now obviously surplus to requirements and consequently moved to York City in May 1961 for a fee of £3,000. Here his career finally blossomed, missing only a handful of games over five seasons, helping York win promotion to Division Three in 1964-65.

In the summer of 1966, he returned to Manchester, joining non-League Altrincham and three years later moving to Droylsden where he was to end his career.

At the end of season 1957-58, United had slipped, not surprisingly, to eight in the table from the second place they held behind Wolves at the time of the crash. The following season, however, with Dennis Viollet and Bobby Charlton back to their best, everyone was pleasantly surprised when they shrugged off their immediate problems and finished as runners up, six points behind Champions Wolves, but five in front of third place Arsenal.

By the start of the sixties, United were beginning to find their feet again, as Matt Busby, slowly recovering physically from the disaster, began to rebuild his shattered team. Not only were established players sought and eventually signed, players such as Noel Cantwell from West Ham United, Albert Quixall from Sheffield Wednesday and Maurice Setters from West Bromwich Albion, the youth team was also restocked with players upon who the club hoped to build its future.

One such youngster brought to Old Trafford with an eye for

the future was Ian Moir, an Aberdonian, who had been sent south by Archie Beattie, the same man who had sent another promising young player to Huddersfield Town. More, however, about that individual later.

Ian Moir had been expected to sign for this home-town club Aberdeen, having trained with them as a schoolboy, but it was to be the red of Manchester United that he was to wear instead.

Upon signing for United on amateur forms as a fifteen year old in 1958, he made rapid progress through the junior ranks, turning professional two years later and was soon turning in some fine performances in the Central League side.

A rather indifferent start to the First Division season of 1960-61, three 3-1 defeats, a 4-0 and a 4-1 defeat, all in the opening nine fixtures, saw Matt Busby ring the changes for the trip to Bolton on October 1st. Nobby Stiles entering the fray at right half and Ian Moir coming in at outside right.

Despite the 1-1 draw, Moir found himself back in the second string for the following fixture, while Stiles was given an extended run in the team. The slimly built Scottish youngster did, however, return to the first team scene before the end of the season, re-appearing on March 4th for the local 'derby' against Manchester City and played in seven of the remaining twelve fixture of that season. He scored his first senior goal a fortnight after the City match, in the 1-1 home draw with Arsenal.

Season 1961-62 brought a further nine first team appearances, four in October and the other five at the end of

March and the beginning of April. Only one of those ending in victory for United.

A poor team performance in the F.A. Charity Shield match against Everton at the start of season 1963-64, which ended in a 4-0 defeat, gave him another opportunity to prove that he was worthy of a first team place. Playing in the opening six League games, scoring two goals, looked indeed like the break that he was after. However, with the emergence of a certain George Best and the tendency of Busby to reshuffle the forward line, he again found himself in and out of the first team picture, adding only a further twelve appearances to his record during that season. All but one came in the opening two months of the campaign.

The following season, 1964-65 saw the signing of John Connelly from Burnley, making Ian Moir's opportunities even more limited, with only one appearance all season, against Blackpool on November 14th.

During this solitary appearance, he must have made something of an impression on the Seasiders management, as three months later, he was transferred to the Bloomfield Road side for a fee of £30,000.

Relegation to Division Two at the end of season 1966-67 brought a minor clear out at Blackpool and Moir found himself transferred to Division Four side Chester for £10,000.

After seven months, he was on the move again, this time to Wrexham, with Chester recouping their £10,000 outlay.

At last, he managed to taste some success, helping the Welsh side to promotion from Division Four in 1970 and to the Final of the Welsh Cup a year later.

In 1972, he joined Shrewsbury Town, under the managership of Harry Gregg, but returned to Wrexham in 1973 for a further two years, before moving to South Africa for three months with Arcadia Shepherds. At the end of this adventure into the unknown, he returned to Chester.

Having finished as runners up in 1958-59, it was something of a disappointment to slip to seventh place in both seasons 1959-60 and 1960-61, especially as in the former some one hundred and two League goals had been scored. This had been reduced to eighty-eight the following term.

Always looking to strengthen his side and as he preferred his teams to play attacking football, forwards were people that

Matt Busby had a passion for and when one of the top centre forwards in the country became available, then the manager pulled out all the stops to sign him.

Leading the Manchester United attack on the opening day of season 1961-62 was new signing **David Herd**. Like many of his goals, Herd was a Scot through good timing more than anything else.

The Herd family home was a mere stone throw from Manchester City's Maine Road ground, where his father earned a living (at one time playing along side Matt Busby). With his wife heavily pregnant and almost due to give birth, Alec Herd despatched her north to family in Hamilton, Lanarkshire, ensuring that the child would be Scottish by birth.

The young David Herd was quick to show his footballing prowess and was soon following his father's footsteps to Stockport County, signing first as an amateur in September 1949 and then as a professional in April 1951.

Like many others throughout this book who have claimed little pieces of history for themselves, or been involved in incidents of note, seventeen year old David Herd found himself in the headlines soon after signing professional for Stockport.

On the last day of season 1950-51, he was selected for the Stockport County first eleven, at inside left, for their match against Hartlepool United, with his father Alec (aged 39) lining up at inside right. Herd junior. marking the occasion with a goal. This is only the second such occurrence of a father and son playing together in the same Football League side.

Alec Herd, as mentioned previously, had played one game for United, as a guest player, in the War League North, during season 1930-40.

David Herd soon established himself in the Stockport side and in 1952 came close to actually joining Manchester United in an exchange deal with Billy McGlen, but the deal fell through.

In August 1954, he did eventually move from Stockport, but it was to Arsenal for a fee of £10,000. Quite a sum for someone who had only played sixteen League games, scoring six goals.

Life in north London did not hold any fears for the Scottish born Mancunian and he was soon scoring freely for the Gunners, finishing seasons 1958-59, 1959-60 and 1960-61 as their leading goal scorer. He also found himself selected for Scotland, much to the joy of his father, making his debut against Wales in Cardiff on October 18th 1958 and scoring in his second appearance, at Hampden, against Northern Ireland the following month.

His ninety-seven goals in one hundred and sixty-six appearances, made him a firm favourite at Highbury, but he became somewhat disillusioned when the Arsenal management tried to use him as bait in order to lure the coveted George Eastham from Newcastle.

So, when Matt Busby made an approach for his services in the summer of 1961, David Herd had no hesitation in returning north, with a fee of £35,000 changing hands. He had an explosive debut in the red of United, scoring the second goal in a 2-0 pre-season friendly against Bayern Munich and almost knocking out one of the German defenders who had got in the way of one of his shots.

He failed to score on his League debut against West Ham United, getting off the mark four days later against Chelsea, but he did finish the season as the club's top marksman, with fourteen goals from twenty-seven appearances. His strong, forceful play giving United the perfect centre forward.

The signing of Denis Law the following summer, created the formation of a deadly partnership, with both individuals repaying much of their transfer fees by scoring the goals which won Manchester United the F. A. Cup in 1963. Herds scoring two, Law the other in a 3-1 win over Leicester City.

Niggling injuries curtailed his opportunities now and again, but his goalscoring ability never waned and between seasons 1961-62 and 1966-67 he averaged twenty-four goals per season.

His goals, while enough to win games, did not beak any records, although on November 26th 1966, he had the distinction of scoring against three different goalkeepers whilst playing for United against Sunderland at Old Trafford. Jim Montgomery went off injured at 1-0. Charlie Hurley let in a second, whilst John Parke let in two, as United romped to a 5-0 win with David Herd scoring four. Season 1966-67 saw him score the 100th goal of his United career (his two hundred and third overall), but on March 18th 1967, he suffered a broken leg while scoring against Leicester City at Old Trafford. This kept him out of the side until January 1968, returning, against Tottenham in the F. A. Cup replay. He was, however, to miss out on the European Cup Final a few months later.

Due to his injury and long spell out of the side, he could no longer command a regular first team place and during the close season of 1967-68, he left United and joined Stoke City.

In November 1970, he moved to League of Ireland side Waterford, managed at the time by his old United team mate Shay Brennan. This move was to last only three months, leaving to re-cross the Irish Sea and become manager of Lincoln City.

His first and only managerial appointment was not without problems and lasted only twenty-one months, due to disagreements with the chairman. Realising that this was not the job for him, he turned his back on the game and set out to carve a successful career in the motor trade.

In the 1990's, a Frenchman arrived at Old Trafford in a swiftly arranged transfer, which caused something of a shock to say the least. The enigmatic talisman was soon to be hailed as 'the King' by countless adoring fans. But, for those who had stood on the Old Trafford terraces during the swinging sixties, he was but a mere pretender to the throne, as there was only, and would ever be, one 'King of Old Trafford'. His name was Denis Law.

If there was ever an unlikely looking footballer as a youngster, then it was the skinny, bespectacled, five foot three Aberdonian, **Denis Law**.

Despite his physical appearance, Law had an inbuilt talent as a footballer and Archie Beattie, a scout with Huddersfield Town saw that special something and quickly recommended him to his brother Andy, then manager with the Yorkshire side.

Impressing in a trial, Denis was signed on amateur forms in April 1955, earning £5 per week, with half of that going on food and rent.

Twenty months later, on December 24th 1956, he made his Huddersfield debut against Notts County. He had a quiet game by his standards, but he now had one foot on the ladder and there was only one way he wanted to go. In the return game against Notts County on Boxing Day, he scored his first of many League goals.

Progressing slowly, his whole career changed dramatically with the appointment of Bill Shankly as Huddersfield manager in 1958. Shankly took Denis under his wing and encouraged him to pace his game and to read situations before they actually happened.

Shankly left Huddersfield a year later and by then, club's were well aware of the talented youngster in the Leeds Road side. Hardly a day went by without Denis law being linked to this club or that – "Everton Mean To Get Law", "Spurs After Young £25,000 Scot", "Birmingham Lead In Hunt For Law", "Arsenal To Step In This Week". Even a certain Matt Busby had shown an interest.

At the end of the day, on March 15th 1960, Manchester City won the race for his signature, having to pay out £55,000, a new British transfer record, to bring him across the Pennines.

A goal on his debut, a 4-3 defeat against Leeds United, gave him the early confidence of being able to fit in at a higher level. City, however, were in the precarious situation of what seemed to be a constant relegation battle. It was only the goals of Denis Law, nineteen in thirty-seven appearances that kept them in the top flight at the end of season 1960-61.

By now, Law was also a regular in the Scotland side, having been selected for his first cap on October 18th 1958, (on the same day as David Herd made his international debut), by the then part time Scotland team manager Matt Busby. Thus becoming their youngest post war debutant. Eighteen minutes into his debut against Wales, he scored what was to be the first of many in the dark blue of Scotland and the first in a 3-0 win. "The biggest fluke you'll ever see" he later recalled.

Entries into the record book were something that would follow Law throughout his career and in January 1961 he established one which will probably never be beaten – scoring six goals in one game, yet finishing on the losing side.

"City's Luck Runs Out After Law Hits Six" proclaimed the headlines the following morning, with the score line Luton Town 2 Manchester City 6 emblazoned underneath. The game, however, was abandoned with twenty-one minutes left, due to the pitch becoming unplayable as the rain poured down.

Scoring a hat trick in each half, Denis was to later say, "It was one of those games where everything I tried came off", but in the end, his goals meant nothing.

In the re-arranged fixture, Luton surprisingly won 3-1! Ironically, Denis scored the only City goal.

His performances with the Maine Road club, like they had been with Huddersfield Town, attracted much attention and with City constantly struggling, bigger club's felt that he could be easily prized away.

The inevitable happened in the summer of 1961, with Italian club's scouring the Football League for players.

The likes of Denis Law were a prime target for the mega-rich Italians and when Torino made City an unrefusable offer of £100,000, it was quickly accepted, making the player the first in Britain to be transferred for a six figure fee.

At Torino, Law team up with Joe Baker, the former Hibs player, who was signed at the same time. Both were soon to discover that there was more to Italian football than sunshine and good money.

A club fine of £200 for refusing to play in Torino's next game followed a sending off against Lanerosi. Something he couldn't do anyway, as he was under suspension. Things then began to go from bad to worse and a car crash, which almost killed Baker, did little to help the situation.

At the end of his first season, Law was at a low ebb, but a message to go to Lausanne to meet Matt Busby gave him some encouragement. Following the meeting, Law quickly returned to his Turin flat, packed his bags and left for what he hoped would be the last time, heading for Britain. Turin, naturally, demanded his immediate return, but Law refused and when Manchester United offered the Italians a British record fee of £115,000 for his signature, they quickly agreed.

Re-united with his former Scotland boss Matt Busby, the swagger and the smiles returned to the Aberdonian's game and he celebrated with a goal, seven minutes into his United League debut, against West Bromwich Albion on the opening day of season 1962-63.

By the end of his first season at Old Trafford, he had played a major part in Manchester United's F. A. Cup success and also finished as the club's leading scorer with twenty-three goals from thirty-eight outings.

His career as a Manchester United player, however, was not all roses, as his fiery Scottish temperament, sometimes as quick as his lightening goalscoring reflexes, often had him in trouble with officials, bringing three lengthy suspensions between 1963 and 1967. Two covered a period of twenty-eight days, the other six weeks.

It was once suggested by team mates, that Denis would time his suspensions so that he could spend the festive period at home in Aberdeen!

The supporters were somewhat blinkered to this side of their heroes play, forgiving his every failure, as the sound of "We'd walk a million miles for one of your goals, oh Dennnnnis", frequently echoed down the terracing, as the Lawman terrorised defences at home and abroad.

European Footballer of the Year, League Championship medals, captain of Manchester United, the honours flowed like the goals, but his daredevil performances also brought injuries. It was to be a knee injury that robbed him of an appearance in the 1968 European Cup Final.

Law bounced back, but by the beginning of the seventies, Manchester United were not the team who had taken the previous decade by storm, they were now on a downward slide.

Now in his thirties, Denis still had something to offer, but with the arrival of Tommy Docherty, his days as a Manchester United player were now numbered. On April 7th 1973, unbeknown to the 48,593 supporters inside Old Trafford for the match against Norwich City, they were watching his last match in the red of United.

At the end of that season, Docherty gave Law a free transfer, amid much controversy, and he returned to Maine Road for the start of the 1973-74 campaign, climaxing in what was to be a dramatic swansong.

1973-74 was a season when United found themselves staring relegation in the face for the first time in thirty-seven years and a local 'derby' against Manchester City in the second last game, of what was a disastrous campaign, was not something they would have wanted on the agenda. Desperate for some return from the game, it looked, with only eight minutes remaining, that United were indeed going to claim a point in an, up until now, uneventful match.

A City attack saw the ball squirm through to an unmarked Law in front of the United goal. Instead of his cavalier approach to goalscoring, he innocuously took a back heeled jab at the ball and was as amazed as the wrong footed Stepney, to see the ball trickle over the line to give City a 1-0 lead. It was also Denis Law's last touch in League football. A pitch invasion duly followed as the clearly distressed figure of Law made his way back towards his own half and as more and more fans streamed onto the pitch, he was substituted.

"It was one of life's incredible ironies that I scored the goal", he was later to say. "I felt sick and have seldom felt so depressed in my life as I did that weekend".

When the dust had settled, it was not Denis Law's goal that sent United down, as other club's results had made relegation for United a certainty.

It is, however, a vision of Denis Law which will never be forgotten, but will always take second place to the sight of the blond headed, red shirted player, with no.10 on his back, white cuffs pulled down and one arm raised in salute of yet another Manchester United goal.

Despite 'that' goal, however, Denis Law will always be 'the King' of Old Trafford, something that was made even more obvious, on Saturday February 23rd 2002, when prior to United's home game against Aston Villa, Denis unveiled a ten foot high bronze statue of himself underneath the stand in the old Streford End. Immortalised forever!

If the Manchester United of the sixties spun round the axis of Law, Best and Charlton, there was another member of that illustrious side who performances more often than not greased the axis to ensure it rotated smoothly. His name was Pat Crerand.

Born in the east end of Glasgow, **Pat Crerand** joined his beloved Celtic from Duntocher Hiberian in August 1957.

The old adage of 'practise makes perfection' was particularly true in the case of the young Celtic player, as he was soon developing into one of the best half backs in Scotland, after making his debut in the green and white hoops in October 1958 in a Scottish League Cup tie against Queen of the South at Celtic Park.

It was not an uncommon sight at Celtic Park to see Crerand attempting to knock over traffic cones from various distances, often seventy to eighty yards, as he honed up on his passing skills.

Season 1960-61 was perhaps his best to date, winning a Scottish Cup runners up medal with the Glasgow side to accompany his Scotland under 23 and full international caps, with back page headlines a year later following a superb display in a friendly against Real Madrid.

Crerand's playing career, however, did not run smoothly and despite his undoubted talent, there was always a slight question mark as to his temperament.

On May 14th 1961, whilst playing for Scotland against Czechoslovakia in a World Cup qualifying tie, he was sent off for fighting with Kvasnak ten minutes before half-time. His Jeckle and Hyde side of his character also surfaced during a five-a-side competition at Falkirk. He was sent off for a second time at international level, whilst playing against Uruguay, a stormy encounter, when an unknown Scottish player punched the referee.

His relationship with Celtic chairman Bob Kelly could certainly be considered as stormy and things came to a head on New Years Day 1963. At half time, during an 'old firm' match against Rangers, he was involved in a flare up with trainer Sean Fallon and was never to play in a green and white hooped shirt again.

Two weeks later, he was trying on the red and white jersey of Manchester United

for size, with Matt Busby quickly agreeing to pay a sum of £56,000 for the talented wing half.

It was a transfer that Crerand knew nothing about until officials of both clubs had completed it. Despite leaving Celtic under something of a cloud, he was later to say, "Celtic will always be one of the great loves of my life". Crerand's Manchester United debut came in a friendly against Bolton Wanderers in Cork, on February 13th 1963, with his talent clearly visible despite playing on a mud covered pitch. "Crerand's forceful and constructive football gave United the plan for victory" wrote one reporter.

Ten days later came his Football League debut, against Blackpool at Old Trafford, "an intelligent and economical performance only exceeded by an exceptional goalkeeping performance by the visitors Tony Waiters".

He soon settled in Manchester and his skill and ball distribution soon made him a favourite with supporters, as well as playing a major part in United winning the F. A. Cup and the end of his first season. "Herd and Law get the goals as Crerand stars" proclaimed the headlines.

His Scotland career, having won sixteen full caps, came to an end in 1966, following various confrontations with the Scottish selectors, but his country's loss was clearly United's gain, as he added League Championship and European Cup winners medals, in 1965, 1967 and 1968, to the F. A. Cup one of 1963. "When Crerand played well, United played well" soon became a common saying. Something that George Best was to back up when he said, "Paddy made the team tick, he always gave United the edge when it mattered".

Despite taking his football seriously, Crerand also enjoyed a laugh. In November 1965, as United travelled to East Berlin to face Vorwarts, with a warning from Matt Busby regarding the strict standards required in that part of the world echoing in their ears, the United wing half filled in his immigration card under the name of "James Bond" with a destination of "Moscow" for the purpose of "espionage".

As the League appearances became fewer at the beginning of the seventies, more time was taken up coaching the younger players at Old Trafford and he was eventually appointed reserve team manager.

With the appointment of Tommy Docherty as manager, Pat Crerand was appointed his assistant, but the relationship soured, with Crerand's position demeaned to watching United's next opponents.

Fed up with the non-day to day involvement, he quickly

T / R

grasped the opportunity to become manager at Northampton Town in January 1976, quitting his £8,500 a year job. Six months in the hot seat proved to be long enough and Crerand severed his connections with club football.

The signing of Pat Crerand was what could be described by the well used clique, 'the last piece of the jigsaw', as Busby completed his rebuilding programme following the demise of his team at Munich.

Reaching Wembley and actually winning the F. A. Cup in 1963 was a major achievement, as United's League form that season had been, at times, abysmal, with two six game runs without a win. At the end of the season, they had only escaped relegation by the skin of their teeth.

The following season, however, saw a complete turn around, with fifty goals split between Denis Law (30) and David Herd (20), helping to take United to the opposite end of the table, finishing runners up to Liverpool.

Twelve months later, they had gone one better and were crowned Champions, following a 3-1 victory against Arsenal in the penultimate fixture of the season. The semi-final stages of both the F. A. Cup and the Inter Cities Fairs Cup had also been reached. United were back!

One youngster who made his League debut during those exciting mid-sixties days, was John Fitzpatrick, a typical looking teenager of the time, with his hair flapping below his collar as he ran around the pitch like a terrier dog, snapping at the heels of opposition forwards.

John Fitzpatrick, like Denis Law was an Aberdonian and was spotted by a United scout whilst playing for his local side Thistle Lads Club and was invited to Old Trafford for trials.

Before signing for Manchester United though, he asked, and was given, permission to play one last game with his old club. During the match, however, he broke his leg, leaving his United dream in ruins. Much to his relief, he made a complete recovery and in July 1962 signed apprenticeship forms.

Two years later, he was one of the stars of the F.A, Youth Cup winning side, alongside other youngsters who would soon be breaking into the first team, like Jimmy Rimmer, David Sadler, John Aston and George Best.

On February 24th 1965, he was given his first team opportunity, following an injury to Nobby Stiles, making his debut against Sunderland at Roker Park. On the last day of the season, he notched up a second appearance at Villa Park.

Appearances the following season, 1965-66, were again few and far between, but he did manage to write his name into the United record books, by becoming their first substitute in League football, replacing Denis Law at Tottenham on October 16th. Due to the performances of Crerand and Stiles though, his first team opportunities were severely limited.

Although there was not much of him, 5'6" and 9st 12lb, John Fitzpatrick was a tough tackler, who never gave less than 100% in whatever position he was selected for.

During 1967-68, he enjoyed his best season, notching up fourteen appearances, with three others as substitute.

Such was his versatility, he could easily adapt to an inside forward role, but mid-way through season 1968-69, Matt Busby decided to employ his defensive strengths in the full back position. Here he confidently played out a fifteen game run in the team, interrupted once, due to his selection at centre forward!

Because of his style of play, and perhaps also because of his appearance, he was often in trouble with officials. On one occasion, when sent off against A C Milan in the away leg of the European Cup semi-final, he had to be given a police escort to the dressing rooms.

1971 saw him sidelined with a second cartilage operation, producing a set back to his hopes of becoming a first team regular. The following year, he underwent five knee operations and eventually had to call it a day, at the age of only twenty-six.

United, in an excellent gesture, paid recognition to his services to the club over a nine year period and presented him with a cheque for £20,000. A special cabaret dinner raised a further £1,000.

1965-66, for the fifth season in a row, saw United reach the semi-finals of the F. A. Cup, but for the fourth of these, it was to be failure with the twin towers beckoning. It was also to be disappointment in the League, with the failure to retain the trophy, as well as in Europe where, with expectations running high, the team slumped to defeat as it had done in the F. A. Cup, at the semi-final stage.

Easy aggregate wins over Helsinki and Vorwaerts in the preliminary and first rounds set up an interesting confrontation against Benfica.

In the first leg at Old Trafford, United secured a one goal advantage with a 3-2 win, but with the majority of people giving them little chance in Portugal. In a superb second leg performance, the doubters were proved very much wrong, as United stormed to an unbelievable 5-1 win.

It was now considered to be United's cup, but a 2-0 defeat in Belgrade, against Partizan, gave them too much to do in the second leg. Especially as they were without the tormentor of the Portugese in the previous round, George Best. A solitary Stiles goal was nowhere near enough and the dream had gone once again.

For a young forward at the club during the mid-sixties, there must have been times when they felt like banging their heads against a brick wall, as United strode to their fourth post war Championship, with the regular forward line of Connelly, Charlton, Herd, Law and Best contributing eighty-three goals and being almost ever present throughout the season.

One of those frustrated youngsters in the Central League side was **Jimmy Ryan**, who had been signed as an amateur from Cowie Hearts, a Stirlingshire junior side, on December 7th 1962. Six weeks later, he signed professional. His first team debut came on May 4th 1966, against West Bromwich Albion away, and a favourable performance saw him retain his place for the remaining three games of that season, scoring in the penultimate fixture, a 6-1 victory over Aston Villa at Old Trafford.

It was back into the reserves at the start of the following season, with only a handful of appearances as United took the title, with a similar story unfolding the following campaign.

With George Best totally unmoveable on one flank and John Aston squeezing past him in the pecking order on the other, appearances were always going to be limited. The signing of Willie Morgan in August 1968 was to add further difficulties to his hopes of securing a regular place or even an extended run in the first team.

At the end of season 1969-70, having made only twenty-one League, three F. A. Cup and two European Cup appearances, with another three in the League as substitute, he was given a free transfer by United. He subsequently moved to Second Division Luton Town, where he was eventually able to obtain a regular first team spot.

Ryan was later to say "I don't think my dedication was what it should have been. When I was a teenager I think I lost my concentration. It was the time of the swinging sixties and I was a young lad growing up. United showed a lot of faith in my ability, but I do not think that I repaid it".

His old form slowly returned, following a lot of hard work and he proved a big asset to the Hatters, as they marched towards the First Division in 1974.

Having made one hundred and eighty three appearances, scoring twenty-one goals for Luton by 1976, he went to America during that summer for a five month loan spell with Dallas Tornados. The five months extended into four seasons, as the loan deal became a permanent move. A further three years were spent on the American indoor circuit with Witchita in Kanas.

An incredible time Ryan recalled, "we rode onto the pitch on the back of elephants for one game.

He then returned to Luton Town, joining the back-room staff, moving up the ladder to become reserve team coach and as he proved his worth over the years he was appointed manager in January 1990.

What could have been a lengthy and profitable appointment came to a rather sudden and unexpected end in June 1991, when he accepted an offer from Alex Ferguson to become reserve team manager at Old Trafford.

As he had done at Luton, Jim Ryan once again made a big impression, guiding the reserves to the Central League title in 1993-94, moving up to first team level as a coach, upon the departure of Steve McLaren in 2001.

Season 1966-67 epitomised Manchester United at their cavalier best. A football team awash with talent, that the crowds flocked to see at every opportunity, in the hope of some magical moment of brilliance from their array of top name players.

The home form was incomparable, scoring over fifty goals at Old Trafford for the fourth consecutive season, with Denis Law and David Herd top scorers for the fourth season out of five.

The Anglo Saxon side of the fifties now had a distinct dash of tartan woven through it.

It wasn't, however, just Manchester United who enjoyed success with a Scottish contingent within its ranks, as back in the sixties, almost every top side had their quota of Scots. In London, Chelsea had one of the games first overlapping full backs in Eddie McCreadie, along with the superb dribbling skills of Charlie Cooke. Across the Thames, Tottenham Hotspur, the first League and Cup double winners of the century boasted a backbone of Scots – goalkeeper Bill Brown, iron man Dave Mackay and the immensely talented John White. A few miles down the road, towards the end of the decade, Arsenal had Frank McLintock, Ian Ure and George Graham.

On Merseyside, the picture was the same, with the emerging Liverpool also being built with a distinct vein of Scottish blood running through the team. In goal was Tommy Lawrence, in the half back line was Ron Yeats (their captain) and Billy Stevenson, with Ian St John up front.

Across Stanley Park, Everton had Jimmy Gabriel, Alex Scott and the still hero worshipped Alex Young.

Leeds had Bremner, Bell and Collins, with Gray and Lorimer soon to follow. Newcastle had Moncur, while Sunderland claimed Jim Baxter and Neil Martin.

Many would have thought it simply fashionable to have the Scots around. Those in the know, were well aware

how much they contributed to the teams and the quality of play they provided.

The Championship of 1967 again gave Matt Busby the opportunity to pit his wits with the best of the continental sides and with his team now undoubtedly at its peak, many believed it to be a case of now or never.

The European campaign opened in September, with a 4-0 win at Old Trafford against Maltese Champions Hibernians, goals coming from David Sadler and Denis Law, scoring two each. The second leg in Malta, was a complete non-event, resulting in a goalless draw.

Round two, produced a much harder task, with the equally unknown Sarajevo the opposition. A second consecutive 0-0 in the away leg, gave the return at Old Trafford an added bite and goals from the left wing pairing of Best and Aston took United through.

The quarter-final opposition of Gornik were always going to produce a tough test, but the 2-0 home leg victory gave United the cushion that they needed and on a freezing, snow covered pitch in Poland, United held out as Gornik won 1-0.

The League Championship was also there to be retained during 1967-68, but two defeats in the last three fixtures – 6-3 at West Bromwich Albion and 2-1 against Sunderland at Old Trafford, saw the trophy make its way across Manchester to Maine Road.

Normally such an event would have been hard to swallow, but by the time Sunderland acclaimed their surprise victory in Manchester on May 11th, the players, management and supporters of Manchester United had more important things on their minds.

Four days later, United were due in Madrid to face old rivals Real, in the second leg of the European Cup semi-final.

A solitary George Best goal at Old Trafford in the 1st leg had given them the advantage, but the Bernabeau Stadium was an awesome arena and this was not considered a big enough lead to ensure a passage into the Final.

On a memorable balmy night in the Spanish capital, goals from David Sadler, Bill Foulkes and an own goal gave United a 3-3 draw and at long last, a place in the Wembley Final.

At the north London stadium, there was only ever going

to be one winner, but it required extra time to clinch the trophy, defeating Benfica 4-1.

It was a campaign of mixed emotions, especially for one youngster who broke into the first team early in September and was an ever present up until April, only to miss out on the crowning glory of the end of season triumph.

Coatbridge born **Francis Burns** had represented Lanarkshire Schools and captained Scotland Schoolboys on three occasions before joining Manchester United as an amateur upon leaving school in June 1964, signing professional the following year.

He soon added Scottish Youth honours to his CV, as he moved through the United ranks to the Central League side. With a first team place now within his sights, he was delighted to find himself included in the United party to tour Australia at the end of season 1966-67, where he made his initial appearance against Auckland on May 28th, playing left back in the 8-1 win.

Having switched from halfback to full back, he did not have long to wait for his opportunity in the League side, as an injury to Shay Brennan in only the third game of season 1967-68, saw him make his debut at West Ham on September 2nd in the left back position, with regular left back Tony Dunne switching to the right flank.

Such were his impressive performances that he added Scottish under 23 honours to those previously won at lower levels.

As season 1967-68 progressed, Burns remained first choice left back, both in the League and in Europe, but with the second leg of the European Cup semi-final on the horizon, manager Matt Busby dealt the youngster a killer blow. Although he had played his part in the first leg victory against Madrid at Old Trafford, Busby left him out of the return, playing the "more experienced" Shay Brennan at right back and switching Tony Dunne back to the left side. This pairing remained for the Final, leaving Francis Burns a very disappointed spectator on the sidelines.

Ironically, the following season saw him notch up only fourteen appearances due to injury problems, but he bounced

back for the start of season 1969-70, with a full Scotland cap being won against Austria in Vienna in November.

Three cartilage operations in eighteen months didn't help his United career, or indeed his international career and season 1970-71 and 1971-72 saw his opportunities limited to thirty-one appearances over the two.

In the summer of 1972, Southampton made an offer of £50,000 for him, which United accepted and he was soon on his way to the south coast. His injury problems were to follow, with a fourth knee operation limiting his appearances to twenty-one.

Former team mate Bobby Charlton, having taken up the managers post at Preston North End, brought him back to Lancashire, where he was to make some two hundred and seventy three appearances during his seven years at Deepdale, playing mainly in mid-field.

In 1981, now in the twilight of his career, he moved across the Irish Sea to join Shamrock Rovers before finally retiring. One unusual accolade that Francis Burns could claim, would be the most used United substitute. A look at the record books will show that he made only thirteen such appearances, a figure easily surpassed by many others, but his "record" is just for one particular match, because during the ninety minutes, he was on and off the pitch five times. Playing against Eintracht Frankfurt in Los Angeles on May 17th 1970, Francis Burns began the match, but was replaced by Steve James. He then returned to the fray taking over from Paul Edwards. He was later taken off with Willie Watson coming on. Before making another re-appearance as a replacement for Pat Crerand!

Season 1967-68 was also to see another young Scot break into the first team picture, but Frank Kopel was only to make two appearances during this time, one as substitute and suffer none of the disappointment of his former Scottish Schoolboy team mate Francis Burns.

Like Burns, Falkirk born **Frank Kopel** joined United upon leaving school and was also converted from a half back to full back in his early days with the club.

Having performed to a creditable standard at reserve team level, he was selected as substitute against Burnley on September 9th 1967, (a game that saw Francis Burns open his

United scoring account), coming on in place of fellow Scot John Fitzpatirck. He was, however, to wait a further couple of months before his full debut, against Nottingham Forest, at the City Ground on October 28th, as a replacement for Tony Dunne. During season 1968-69, he managed seven appearances, plus one as substitute, in the opening half of the season, but with the switch of John Fitzpatrick to full back, he was to find another barrier in his way as the yearned for a first team place.

In March 1969, an enquiry by Blackburn Rovers led to his transfer to Ewood Park for a £25,000 fee, but once again, he struggled to secure a regular place. Making only twenty-five appearances in around two and a half seasons.

Everyone needs a little bit of luck at sometime or other and for Frank Kopel, it came in the shape of a move back to Scotland. In February 1972, he left Lancashire, his home for the past eight years and moved to Tayside, joining Dundee United.

In a ten year career at Tannadice, he amassed two hundred and eighty four appearances, plus a further seven as substitute, winning Scottish League Cup runners up medals in 1980 and 1981 and a Scottish Cup runners up medals in 1974 and 1981.

Season 1981-82, at the age of thirty-one, he moved down a couple of divisions to see out his career with Arbroath, where he made a further sixty-two appearances, with one as substitute.

With United having such a regular team in that successful sixties period it was difficult for the likes of Ryan, Kopel and to a certain extent Fitzpatrick to break into the team and secure a permanent place. For others, like Best, Aston and Kidd, they did manage to establish themselves after making the breakthrough.

There was also the danger of a new signing arriving at the club, pushing reserve team players further down the pecking order, especially if the signing cost a considerable fee and was destined to be a future internationalist.

One such signing was **Willie Morgan**, a £110,000 signing from Burnley in August 1968. Morgan, born in Sauchie, near Alloa, had joined Burnley from Fishcross Boys Club in May 1960, signing professional forms in October of the following year. He made his initial breakthrough at Turf Moor in April 1963, but following John Connelly's transfer to United during season 1963-64, he came more to the fore and slowly began to make a name for himself. His dribbling skills and natural

talent earned him Scotland under 23 caps and one full cap, against Northern Ireland in 1967. It also prompted Matt Busby to sign him immediately following the European Cup Final success in 1968.

Upon his arrival, he took over the No. 7 shirt, which George Best had made his own, with the Irishman switching to the opposite flank.

Best by now was the pin-up boy of British football and Morgan, with his similar hair style and fashion sense seemed to harbour a personal ambition to attempt to emulate the multi-talented Belfast Boy. However, setting up his own fan club before Best, was about the only time he was to manage the upper hand.

More of a goal maker than a goal taker, he scored only thirty three in two hundred and ninety one games, plus three as substitute, it had taken Morgan some time to settle at United.

He was to find himself out of favour for a while during Wilf McGuinness's short reign as manager, but with the beginning of the end of the wayward George Best's career now clearly looming on the horizon and also the appointment of Frank O'Farrell into the United hot seat, he found himself back in the frame of things during 1971-72. His regular, solid performances in the United team also earned him a recall into the Scotland squad, bringing him a further twenty caps.

As United began to struggle performance wise, it was Morgan who became relied upon more and more during the reign of Tommy Docherty. It was to be a period, which despite the team's short comings, perhaps saw the best of Willie Morgan.

As United slid towards the Second Division in 1973-74, Morgan, by now employed in more of a mid-field role, played in all but one of the League fixtures, scoring only two goals. A total perhaps not to be considered so bad, when it is taken into consideration that the club's top scorer only had six!

Morgan added a Second Division Championship medal to his collection of honours, as United stormed to the 1974-75 title. However, his Manchester United days were numbered, as his relationship with Tommy Docherty, a man he had recommended for the managers job at Old Trafford, hit a sour note in October 1974. He was substituted, much to his disgust against Southampton, leaving the ground before full time, signalling the beginning of the end of his United career. His position was clearly under threat, when Docherty brought Steve Coppell to the club in the latter days of that somewhat memorable Second Division campaign.

It was also a season which he almost never started, as he suffered a serious eye injury whilst playing tennis.

The sweet and sour relationship with Docherty came to an end during the summer of 1975, when he was allowed to leave United and re-join his previous club Burnley. This was to be a brief re-acquaintance, making only thirteen appearances, before moving across Lancashire to join Bolton Wanderers.

At Burden Park, he was to enjoy four successful seasons, winning another Second Division Championship medal in 1978, as Bolton returned to the big time.

One appearance that Morgan had not planned for in 1978 was in court, facing his former friend and manager, Tommy Docherty.

Following a Granada TV programme, Docherty took out a libel action against the company and Morgan in a much publicised case. Amid furious accusations from both sides, Docherty eventually admitted that he had lied under oath and the case collapsed.

Like many other talented players during the late 1970's early 1980's, he was lured to America for summer football, where he played in the NASL for Chicago Sting and Minnesota Kicks.

Seasons 1980-81 and 1981-82 saw him at Blackpool, who were to be his final League club, where he played forty-two games, before retiring from the game at the end of the latter season.

THE WINDS OF CHANGE

Following the European Cup success of 1967-68, United once again reached the semi-final of the tournament in 1968-69, but slumped to eleventh in the First Division. The retention of the prestigious European trophy looked a probability, until the semi-final stage, with a 2-0 defeat in Milan giving them much to do back in Manchester.

Leading 1-0, the Milan goal was under constant siege for the final twenty minutes. A Crerand chip was prodded goalwards by Law, whose upraised arm, in front of a bellowing, throbbing Stretford End, signalled what was thought to be the equaliser.

To everyone's (except the Italians) disappointment, the referee waved play on as a Milan defender kicked the ball away from the open goalmouth. The dreams of a second European Final faded in the Manchester mist.

It was now becoming clear to even the most devoted Manchester United supporter that many of the team, who had brought the club so much success, were now coming towards the end of their careers and replacements were desperately required. Surprisingly, very little was done about it.

The appointment of Wilf McGuinness as manager in April 1969 did little to signal the beginning of a revival or a re-building process and during his brief spell as team manager, he made only one signing, bringing centre half Ian Ure from Arsenal. The signing surprised many, as the player was nearing his thirtieth birthday and was seen as nothing more than a stop gap.

Born in Ayr, **John Francombe Ure** (to give him his real name), began his senior career with Ayr Albion and then Dalry Thistle from where he was signed as a nineteen year old by Dundee. A former member of the Scottish National Association of Boys Clubs team, he gained a regular place in the Dens Park side during 1960 and played an important part in Dundee's League Championship win two years later. Doing likewise in their European Cup campaign of the following season, which saw the Dens Park side reach the semi-final stages, losing to eventual winners A C Milan. At just over 6' tall and weighing 12st 10lb, he was an imposing figure in the heart of the Dundee defence, with his mane of blond hair making him stand out even more.

Due to Dundee's success and his own outstanding performances, he won Scotland recognition at both under 23 and full international level, winning his first cap at this level against Wales in 1962. Numerous club managers were now also beginning to show him more than a little attention.

In August 1963, a tussle for his services was won by Arsenal, who paid Dundee a fee of £62,500, a then record fee between two British clubs, to take him to London. His move south proved a major success and a further three Scottish caps were won during his five years at Highbury, where he also took part in two Football League Cup Finals, but had also endured two cartilage operations and suffered ongoing pain in his right knee, as well as two broken jaws.

A very physical and aggressive player, which two broken jaws during his Arsenal days would signify, Ian Ure perhaps first came to the attention of the Old Trafford faithful during season 1966-67. During a tempestuous match on October 29th between United and Arsenal, he was sent off along with Denis Law, after a running feud ended with punches being exchanged in the centre of the pitch.

With Bill Foulkes, at the end of his Manchester United playing career, a replacement central defender was urgently required and Wilf McGuinness paid Arsenal £80,000 in August 1969 for Ure.

He immediately added a hint of stability to the United defence, following his debut in a 0-0 draw at Wolves on August 23rd. However, it was to be something of an Indian summer for the big, twenty-nine year old defender.

The following season, 1970-71, saw him lose his place, mainly due to injury and his knee failing to stand up to the physical demands of First Division football. He made the last of his sixty five appearances for United at Derby County on Boxing Day 1970, in what was his first senior game for United in two months.

At the end of 1971-72, following a whole season in the reserves, he was given a free transfer and on August 4th, he

T / R

returned to Scotland joining St Mirren at the age of thirty-two, as a replacement for Gordon McQueen who had been recently transferred to Leeds United. But he was only to start three first team games with the Paisley side.

Prior to the end of 1972-73, he retired from playing and took over the manager's job with junior side Cumnock, moving to East Stirling in a similar position, where he took over from Alex Ferguson. A year later, he took up a coaching post in Iceland with FH Hafnarfjorduri, but this was to last less than a year, despite being offered an extension of his contract, as he decided to put his family first and left the game for good.

Wilf McGuinness found the task of replacing Sir Matt Busby a difficult one, with the fact that he had played alongside many of those now having to regard him as "the boss", proving something of a stumbling block.

To his credit though, McGuinness gave the job everything he had and his dedication to the club and the job brought him something of a reward with semi-final appearances in both the F.A. Cup and the Football League Cup in his first season. A second League Cup semi-final appearance followed during 1970-71. Success in many minds and at many clubs, but not Manchester United.

Perhaps the fact that it was a Third Division club, Aston Villa, who had marched into the Football League Cup Final of 1970-71, played a significant part in the board reconsidering his appointment as manager. Amid rumours of an unsettled dressing room, McGuinness was demoted and Busby re-instated as manager.

One young Scot did have cause to be grateful to Wilf McGuinness during his period in charge of team affairs, as the United manager of eighteen months had given him his initial taste of first team football.

Willie Watson, a Motherwell born full back had been brought into the side at right back against Blackpool at home on September 26th 1970, in place of Paul Edwards, who had began the season in this position. Before the managerial re-shuffle took place, he was to manage a total of eight League and two League Cup appearances.

A former Scotland Schoolboy international, Watson

joined Manchester United in the summer of 1965, signing professional the following year. By 1968, he was a regular in the Central League side, but always found his path to the first team blocked.

Towards the end of season 1969-70, former United defender Ian Greaves took the youngster to Huddersfield Town on loan, but he failed to make any first team appearances at Leeds Road.

Having been allowed to go out on loan, there were suggestions that he might be released by United, but he was re-called to Old Trafford and eventually got his big break, an opportunity he thought at one time he would never get, having suffered a broken leg in a youth competition.

Upon Busby's re-appointment as manager, it was back to the reserves for Watson and he did not feature in the first team again until a three match run in October 1972, under Frank O'Farrell.

In the summer of 1973, he went to America to play for Miami Toros and upon his return considered going to play in South Africa, having been released by United.

A trial with Burnley failed to produce a contract and when the opportunity arose to return to his native Motherwell, in September 1973, he jumped at the chance.

Four days after Willie Watson made his second United appearance, a second young defender from north of the border, **Ian Donald** stepped into the first team for his debut, at right back against Portsmouth in a Football League Cup tie at Old Trafford on October 7th 1970.

Sadly for both Watson and Donald, Paul Edwards regained his fitness almost immediately and stepped back into the right back slot. Allthough Watson, as previously mentioned did manage further appearances during that season, Ian Donald failed to make the first eleven again until September 23rd 1972 against Derby County at home, almost two years later.

Born in Aberdeen, another former Scotland Schoolboy internationalist and later a youth internationalist, joined United in 1968 from Gordon's College, whilst having played a few games for the Bank's O' Dee 'A' juveniles. His career failed to blossom as expected in Manchester and his four League and one further Football League Cup outing, spread between mid-September and the beginning of November 1972, were all he was to amass.

Following Tommy Docherty's arrival, the playing staff was severely primed and Ian Donald was one of the unlucky ones who were given a free transfer. Returning to Scotland, not surprisingly a little disillusioned, he joined Partick Thistle for a brief spell before moving to Arbroath, where he was to stay for two years.

In 1990, he followed in his fathers footsteps onto the board of Aberdeen F.C., later serving as Chairman and vice-Chairman. It is interesting to note that it was Ian's father Dick, who appointed a certain Alex Ferguson as manager of Aberdeen in June 1972.

The return of Sir Matt Busby to the helm in December 1971 possibly saved the club from finishing at the wrong end of the table some months later and a similar position to that of the previous season, eighth was finally secured much to everyone's relief.

Busby, however, was more than happy to step down from the enforced position of manager at the end of 1970-71, following the appointment of Frank O'Farrell. The quite spoken Irishman, in hindsight, would have been better staying with Leicester City. His first season in charge ended with the team in a similar position to that of the previous two seasons – eighth, but there was to be little in the way of progress.

The following season of 1972-73 stuttered and started. Three defeats in the opening three fixtures were followed by three draws, then a further two defeats. A 5-0 defeat at Crystal Palace on December 16th, with only five

victories all season, ultimately brought to an end O'Farrell's reign at Manchester United.

Perhaps if the circumstances had been better, with no distractions from George Best, things would have worked out better for Frank O'Farrell, with the signings of two Scotsmen possibly the key to what could have been success.

One of those players arrived at the beginning of March 1972,when O'Farrell made an excellent signing and one that was to pay dividends for Manchester United, long after the quietly spoken Irishman had left the club. The player in question was Martin Buchan, who cost £125,000 when signed from Aberdeen, and was someone who was to etch his name into the history of the club in the years ahead.

Martin Buchan was born in the 'Granite City' and into a footballing family, as his father had played for the home town club and Dundee United, before spending ten years in the Highland League with Buckie Thistle.

At Cummings Park School, their team which included the young master Buchan did not loose a game for three years, but upon moving to a rugby playing grammar school he had to look elsewhere to play competitively. He found a place in the local Boys Brigade side and from there progressed into the Aberdeen Youth League with Banks O' Dee, a team he was to captain to numerous honours.

At the age of seventeen and a half, he had to make the big decision of whether to continue his studies or join Aberdeen. "I wondered if I would be good enough", Buchan was to relate later. "I had seen many promising players fall by the wayside at professional level, but I had always wanted to be a footballer and so I joined Aberdeen. Although I did tell them that I would give it until I was twenty-one before finally deciding what I wanted to do".

A token fee of £250 was paid to Banks O' Dee by Aberdeen in 1966 for the tall and talented defender and six months after signing progress was certainly being made, as he was a member of the Scotland Youth team, alongside future team mate Lou Macari.

He made his debut against Dunfermline a couple of months after signing and managed three other first team outings during that season. Five years later, he was not

T/R

only a first team regular, but also club captain and by his 'deadline date', he had led Aberdeen to a Scottish Cup win over Celtic, becoming the youngest to ever to achieve such an honour. While a year later, in 1971, he was voted Scottish Player of the Year, while also winning his first full Scotland cap against Portugal, coming on as substitute for Eddie Colquhoun .

Frank O'Farrell certainly signed a player of quality and Martin Buchan quickly settled at Old Trafford, becoming an integral part of the team, following his debut against Tottenham Hotspur at White Hart Lane on March 24th 1972. He was to make the number six shirt virtually his own for almost eleven years, although all his appearances during his initial two months at the club were made with the number four on his back.

Martin Buchan was soon regarded as Manchester United's most influential player, with his cool, no nonsense approach to the game and his on the field leadership. Tommy Docherty, upon his appointment as manager, had no hesitation in appointing him captain and by 1977, having given him his first full Scotland cap against Portugal at Hampden in 1972. The classy defender then guided Manchester United to both the Second Division Championship and the F.A. Cup, becoming the first player to captain a side to the latter and also the Scottish equivalent.

He was a model professional, but was not afraid to speak up to anyone in authority if he thought that they were wrong and he also expected his fellow team mates to show a similar dedication to the game as he did.

During one match at Old Trafford, with United fighting for the points, he unceremoniously slapped team mate Gordon Hill across the head for some slack defending. On another occasion, he refused to hand over his passport to club officials prior to a pre-season tour, telling them that he was quite capable of looking after it himself.

This side of his personality was not something that he had developed since joining Manchester United, as similar examples of his thoughts and actions had been noted whilst with Aberdeen.

"A rebel" were words that he had used to describe himself while at Pittodrie and once, during a half time team talk, he was to tell Aberdeen manager Eddie Turnbull, that he was "talking rubbish". He also admitted that he would rather join Celtic than "the inflexible Rangers".

Never afraid to speak out, his club and country bosses of the time also received comments from the seemingly unflappable Aberdonian.

Willie Ormond was Scotland manager in May 1975 when Martin Buchan packed his bags at walked out on the team prior to a match against England at Wembley, after the manager had "promised him a place", then omitted him from the team. Sitting in the stand, he watched Scotland comprehensively beaten 5-1, after the match being quoted as saying "Willie Ormond made a fool of me and I do not like anyone doing that". He later refused to play against Rumania, a move that could have brought a premature end to his international career, but he not only returned to the side, but returned as captain, such was his influence.

With Tommy Docherty, he also had his moments, being sent off by the United manager during a practice match at the Cliff for "speaking his mind".

One other incident, which exemplifies the player, came following a new boot deal at United with a manufacturer that he did not use. Nor did he care to use, as he refused to accept the money that came with the deal and continued to use his own preferred make of boot.

Goals were a rare commodity in Buchan's make up, with only four in over four hundred and fifty appearances for Manchester United, but he rarely strode up-field to be a danger to opposition defences.

An injury during season 1980-81 put him out of action for twelve games and the following season he again missed games because of a similar problem. Season 1982-83 saw him start only three games, spread between the opening four months of the season and because he could not reach the high standards that he set himself, he decided to leave United.

Joining Oldham Athletic on a free transfer, having been

awarded a testimonial by United in August 1983, he only managed twenty-eight games for the Boundary Park outfit, over a two season period. Injuries were again the cause of the missed fixtures and after only a further four games during 1984-85, he decided to call it a day.

Burnley managed to entice him into management, but after only one hundred and nine days in charge he resigned. Later saying, "I have not been happy with my own performance. There were also aspects of the job that I could not handle" and walked away from club football for good.

In the 1960's, the name of Manchester United was associated with goals, as their free scoring side clawed their way from relegation candidates to European Cup winners over a five year period, when the likes of either Law, Herd, Charlton, Best and Connelly could find the back of the net on a regular basis.

We are now in the 1970's, however, and the likes of Herd and Connelly have long since gone. Charlton was beginning to find each game harder, leaving Law and Best to give the 'goals for' column a healthy and respectable look. Compared to the 1960's, Manchester United were now scoring twenty goals per season less!

As the opening games of season 1972-73 showed, United were clearly lacking an out and out goalscorer, having scored only four in the opening nine fixtures. Best scoring two, Law and Ian Storey-Moore the others.

Aware to the problem, manager Frank O'Farrell finally decided that something had to be done and the player to solve his main problem within the team was Bournemouth's Ted MacDougall, a prolific scorer in the lower Divisions with the south coast club.

Although born in Inverness, **Ted MacDougall's** family had moved to the Widnes area when he was just a youngster. Following a short spell with ICI Recs. in Widnes, he joined Liverpool in 1964, signing professional two years later. The closest he was to come to a first team appearance with the Anfield side, was a place on the substitute bench for one game. The lack of first team opportunities and the chance of regular football at York City prompted a £5,000 transfer in 1976.

At York, he soon found himself amongst the goals, (thirty-

four in eighty-four games) and two years after moving to Bootham Crescent, he was on the move again, with a £10,000 fee taking him to Bournemouth. It was here that he really made a name for himself as a goalscorer and by Christmas 1970, his was the name on everyone's lips. His goals played a major part in Bournemouth's promotion to the Third Division at the end of 1970-71 and on November 20th 1971, he wrote himself into the record books, by scoring nine of his team's eleven goals against Margate in the F.A.Cup. His one hundred and three goals in just over one hundred and forty games for the Dean Court side had alerted numerous club's to his undoubted potential. It was Manchester United's Frank O'Farrell, however, who stepped in first, paying £195,000, a record for a Third Division player, to take him north to Old Trafford.

"I hope the fans do not expect miracles" said MacDougall upon signing. Expectations were high, but goals would suffice.

He made his United debut at West Bromwich on October 7th 1972, but he had to wait until the following Saturday against Birmingham City at Old Trafford, before notching his first goal for his new club, scoring the only goal of the game.

Despite his arrival, United continued to struggle, with MacDougall getting few breaks, much to the crowds growing concern, although the second goal in a 2-0 win over Liverpool, did endear him to the fickle Old Trafford support.

United and MacDougall continued to stutter along and two further goals in five games were not enough to save O'Farrell's job, as he was sacked on December 19th,following the 5-0 defeat at Crystal Palace.

Into the hot seat came Tommy Docherty and despite scoring the only goal in the new managers first game in charge, a 1-0 win over Leeds United at Old Trafford, MacDougall's days were clearly numbered.

"After Tommy Docherty was appointed as manager, I felt that my face would not fit. With some managers you know you are not going to be wanted", MacDougall was to say. The manager indeed made it clear that the player was available for transfer and in February 1972, only five months after joining Manchester United, he was sold to West Ham for £170,00.

Perhaps MacDougall was unlucky in the fact that United did not utilise his strengths to their advantage or perhaps he was just not a Manchester United player.

At West Ham, he again found his appearances limited, with his twenty four outings bringing only a mere five goals and during 1973-74 he was suddenly on the move again, to Norwich City, a transfer that was to put the smile back onto his face and start the goals flowing again on a regular basis. With the East Anglian club, he was to score fifty-one goals in one hundred and twelve appearances and also confounded his critics by breaking into the Scottish international side, winning seven caps between 1975 and 1976, scoring on his debut against Sweden.

Season 1976-77 saw MacDougall return to the south coast, joining Southampton and in his two years at the Dell, he scored forty-two goals in eighty six appearances. Once again proving to his critics that he could score goals if given the service and the opportunity.

Since his departure from Old Trafford, Ted MacDougall made a point of getting on with his career, despite a behind the scenes wrangle continuing between Bournemouth and United, as the former pressed for payment of money they claimed to be owed as part of the original transfer fee. In November 1978, at a time when the player was about to rejoin Bournemouth on a free transfer from Southampton, Manchester United were ordered by the Law Courts to pay £22,000 to the Cherries, as part of the original deal.

His return to Dean Court yielded only sixteen goals in fifty two games between 1978-9 and 1979-80 and a later move to Blackpool, where he was to become player coach and assistant manager, he failed to score in thirteen appearances. A journey around non-League football for a short spell eventually saw him hang up his boots in December 1983, having tasted summer football in both Canada and South Africa.

Looking back on his playing career, it could well have been a case of 'what might have been', if things had turned out different for him at Old Trafford. But, with some two hundred and fifty six League goals, he could always say that he was the first Scottish player since Denis Law to score over two hundred. He might also claim that his Old Trafford career might have been different if it had not been for the arrival of Thomas Henderson Docherty in December 1973.

One of football's larger than life characters, **Tommy Docherty** was born in Glasgow and always harboured dreams of pulling on the famous green and white hooped shirts of his boyhood heroes Celtic.

As a teenager, he played with St Paul's Shettleston BG and Shettleston Juniors before joining the army, serving with the HLI, where he progressed to the rank of sergeant. Demobbed on July 12th 1948, he signed for his beloved Celtic two weeks later. Although a tough tackling centre half, he was somewhat surprised to be given his debut at outside right, and so soon after signing, against arch-rivals Rangers on August 21st. Not surprisingly, he did not make too much of an impression in that unfamiliar role and was back in the reserves the following week, not re-appearing in the Celtic first team again until October 23rd of that year. This time, it was in his natural position, taking over from the regular No.5 Bobby Evans, who was on Scottish international duty in Wales.

Having made only nine League appearances, scoring twice, for Celtic, he suddenly found himself a transfer target of Preston North End. On November 4th 1949, he left Glasgow and headed south to Lancashire, after Preston had paid £2,000 for his signature. "When I was transferred, it was one of the biggest disappointments of my life" he was later to say.

At Deepdale, however, he never looked back, as his career quickly took off and during his nine seasons with Preston he helped them to the Second Division title in 1950-51 and to runners-up in the 1954 F.A. Cup Final, when they lost to 3-2 to West Bromwich Albion. His performances also gained him full Scottish representative honours, making his debut against Wales in 1952 and winning a total of twenty-five full caps, (plus a further two in 'B' internationals), with the added distinction of being selected as captain.

In August 1958, following a brief loan spell with Third

Lanark in 1956, Tommy Docherty once again moved south, this time to London, signing for Arsenal in a £29,5000 transfer. With the Gunners, he added a further three Scottish caps to his impressive total, but achieved little else, before moving across London to join Chelsea in February 1961 in a player-coach, having helped out at Oxford University and Barnet in a part-time coaching capacity, whilst still a player at Highbury.

The following September, he was appointed manager, but could little to prevent the club from finishing bottom of the table and dropping into the Second Division.

Twelve months later though, he had guided them back into the top flight and to a regular top five placing between 1965 and 1967. There was also three successive F.A. Cup semi finals, reaching Wembley and lifting the trophy in 1967 A semi final spot in the Inter Cities Fairs Cup of 1965-66 and a Football League Cup triumph during 1964-65.

After building such a good side, Docherty surprisingly resigned in October 1967, taking over the manager's post at Rotherham United the following month. Under the new manager, although in the lower half of Division Two, they reached the last eight in the F.A. Cup and regularly had gates of around the 20,000 mark.

One year later, the nomadic Docherty was on the move yet again, this time to Queens Park Rangers, for what was to be his briefest managerial appointment.. Appointed on November 6th 1968, he left on December 5th, twenty-nine days later.

Within a fortnight he was trying the chair in the Aston Villa's managers office for size, this time staying in the job long enough to unpack a few suitcases. He was to find the going tough in the Midlands, narrowly avoiding relegation in his first season, but being unable to turn around the team's fortune during 1969-70 and prevent relegation into the Third Division.

In January 1970, with Villa looking capable of making a return to the Second Division, Tommy Docherty was sacked and shortly afterwards took up an appointment with F.C. Oporto in Portugal.

By April 1971, he was back in Britain, taking up the post of assistant manager, under Terry Neil at Second Division Hull City. Two months later though, he was appointed caretaker manager of the Scottish national side and in November 1971, he was given the job on a full time basis, laying the basis of the World Cup qualifying side of 1972.

An approach was made by Manchester United in December 1972, inviting him to take over from the sacked Frank O'Farrell and he jumped at the chance. In his first season, he saved the club from relegation, but twelve months later the drop into the Second Division became a reality.

In the unfamiliar surroundings of the lower Division, United played some of their best football in years and romped to the Championship at their first attempt. Season's 1975-76 and 1976-77 brought appearances in the F.A.Cup Final, losing to Southampton, unexpectedly, in the former but defeating Liverpool 2-1 in the latter.

On the outside, everything at Old Trafford looked fine. There was a trophy in the cabinet, the team was playing exciting attacking football, but a few weeks after the Wembley triumph, the 'Doc's' career was again in disarray. Unknown to anyone, he had been having an affair with the wife of club physiotherapist Laurie Brown, and amid much newspaper speculation and following a board meeting on July 4th 1977, Docherty was sacked.

From then on, the managerial career of Tommy Docherty was a series of brief appointments and could fill numerous more pages of this book.

Upon leaving United he took over at Derby County in September 1977 and in the following eleven years held either the managers post or a coaching role at Queens Park Rangers (where he was to leave on May 6th 1980 only to be re-instated nine days later), Sydney Olympic, Preston North End, Melbourne, Sydney Olympic (again), Wolves and Altrincham.

His career in Management was always stormy, dropping established stars, fining others and sending players home from away trips. On the other hand, he always showed an eye for some shrewd buying in the transfer market, signing many talented players for bargain fees.

With every club he has been with he seemed to achieve something, whether it be a trophy or relegation, leaving a club in disarray or giving it hope where none really existed. Wherever he went, you certainly knew that 'the Doc' had been there. Whether you liked him or hated him, you certainly could not ignore him or keep him out of the headlines.

Docherty in his own individualistic style jumped into the Old Trafford managerial seat and wasted no time in creating his 'Manchester United'. Within days of his arrival, the cheque book was out and the re-building work had began.

The first of what was to be numerous signings was George Graham, from Arsenal for a fee of £120,000.

"From the moment I took the United job' he was later to say, "I wanted George. He has always played well for me. He was one of my best bargains at Chelsea, when I signed him from Aston Villa for £6,000.

"I didn't want to sell him to Arsenal for £75,00, but circumstances at that time forced me to do so.

"When I became Scotland team manager, I had no hesitation in picking him for my World cup squad. Again he did a marvellous job and I am confident that he will do a vital job for us".

George Graham was born in Bargeddie, Lanarkshire, but played all his football south of the border.

The former Coatbridge schoolboy player joined the Aston Villa ground staff, as a fifteen year old, in 1959, signing professional two years later. In his early days with the Midlands side, he gained Scottish Youth honours and also represented the Rest of the U.K. against England. He made his Football league debut during season 1962-63, but managed only eight appearances in two seasons, before joining Chelsea in June 1964.

Despite being more of a playmaker, he scored thirty-five goals in seventy-two appearances, as Tommy Docherty transformed the Stamford Bridge side, taking them to

Football League Cup success over Leicester City in 1964-65. A competition where George Graham had been a losing finalist two years earlier with Villa.

In October 1966, he crossed London to join Arsenal and as he had done on his debuts for Villa and Chelsea, he scored. During his six years with the Gunners, he played what was to be the best football of his career, helping them to successive Football League Cup Finals in 1968 and 1969 and playing his part in the 'double' success of 1970-71. Winning the 'man of the match' award in the Wembley Cup Final. The following year, he was to win the first of twelve Scottish caps against Portugal.

On December 28th 1972, six days after Tommy Docherty's appointment as manager, George graham became a Manchester United player, with the new manager hoping that his steadying influence would help save United from the drop into Division Two.

"I could have joined Everton or West Ham", said Graham at the time, "but when the chance came to join the old magician at Old Trafford, I didn't really need to stop and think. It took me ten minutes to sign for him when he was Chelsea's manager and it took me half that time with the move to Manchester United".

Ironically, Graham made his debut against his former club Arsenal (a game United lost 3-1), but went on to play a major part in keeping the club in the top flight, taking on a more defensive mid-field role, something that was dictated more by the plight of the team than the players talent.

Upon the departure of Bobby Charlton, George Graham was made team captain, but as United's form went from bad to worse, his own form subsequently suffered and he became the main target of the disgruntled supporters.

He lost his regular place in the team in mid-January 1974 and managed only a rare outing before being involved in a player exchange deal with Portsmouth's Ron Davies, one of Docherty's stranger transfer deals.

In a two year spell at Portsmouth, Graham made sixty-one appearances, scoring five goals, before returning to London to join Crystal Palace. A club he helped into the Second Division and where he was later to become Youth Team coach upon his retiring from playing in May 1980.

He took up a similar post at Queens Park Rangers the following year and in December 1982 stepped into the

vacant manager's job at Millwall, beginning what was to be a highly successful career in such positions. With the south London club, he steered them to a Football League Trophy win in 1983, followed by a place in the F.A. Cup quarter-finals and promotion into the Second Division in 1985. Setting the club up for its push towards the top flight for the first time in their history.

The rewards, however, were not to come until he returned to Highbury in may 1986, when he made footballing history by becoming the first person to play for and manage a team who won the League Championship, F.A. Cup and Football League Cup.

In 1993-94, he also added the European Cup Winners Cup to his list of managerial honours.

Later events would somewhat sour his achievements as a manager, but there is certainly no denying that George Graham was a success both on and off the pitch.

Two days after George Graham's arrival at Old Trafford, a fellow countryman and another player who had been associated with Arsenal joined him.

Alex Forsyth's spell at Highbury, however, had only been brief, joining them as a schoolboy in 1967, from Possil YMCA. He returned to Scotland, rather disillusioned, the following year to sign for Partick Thistle.

He made his debut for the Firhill side during their Second Division Championship winning season of 1970-71, but it was not until the following season, after beginning the campaign as substitute, that he managed to obtain a regular place in the team, reverting from outside left to full back.

1971-72 was a season to remember for everyone connected with the 'Jags', not just Alex Forsyth, as they swept forward to Scottish League Cup success, unexpectedly beating Celtic 4-1 in the Final.

His performances during that historic season earned him a

T / R

place in the Scotland squad for the close-season tour of Brazil, which brought him his first international cap against Yugoslavia in Belo Horizante. A fine performance saw him keep his place for the following two games in South America and also a match against Denmark a few months later.

Having caught the Scotland manager's eye in Brazil, it was no real surprise when Tommy Docherty brought him south to Manchester, paying Partick Thistle £100,000.

He took a few games to find his feet in the different environment, but soon showed his talent as an attacking full back, who also possessed a powerful shot. He played in all but three of the games during the Second Division Championship winning season and established himself in the Scotland side.

Upon the return to the First Division in 1975-76, he began as first choice left back, but lost his place to Jimmy Nichol between September and November. He then returned to the side for the remainder of the season.

At the start of season 1976-77, he found himself omitted from the starting line up and only managed a further five appearances up until the time he left the club.

Surprisingly, he was seemingly content to remain in the Central League side, especially when youngsters such as Jimmy Nicholl and Arthur Albiston were making their mark in the first team.

At the end of season 1977-78, he was put up for sale and to the surprise of many, secured a loan deal with Glasgow Rangers, before obtaining a permanent move. At Ibrox, he made twenty-five appearances over a two year period, before seeing action with Motherwell, Hamilton and Queen Of The South, before hanging up his boots in the mid-eighties.

Determined to rebuild the ailing Manchester United and determined to do so as quickly as possible, Docherty seemed to keep the chequebook lying constantly open on his desk. With January only ten days old, he was scribbling out yet another, paying Shrewsbury Town £80,000 for an unknown twenty-one year old.

The youngster was not to remain unknown for long, as within a few weeks, **Jim Holton** was the new terrace hero of Old Trafford.

Although born in Lesmahagow, just south of Glasgow, Holton like George Graham, played all his football in England, having failed to make any impression whilst on Celtic's ground staff.

Rejected at Parkhead, the sixteen year old headed south to West Bromwich Albion for trials, determined to make the grade as a professional footballer. His displays in the Midlands were more impressive than they had been in the east- end of Glasgow and he was signed as an amateur in December 1967, winning his sought after professional contract four months later.

He made steady progress over the following three years, progressing through the junior and youth teams, but somehow failed to make it beyond the Central League side. Eventually, at the end of season 1970-71, he was given a free transfer.

Uncertain about his future, he was soon offered terms by former United goalkeeper Harry Gregg, now manager of Shrewsbury Town, who had watched him in Albion reserve team games and it wasn't long before he was a regular in the first team, after making his debut at Bournemouth on the opening day of season 1971-72.

Gregg had told the rugged youngster upon signing, "You're going to make it. I'm sure you can make it right to the top too".

A letter from Shrewsbury to the SFA offices in Park Gardens, Glasgow, alerted new Scotland manager Tommy Docherty to the promising youngster in the heart of the Shrewsbury defence, pushing him forward as a possible candidate for the national under 21 side. A visit by Docherty to Gay Meadow, confirmed the contents of the letter and the name of Holton was pencilled into the Scotland managers notebook.

Upon taking over at Old Trafford, 'the Doc', remembering the talented Holton's performances, sent Pat Crerand to run his eye over the youngster and upon his return to Manchester, the assistant manager confirmed everyone's opinion.

So, after only sixty-seven appearances for Shrewsbury, Jim Holton made the big step up from the Third Division to the First, determined to make the most of his opportunity.

On January 20th, he made his United debut against West Ham United, taking over the number five shirt from David Sadler and two months later was pulling on the dark blue of Scotland as he made his debut at under 23 level against Wales. Another two months down the line, he was making his full international debut, again against Wales.

Jim Holton's career in the dark blue of Scotland ran on a parallel to that in the red of Manchester United and he was one of the successes in the 1974 World Cup in West Germany, after scoring one of the goals in the deciding qualifying tie against Czechoslovakia at Hampden.

Few players can have made the same impact on the Old Trafford crowd in such a short space of time as this big fellow. His physical appearance and determination, along with his 'take no prisoners' attitude, made him a firm favourite and the terraces were soon vibrating to the sound of "Six foot two, eyes of blue, big Jim Holton's after you". The first and the last statements were the only ones that were true.

The physical nature of his play and at times over exuberance saw him fall foul of referees and he was sent off twice in his first nine games for United. Firstly in a friendly against F. C. Porto and in the League against Newcastle United. To many outside Old Trafford, he was considered a dirty player, an opinion that was strongly rebuffed by Holton himself.

"I was pretty raw when I joined United", he was to explain, "and I was pitched right in at the deep end. Every match was a battle and we were fighting for our lives. It was for those reasons that I got the reputation of being a dirty player. That's something that I have never been. I'm a big fella and I play the game with total commitment. I play hard, but I am not dirty".

Perhaps it was more than a little coincidence that United won only one of the eight fixtures that he missed during the relegation season of 1973-74 and it came as no surprise when he was voted the supporters Player Of The Year. He was also awarded the Scottish Football Writers Player Of The Year award, the first Anglo-Scot to do so.

In the Second Division, Holton's presence was going to play a major part in the plans for an instant return to the big-time, but a broken leg in the 4-4 draw at Sheffield Wednesday on December 7th 1974 brought a premature ending to the big man's season.

In reality, it also brought an end to his Manchester United career.

He returned to the first team during the close season tour of 1975, but a knee injury prior to the pre-season friendly against Red Star Belgrade, in August of that year set him back again. Upon returning to fitness, he was to suffer a second broken leg, against Bury, in what was only his second reserve match of his come back.

By now, Brian Greenhoff had taken over the number five shirt, with Colin Waldron signed as cover, Jim Holton was out in the cold.

During the summer of 1976, he went to the United States, to play for Miami Torros and upon his return joined Sunderland in September, on a one months loan deal, before signing a permanent contract on a £40,000 move.

On Wearside, he only managed fifteen appearances in five months and in March 1977, he joined Coventry City in another £40,000 deal, where his career enjoyed something of a re-birth, playing in some ninety-one games, over a three year spell. A return to the States in the summer of 1980 with Detroit Express, was sandwiched in between.

In May 1981, he signed for Sheffield Wednesday, but persistent injury problems saw him fail to make any first team appearances with the Owls an he decided to retire in the summer of 1982.

Upon retiring, he returned to Coventry, taking over a public house, which became a regular haunt for visiting United supporters. Sadly, his life, like his United career was to be brief, as he died from a heart attack at the age of 43, in October 1993, whilst at the wheel of his car as he returned from a keep fit session.

Alongside Jim Holton on his debut for Manchester United against West Ham United on January 20th 1973, a game that saw the United team contain eight Scots, was another one of Tommy Docherty's new signings, the diminutive **Lou Macari**.

Born in Edinburgh with Italian parents, Macari won Scottish Schoolboy honours before joining Celtic in July 1966 from Kilwinning Amateurs, making his first team debut in the green and white hoops against Ayr United in a Scottish League Cup tie in September 1967, coming on as substitute and scoring.

In an honour strewn seven years at Celtic Park, he was a member of the Scottish League Championship sides of 1970 and 1972, the Scottish Cup winning sides of 1971 and 1972 and won runners up medals in the Scottish League Cup Finals of 1971, 1972 and 1973.

Being part of a successful Celtic team also brought him international honours, winning the first of fifteen Scotland caps, alongside future United team mates Denis Law and Martin Buchan, when he came on as substitute for John O' Hare against Wales at Hampden on May 24th 1972.

Prior to United sealing the record breaking £200,000 transfer, Macari could have moved to the League leaders of that time, Liverpool, but surprisingly opted for a move to the club sitting at the opposite end of the table. "I picked United because I know I will feel at home here", said the new signing. "There are other members of the Scottish International squad here and I know this will help me settle in easier".

Celtic manager Jock Stein was quick to add, "I don't think Lou has been happy since he came back from Scotland's close season trip to Brazil. It would be true to say that I have not been totally happy with his form this season. I never had any doubt that he wanted to go to Manchester United".

Macari's Manchester United career almost came to an end, before it had even begun. Along with United manager Tommy Docherty and his assistant Pat Crerand, Macari had a very narrow escape whilst travelling south from Glasgow after having signed, on January 18th.

A mile or so from the Scotland/England border near Gretna Green, on a very foggy night, with a multi-vehicle pile-up immediately in front, a heavy goods lorry ploughed into the back of Docherty's three day old Merecedes, before scapping along its side, unable to brake in time. All three occupants had a fortunate escape. The United manager was later to joke that the diminutive Macari had jumped into the glove compartment for safety.

Although small in stature, Macari was big in heart and he immediately set about repaying his transfer fee almost immediately, scoring an eightieth minute equaliser against West Ham on his debut, earning United a 2-2 draw and adding a further four as they fought to avoid relegation. There was little Macari could do to help avoid the drop to Division Two during the following campaign, scoring a meagre five goals in thirty four appearances as United went down. In Division Two, a more productive eleven goals from thirty-six games, helped the promotion push. One of those being a vital strike in the 1-0 victory at Southampton, when there was only three games left. This was his fourth goal in the same number of games.

On returning to Division One, Macari finished only one goal behind Stuart Pearson in the scoring charts, with twelve and played a major part in the F. A. Cup success of 1977. His shot at the Liverpool goal being deflected off Jimmy Greenhoff's chest, to give United their 2-1 win. By now, he was playing in a more midfield role than when he first joined the club.

The following year, following the World Cup, Macari's Scotland career came to an end, when he was suspended by the SFA for stating that he no longer wanted to play for his country again.

During Macari's early days at Old Trafford, he must have often wondered if he had indeed made the right move, opting for United instead of Liverpool, as ten months after signing, he and Docherty were at loggerheads.

On a charge of "breach of club discipline", Macari was fined two weeks wages and placed on the transfer list by the manager after a flare up prior to a match at Mossley. Selected to play in a team made up mainly of reserves, Macari was perhaps justified in his request to be left out, as this would have been his fourth game in seven days.

Upon arrival at the non-League club's ground, he was told not to bother getting changed, as he was not playing and a verbal flare up followed.

By the end of the month, the episode was forgotten about

(officially at least) and the name of Macari taken off the transfer list, with Docherty saying that Lou had regretted refusing to play in the match at Mossley!

On May 13th 1984, a crowd of 40,140, a record for a testimonial match in England, gave Macari an £85,000 send off, as United faced his old club Celtic in a testimonial match to mark his ten years as an Manchester United player. Beginning the match in a red jersey, he swapped shirts and dressing rooms at half time, playing the second forty-five minutes in the green and white hoops and supplied the vital touch to the ball for Tommy Burns to score the equaliser in a 1-1 draw.

Two months later, Lou Macari was appointed player-manager of Swindon Town and in the months that followed, controversy was never far away, seemingly following him like a shadow.

April 1985 saw him sacked, along with his assistant, former United goalkeeper Harry Gregg, as the pair could not reconcile their differences. However, Macari found himself re-instated six days later.

He guided Swindon to promotion from the Fourth Division at the end of 1985-86. Promotion again followed, courtesy of the play-offs, but amid allegations of illegal payments, they were swiftly demoted with an Inland Revenue investigation to follow. He also ended up in trouble in January 1988, after placing a bet on Swindon to lose an F.A. Cup tie against Newcastle United, a match that was lost 5-0! He was fined £1,000 and the club £7,000.

He left the Wiltshire club under a dark cloud, but sprang back into life in the summer of 1989, when he was appointed manager of West Ham United. But a betting scandal was soon to surface and he found himself heading out of London in February 1990, making the move to Birmingham City, where he again took up the post of manager.

At St Andrews, he took them to Wembley in 1991, where they won the Leyland DAF Trophy and the following year he was to return to the twin towers for the Final of the Autoglass Trophy. This time, it was as manager of Stoke City, whom he had joined only four months after taking up the Birmingham post.

Court appearances soon became as regular as those at Wembley, with charges of defrauding the taxman and running an illegal betting shop following each other within a three month period. Macari, was cleared of both.

The lure of the Celtic managers job, was always going to prove too strong and he left the Potteries when the vacancy at Parkhead occurred, hoping to guide his former club to the success they yearned for and the possibility of overtaking their arch-rivals Rangers.

Internal boardroom conflict, lack of cash and various other matters clouded his return to his spiritual home and after only eight months in the Celtic hot seat, he was sacked by Fergus McCann, who cited "infrequent attendance and inadequate supervision" as the main reasons for Macari's dismissal.

He subsequently returned to Stoke City, but was later to replace another former United player, Steve Bruce, as manager of Huddersfield Town.

The Doc's immediate surgery rejuvenated the team and despite defeats in his first three games in charge, enough points were accumulated in the final months of the season to ensure First Division football again in 1973-74.

In May 1973, Docherty increased his Scottish clan at Old Trafford by one, but for once, there was no money involved, with George Buchan arriving from Aberdeen on a free transfer.

George Buchan was the younger brother of Martin and after playing alongside him at school, he followed him to Aberdeen via the Banks O' Dee junior team.

He made his debut for the Dons in March 1969 and played his part in helping them to Scottish Cup success the following year. Mainly a fringe player, making only sixty-nine appearances, including those as substitute, over a period of four years, he was given a free transfer at the end of 1972-73.

He was signed by United purely as a back up player and during his year at Old Trafford made only four substitute appearances, making his debut against West Ham United on September 15th 1973.

August 1974 saw him move to Bury, again on a free transfer, where he remained for two years, making over sixty appearances, before returning to Scotland for a brief spell with Motherwell, where he finished his career in 1976.

Tommy Docherty supplemented his collection of Scots with almost an equal number of Irishmen, bringing Gerry Daly, Mick Martin and Trevor Anderson into the team for the opening fixture of 1973-74, but along with five from north of Hadrians Wall, they could do little to stop Arsenal from winning 3-0.

The season progressed in a similar fashion, with only four victories in the opening twenty-one fixtures. There were problems throughout the team, with the defence leaking twenty-seven goals and the forwards scoring only eighteen. Well, to be honest, that last statement is totally wrong, as Brian Greenhoff, Tony Young, Jim Holton and Steve James had all found the net and at one point, the team's leading goalscorer was goalkeeper Alex Stepney with two, both penalties!

In order to stem the flow of goals conceded, Docherty once again moved into the transfer market, bringing full back **Stewart Houston** to the club from Brentford.

A native of Dunoon, Houston was another player who had always plied his trade as a professional south of the border, having joined Chelsea (under the managership of one Tommy Docherty), from Port Glasgow Rangers, as an eighteen year old in August 1967.

Injuries hindered his progress at Stamford Bridge and after only nine first team outings in four years, he moved across London to join Brentford for a modest fee of £17,000, following a brief loan spell, in March 1972.

At Griffin Park, he spent two enjoyable years, making a total of seventy-seven appearances, often playing in attack. He was to score twice during their Fourth Division promotion winning season of 1971-72, before Docherty

resigned him in December 1973 for a fee of £55,000. Stepping up a few levels caused no problems for the cultured full back and he immediately became the automatic choice for the number three jersey following his United debut at Queens Park Rangers on January 1st 1974.

He went on to help United out of the Second Division in 1975 and to the Cup Final the following year. His performances with United in 1976 also earned him his one and only Scotland cap against Denmark.

Despite his sterling performances for United, he will most probably be remembered by the Old Trafford supporters as the unlucky player who missed the 1977 F.A. Cup Final, due to a broken leg received at Bristol City, a couple of weeks before the Wembley show piece.

Unfortunately, following his leg break, he was no longer an automatic first team choice and drifted in and out of the team, sometimes filling in as a central defender.

At the end of season 1979-80, he was given a free transfer and shortly afterwards joined Sheffield United, where he went on to win a Fourth Division Championship medal in 1982.

A year later, in August 1983, he joined Colchester United as a player-coach and what was to be the start of a successful career in this field, later serving Plymouth Argyle, Arsenal, Queens Park Rangers and Tottenham in coaching and assistant manager capacities.

As season 1973-74 progressed, United were clearly a club in turmoil, winning only one game between January 1st and March 23rd and with each dropped point, relegation became more and more of a possibility.

With the games becoming fewer and fewer and points becoming more desperate, the manager had no qualms of once again making a plunge into the transfer market in the hope that new blood could invigorate and revitalise the team. Once again, he signed a player with whom he was familiar, another of his former Chelsea starlets, **Jim McCalliog**.

McCalliog, a former Glasgow schoolboy, had originally joined Leeds United as an apprentice, in May 1963, but failed to make the grade at Elland Road and returned home disappointed. Four months later, in September 1963, he once again took the road south in the search for

soccer stardom, this time with Chelsea. Under the guidance of Tommy Docherty, he won Scottish Youth honours, but after a mere seven appearances, in which he scored two goals, he was told that he was being released and made available for transfer.

In October 1965, Sheffield Wednesday paid £37,500, a record fee for a teenager, to take him to Hillsborough. With Wednesday, he proved both Leeds and Chelsea wrong and shortly after moving to Yorkshire, he was playing, and scoring, in the F. A. Cup Final. Unfortunately, he was to pick up a runners-up medal, as opponents Everton ran out 3-2 winners.

Some of his performances with Wednesday were outstanding and he soon found himself in the Scotland under 23 side. After only two appearances at this level, he graduated to the full international side, winning the first of his five caps against England at Wembley in 1967, in what turned out to be a memorable encounter. Not only did the Scots become the first team to defeat the then World Champions, but Jim McCalliog scored the third Scottish goal in a 3-2 win.

The summer of 1969 saw Wolverhampton Wanderers pay Sheffield Wednesday £70,000 for his signature, But the dream move, after an excellent first three years, turned into disappointment as he began to miss numerous games due to injuries. One such injury in 1974, causing him to miss a Wembley Cup Final return, and Wolves 2-1 victory over Manchester City in the Football League Cup.

Within a fortnight of missing this Final, he was packing his bags for a move to Manchester United, with Tommy Docherty paying out £60,000, in the hope that the

experienced and still talented inside forward could steer United clear of relegation. This could be considered as something of a delayed transfer, as the player had at one time been high on Matt Busby's shopping list. McCalliog considered it better late than never, saying "This is a tremendous move for me. Regardless of their position, a move to United suits me fine".

United lost their first two fixtures with McCalliog in the side, but suddenly it began to look as though 'the Doc' had pulled off a masterstroke of a signing and one of his best ever plunges into the transfer market.

Chelsea were beaten 3-1 at Stamford Bridge, a point was taken in a six goal thriller with Burnley at Old Trafford, Norwich City were beaten 2-0 at Carrow Road and then Jim McCalliog went on some thing of a one man crusade.

On April 13th, with six games remaining, he scored the only goal of the game against Newcastle United, notching a double two days later in the 3-0 win over Everton. Another goal was enough to earn a point at Southampton the following week.

Sadly, that was to be it. In the three games United had left to save themselves from relegation, they failed to score, losing each game 1-0. They were down!

McCalliog failed to see out the Second Division campaign with United, after playing in all but four of the opening twenty-one fixtures, returning to the First Division in February 1975 with Southampton for a fee of £40,000. Ironically, he played a major role in Southampton's F. A. Cup run the following year, which saw him pick up a winners medal as the Saints defeated United 1-0 in the Final.

April 1977 saw him move to America for a summer stint with Chicago Sting, before playing a season in Norwegian football. This was followed by a player/coach position with Lincoln City and a period as player/manager with Runcorn between September 1978 and 1990.

A brief spell as caretaker manager and manager with Halifax Town between 1990 and 1991 brought an end to his career in football.

Relegation to the Second Division, for the first time since 1936-37, was a hard pill to swallow, but right from the first whistle of the opening fixture of season 1974-75, United showed that they had no intentions of staying longer than the necessary one season.

On the opening day of the season at Orient, Docherty had seven Scotsmen in his starting line up and all of them, with the exception of McCalliog, who was transferred and Holton who was injured, played in more than thirty games each. But for one young Scotsman, he was simply grateful to make the senior squad and play in two League fixtures and one Football League Cup match. Little did he know then, that he was to go on and become the longest serving Scotsman in the club's history, amassing some four hundred and sixty-four appearances over a fourteen year period.

The player's name was **Arthur Albiston**, an Edinburgh born former Scotland Schoolboy internationalist, who joined United as an apprentice in July 1972, signing professional forms a year later.

In just over two years, he was making his first team debut and few could have had a more demanding baptism than a Football League Cup tie against local rivals Manchester City in front of a packed Old Trafford on October 9th 1974. The experience wasn't entirely alien to him, as he had made his initial appearance for the first team during Tony Dunne's testimonial match against City on October 24th 1973.

The seventeen year old came through his competitive debut with a notable performance in United's 1-0 win, but following his League debut six days later, against Portsmouth he found himself back in the reserves following Houston's recovery from injury. He was to make one further appearance during 1974-75, again replacing Houston, and two (with one as substitute) during 1975-76.

Season 1976-77, however, brought a scattering of appearances up until the final month of the season, when he was to suddenly find himself thrust into the limelight following Houston's leg break at Bristol City.

It was not just a case of standing in for the final few League games of the season, there was the small matter of an appearance in the F. A. Cup Final at Wembley, against Liverpool. Many felt that the big occasion would prove too much for the rather inexperienced defender, but United, who were the underdogs on the day, defeated Liverpool 2-1 to record a memorable victory.

Goalkeeper Alex Stepney was to say at the time, "He was just a kid, but he never put a foot wrong".

Albiston began the following season, 1977-78, as first choice left back and over the next nine years was the automatic choice in this position.

Despite seven appearances for the Scotland under 21 side, following his four Schoolboy and two Youth caps, Arthur was constantly ignored for the full international side and had to wait until 1982 before winning his first of fourteen caps against Northern Ireland in Belfast. Surprisingly, he was omitted from the squad for the World Cup Finals later that year.

Arthur Albiston's Manchester United career spanned the reign of four managers and each one knew that they could depend on the dark curly headed full back as his level of consistency was always very high. On February 13th 1988, however, he was to pull on the red No. 3 jersey for the last time, against Chelsea at Stamford Bridge for what was his three hundred and sixty fourth League match (plus another fifteen as substitute).

Taking his appearance record into comparison with other former United players, he stands in sixth place in the all time chart, behind such illustrious names such as Charlton, Foulkes, Stepney, Dunne and Spence. One record he did make was that he was the first United player to win three F. A. Cup winners medals.

All good things, however, have to come to an end and n August 1988, having lost his place early in Alex Ferguson's reign and following a hernia operation, he rejoined his former manager Ron Atkinson at West Bromwich Albion in the Second Division, on a free transfer. Things at the Hawthorns were satisfactory until Atkinson left, as new manager Brian Talbot considered him surplus to requirements.

The following August, he joined Dundee, but returned south to join Chesterfield, on loan, in November 1990, having made only ten appearances for the Dens Park club, during a very unhappy two years.

The Dundee manager Gordon Wallace surprisingly

branded him "a cheat" and "a disgrace" following a reserve game. "Humiliating" was how Arthur Albiston described it later, having been spoken to in such a manner in front of a bunch of kids.

In the next game, he broke his ribs and suffered a collapsed lung and had to drive himself to hospital. Strangely, he was sent home, but was soon recalled, as x-rays showed some serious damage and he was admitted to hospital for five days.

The loan period at Chesterfield also had its problems, playing in only ten games, before the manager turned against him.

From Chesterfield, he moved to Chester in August 1991, making sixty-eight appearances over a two year period before sampling overseas football with a short spell in Norway, with FC Molde. He returned to Chester, before another brief spell with the Norwegian club.

Before finally hanging up his boots, he played one match with Ayr United under George Burley, but the manager was sacked before any deal could be done.

The swashbuckling football that swept United through the Second Division continued, to a certain extent, upon the return to Division One for season 1975-76. Nine goals were scored in the opening three games and a satisfactory third place in the table achieved along with an appearance in the F.A.Cup Final, the first since 1963.

Opponents at Wembley were Southampton and surprisingly they managed to pull off a surprise 1-0 win. Twelve months later, the disappointment was forgotten, as United returned to Wembley and defeated the much fancied and arch rivals Liverpool 2-1, a match that was to bring down the curtain on Tommy Docherty's United career.

During Tommy Docherty's final season in charge, he introduced yet another Scot into the first team, the ninth of his reign. This time though, there was no splash into the transfer market as the debutant was a product of the United junior sides.

Eighteen year old **Steve Paterson** had been signed two years earlier, in July 1974, from Nairn County, a Highland League side and had progressed favourably through the various junior sides at the club, playing as a fifteen year old

for Scotland's under eighteen side and as an eighteen year old for the under twenty-one's, before establishing himself in United's Central League team.

Few could have more illustrious debuts than the 6' 2" central defender from Mostodloch, near Elgin, coming on as a substitute for Gordon Hill in the UEFA Cup 1st round 2nd leg tie against Ajax at Old Trafford on September 29th 1976. His second outing was even more daunting, again as substitute in a UEFA Cup tie, this time replacing Lou Macari, against Juventus on November 3rd in the away second leg in the next round of the competition.

His League debut followed a week later, on November 10th against Sunderland at Old Trafford, playing in the centre of the defence and he was to retain his place the following week, although changing shirt numbers from five to six. However, he had to wait until April 30th 1979 before making his next start, with only two substitute appearances being made earlier that season.

An ankle injury and the signing of Gordon McQueen, did little to help his claims for a first team place and he made what was to be his final United appearance on August 25th 1979 as a substitute against Arsenal.

Released by United in the summer of 1980, with United having picked up £50,000 insurance from his ankle injury, he was promptly offered a contract by Sheffield Wednesday, but following a medical at Hillsborough, he was not registered with the club.

Somewhat disillusioned, following what he described as "a messy affair", he set off for Hong Kong, later moving to Japan, to re-establish his career in a quieter, not so physical environment, or so he thought at the time.

With Yomuiri, he became Japan's first European professional footballer (ahead of Gary Lineker) and soon became something of a minor celebrity, with free cars, shop openings, guest appearances, the complete works, along with being presented with a League winner's medal from the Emperor himself.

A short spell in Australia followed before deciding to go back home to Scotland in 1986, where, returning to his roots in the Highland League, he joined Forres Mechanics in a player manager capacity, winning the Highland League in his first season.

Football now was not full time, with his role as a social worker in an Elgin children's home becoming his main source of income, but it did not prevent him from making a name for himself amongst the mountains and glens of northern Scotland.

Moving to Elgin City, he won the McEwans North of Scotland Cup, the Scottish Qualifying Cup and the Highland League in 1990, after having taken them to the Scottish Cup quarter finals in 1989, but when offered a rise of £10, taking his salary up to the pricey sum of £50, he decided to change clubs again, moving to Huntly. Here he guided them to their first Highland League title since the 1930's, remaining with them for five years.

Today, he is Scotland's longest serving manager, with Inverness Caledonian Thistle, whose move from the Highland League into the Scottish League itself, has seen the club progress through to the First Division.

An amazing Scottish Cup victory over Celtic at Parkhead in 2000 not only showed that the club had established itself amongst the top sides out with the Scottish Premier League, but it also established Steve Paterson as one of the games up and coming managers.

Tommy Docherty was replaced as manager by Dave Sexton in the summer of 1977 and United's style of play became more cautious, with mid-table positions achieved in the following two seasons, along with a return to Wembley in 1979, where Arsenal grabbed a last gasp winner after United had clawed their way back from 2-0 down to 2-2 in the last five minutes.

Unlike Docherty, Dave Sexton did not dive immediately into the transfer market, giving the players at his disposal the time to show how they were able to perform under a new manager and adapt to a different style. When he did finally decide that the team required some new blood in the early months of 1978, it was to Scotsmen like his predecessor, that he turned.

First to arrive was **Joe Jordan** who cost a record fee of £350,000 from Leeds United.

Jordan came from the same village as former United winger Jimmy Delaney, who would often watch the youngster play for his school team as a left half. Upon leaving school, he joined junior side Blantyre Victoria, before being snapped up by Morton in October 1968.

His early days at Cappielow were little different to that of countless other hopeful teenagers beginning their career at a League club, but things were soon to change drastically. Within three weeks of signing professional forms at £7 per week and having played only a dozen first team games, scoring a couple of goals, he was approached by Leeds United manager Don Revie and asked to join the Yorkshire side. Revie saw him as "an asset for the future", but Joe wasn't so sure about giving up a career as an architect for football on a full time basis. Especially for one so far from home.

His boss, however, stepped in and told him that if he didn't make the grade or settle within a given period of time, then he could have his job back. His position appeared in the 'Situations Vacant' columns shortly afterwards, with Leeds United paying £15,000 to take him south.

At Elland Road, Jordan became a firm favourite with the supporters, as a no holds barred striker, winning a League Championship medal in 1974 and European Cup runners up medal in 1975. A European Cup Winners Cup runners up medal was also won in 1973 as well as breaking into the Scottish International side that same year, coming on as substitute for Lou Macari, against England at Wembley. In 1974, his memorable diving header at Hampden, against Czechoslovakia took Scotland to the World Cup Finals for the first time since 1958.

Never a prolific scorer, two from twelve at Morton, thirty five from one hundred and sixty nine at Leeds, Sexton's first signing was considered a strange one and three goals in his first fourteen outings during the second half of season 1977-78 did little to change that impression.

Jordan didn't make his Manchester United debut immediately after signing, as he was serving a three match suspension at the time and had to wait until Bristol City's visit to Old Trafford on February 8th. His aggressive play soon endeared him to the Old Trafford support and while not scoring himself, set up numerous chances for his team mates.

Season 1980-81 was perhaps Joe Jordan's best with United, scoring fifteen goals in thirty-three games, two better than the previous season, playing one game more. But it was also to be his last, as the Italian lure of the lire proved too strong. A fee of £175,000 took him to AC Milan, in July 1981, with a weekly wage of £2,000 playing a big part in persuading him to move abroad.

Two seasons with Milan were followed by a season with Verona before returning to Britain in 1984 to join Southampton.

February 1987 saw a £50,000 deal taking him to Bristol City, where he combined playing with the manager's job, retiring from playing altogether in March 1988. One rather surprising fact emerging from Jordan's playing career is that despite his fearsome, toothless scowl and aggressive play, he was never once sent off at League level, at home or abroad and only once at International level.

In September 1990 he returned to Scotland to become manager of Heart of Midlothian, moving to Celtic as assistant manager three years later. This was followed by several managerial or assistant managers posts around the country with the likes of Stoke City, Bristol City (again), Northern Ireland and Huddersfield Town.

Hot on the heels of Joe Jordan's arrival at Old Trafford was that of former Leeds United team mate **Gordon McQueen**.

Born in Kilbirnie, Ayrshire, McQueen had trials with both Rangers and Liverpool, before joining St Mirren in May 1970.

With the Paisley side, he made over fifty appearances between 1970-71 and 1972-73, before joining Leeds United, to be groomed as Jackie Charlton's successor in a deal of around £35,000.

His career ran along similar lines to that of Joe Jordan's, winning his first full cap in 1974 (replacing Jim Holton in the Scotland side against Belgium on June 1st) and adding the same medals to the trophy cabinet as his friend and fellow team mate.

At 6' 4", he was a towering presence in the penalty area at either end of the pitch and a few weeks after signing Jordan, Dave Sexton made the return journey across the Pennines to Leeds for McQueen, paying out £495,000 for his signature.

Alongside Martin Buchan and later Kevin Moran, he formed a formidable rearguard for United, enjoying mixed success. Injuries and suspensions kept him out of the side from time to time, following his debut at Liverpool on February 25th, but his career was to span the reigns of both Sexton and his replacement, Ron Atkinson.

At Anfield, in January 1984, he sustained an injury that saw him miss the remainder of that season and one that virtually ended his United playing career, as he managed only another twelve games, before leaving for Hong Kong where he became player-coach of Seiko in August 1985.

McQueen returned to Britain in June 1987 and took over as manager of Airdrieonians, two years later rejoining his first club, St Mirren as coach. In 1994, former United team mate Bryan Robson invited him to join him at Middlesborough as a member of his coaching staff, a position he held until Robson's departure in 2001.

Breaking into the Manchester United first team during the early weeks of season 1980-81 was a young Scot with a distinctive head of curly blond hair and an eye for goals. His name was **Scott McGarvey**.

Glaswegian born McGarvey was a member of the Celtic Boy's Club side before joining United as an associated schoolboy in November 1978. A year later, he was to sign apprentice forms and in April 1980 he became a professional.

Ideally built for a forward at 5' 11" and weighing 11st 9lbs,

T / R

McGarvey earned a favourable reputation at junior and reserve team level with his goals return tally. His displays at this level brought him international recognition, with selection for the Scottish under 21 side, coming on as substitute against England in April 1982, before making a goal scoring full appearance against Belgium in December that same year.

By then, the name of Scott McGarvey had appeared in the Manchester United first team, with substitute appearances against Leicester City, at Old Trafford, on September 13th 1980 and Coventry City, also at home, two months later.

The following season, brought his first start at this level, with his full debut against Everton, again at Old Trafford, on January 6th, replacing Gary Birtles. Four substitute appearances followed over the next couple of months, but he was to reappear in the starting line up at Leeds on April 3rd and kept his place for the next eight games, scoring his first senior goal against Tottenham Hotspur a fortnight later. Season 1982-83 found him knocked back in the pecking order, by the emergence of Norman Whiteside, making only three full appearances, plus four more as substitute, scoring once. Further selection for the Scottish under 21 side added to his frustration at the lack of first team opportunities and in March 1984, he joined Wolves on loan after the Midland side made an approach enquiring about his availability, scoring twice in thirteen outings.

Returning to Old Trafford in May 1984, he realised that his United days were numbered and decided to up his roots and join Portsmouth in an £85,000 deal.

On the south coast, he again struggled for first team opportunities, making only twenty three, scoring six goals, before moving to the opposite end of the country, joining Carlisle United on loan in July 1986, making the move permanent the following January.

Over the next four years, McGarvey played for Grimsby Town, where he was to enjoy an extended first team run for the first time, Bristol City, Oldham Athletic and Wigan Athletic before leaving Britain for a spell with Hiroshima Mazda in Japan, where he won a Championship medal in 1990. Aris Limassol in Cyprus followed two years later.

As the 1990's progressed, Scott McGarvey served Derry City in a player-coach capacity and also played for Witton Albion and Barrow, as his unfulfilled, potentially promising career came to an end.

Under Dave Sexton, Manchester United came close to success in both the League and F.A.Cup, finishing as runners up in both in 1980 and 1979 respectively. In the summer of 1981 despite a run of seven straight wins at the tail end of the season, finishing in eighth position in the First Division, Sexton was sacked.

Many supporters had voiced their disappointment in Sexton's style of play, compared to the devil may care, attacking teams fielded by Tommy Docherty. The board appeared to listen to the terrace unrest and noting Sexton's failure to maintain the challenge for honours for a second season, brought an end to his contract.

Appointed in his place was Ron Atkinson, who had produced an exciting and talented side at West Bromwich Albion. Like 'the Doc', a larger than life character, who liked his teams to entertain.

Like Sexton and Docherty, Ron Atkinson relied on the Scottish backbone to his team for the early days of his tenure, retaining the likes of Albiston, Buchan, McQueen and Macari, but by the end of season 1981-82, only Albiston had appeared on a regular basis, the others fallen by the wayside. Atkinson also enjoyed the odd dabble in the transfer market, as his signing of Bryan Robson and Remi Moses from his old club West Bromwich, in the early days of his managerial reign showed. He did, however, also enjoy bringing through young players, with Grimes, Davies and Whiteside all making their debuts.

Throughout United's illustrious history, there has been a glut of talented wingers, who have thrilled the crowds with their escapades along the touchlines. Many of the names trip off the tongue easily, Meredith, Wall, Delaney, Berry, Pegg, Connelly, Best, Beckham and Giggs, the list is seemingly endless. However, with the style of football slowly changing, an out and out wingman was slowly becoming a thing of the past. Ron Atkinson preferred his teams to show some flair and imagination and also be an attacking force and to do so you required players capable of taking on defenders and supplying the forwards with plenty of scoring opportunities.

In August 1983, Atkinson signed a player, perhaps not graced with the same talents of any of the aforementioned individuals, but an winger, who had the speed and ball control to give any defender a run for his money, while at the same time manage to score a few goals into the bargain.

Arthur Graham cost the United manager a fee of over £45,000 when bought from Leeds United, where he had spent six favourable years.

Born in the Castlemilk area of Glasgow, Graham had begun playing in junior football with Cambuslang Rangers upon leaving school, but was soon snapped up by Aberdeen during the 1969-70 season.

His arrival at Pittodrie coincided with a Scottish Cup run, which cumulated with Aberdeen defeating Celtic 3-1 in the Final at Hampden. This gave the eighteen year old his first senior honour in the game, after only six senior outings and two months at the club.

Further honours were soon to follow, with a League Cup runner up medal and Scotland under 23 and Scottish League caps to go alongside the already won Scottish Youth caps. Having played at a highly consistent level, with almost three hundred appearances for the Dons, it was now only a matter of time before he was prised away by a bigger club and in July 1977, Leeds United secured his transfer for a fee of around £125,000.

Shortly after joining the Elland Road side, for whom he was to make two hundred and twenty three appearances and become a big favourite with the supporters, he won the first of his ten full Scottish caps against East Germany. An honour, which at one point, looked like passing the player by.

In September 1975, whilst with the Scottish squad in Gothenburg for an international against Sweden, an incident in a night club saw five Scottish players, including Arthur

Graham banned for life from playing for their country. Graham, long protested his innocence, claiming that he was the "wrong man" and was never involved. Two years later, the SFA lifted the ban on the effervescent winger.

With Leeds United, his explosive pace quickly saw him become a firm favourite and he complemented his performances by scoring thirty seven goals, including three hat tricks, during his six years there. Not bad for a winger!

By the time he joined Manchester United, he was thirty years old and was obviously considered as a short term signing, but he still had his pace and the ability to deliver the perfect ball to supply his fellow forwards with goalscoring opportunities.

He made his United debut in the F.A. Charity Shield match of 1983, against Liverpool, and went on to make forty six appearances, (plus five substitute), scoring seven goals during what was to be his only season with United.

The signing of Jesper Olsen, perhaps curtailed his stay in Manchester and in June 1985, he joined Bradford City, making thirty one appearances and going on to become reserve and junior coach two years later, before having a spell as caretaker manager during the first two months of 1989.

Ron Atkinson made a notable start to his United management career and quickly won over the fans by lifting the team to third in the League at the end of his first season in charge.

Season 1982-83 saw United finish third in the table for a second consecutive season and it also saw them make two Cup Final appearances at Wembley. In the F. A. Cup, they defeated Brighton and Hove Albion 4-0 in a replay, after a 2-2 draw. While the League Cup was lost 2-1 in extra time to Liverpool.

The future under the flamboyant Atkinson looked bright and with a little more luck might have saw success in the 1983-84 European Cup Winners Cup, losing out 3-2 on aggregate and by a last minute, goal to Juventus at the semi-final stage.

For one United youngster, the European campaign of 1983-84 had mixed memories, as **Graeme Hogg** not only had he made his first team debut in January, but by April,

he had played in both legs of the quarter and semi-final ties, against European giants Barcelona and Juventus.

The home leg of the semi-final against the Italians particularly sticks in his mind, because of Rossi's last minute shot took an unavoidable, slight deflection off him, to give Juventus a 1-1 draw.

Hogg, whose father had played for the same Aberdeen side as Martin Buchan, had trained with the Pittodrie side for a brief period, before signing for United in July 1980.

Graduating through the junior ranks, an injury to Gordon McQueen against Liverpool at Anfield during the first league match of 1984 presented him with his first team debut against Bournemouth in the F.A. Cup third round, five days later. Atkinson had no qualms about throwing the well built defender in at the deep end, but it was not to be a headline making debut for Hogg, as the following day, the only headlines were "United Crash in Cup Sensation", following Bournemouth's surprising 2-0 victory.

The debutant, however, kept his place in the heart of the defence for the remainder of that season, enjoying the experience, particularly the European interludes.

Season 1984-85 saw him start as one of the first choice central defenders, but was to miss several games in mid season due to injury. Indeed, it was an injury that was to bring him much disappointment, as having played in all of that season's F. A. Cup ties, except for the revenge third round victory over Bournemouth, he was to miss out on the Final itself.

His defensive displays won him four Scottish under 21 caps, but his major opponent was always going to be injuries.

After once again beginning a season as a first choice, (1985-86), he lost his place due to his appearances on the treatment table, playing in only two League matches between January and the end of the season.

There were only scattered first team appearances during the opening months of 1986-87 and over the next year and a half, which also saw him spend a brief loan spell with West Bromwich Albion towards the end of 1987.

With the arrival of Steve Bruce at Old Trafford, it was obvious that first team opportunities were going to be severely limited and with season 1988-89 just about to get under way, he decided to gamble on his future by accepting a move to Portsmouth, with a fee of £150,000 exchanging hands.

Hogg could not be too disappointed with life on the south coast, making one hundred appearances between 1988-9 and 1990-91, scoring a couple of goals. In August 1991, he made the return journey to Scotland and joined Hearts, but here, injuries again limited his appearances, making only fifty-eight over a three year period.

Spells at Notts County and Brentford followed between 1994 and 1998 before hanging up his boots, wondering what might have been if it had not been for those injuries.

Alongside the commanding figure of Graeme Hogg in the United line up for the opening day of season 1984-85 were two other Scots, newly signed by the club. One was Alan Brazil, the other, the diminutive red haired figure of Gordon Strachan.

Born in Edinburgh, **Gordon Strachan** was a former Scottish Schoolboy internationalist and joined Dundee in October 1971, straight from school. As a fourteen year old, he had been offered trails with Manchester United, but turned them down, as he had previously agreed to go to Dens Park.

The opportunity had also been there to join his beloved Hibernians, a team whom he had supported since the age of five, but a dispute with the Hibs manager Eddie Turnbull over expenses for his boots ruled out his joining the Edinburgh side.

The young Gordon Strachan's playing career was almost over before in had even began, due to an accident at school. Whilst involved in a playground kick about, he fell following a tackle and unfortunately had a pen in his hand at the time. This went into his eye as he fell, damaging an optic nerve and he was within a thousand of an inch of losing his sight.

At Dundee, his career, after the initial setback, began to prosper and he made his League debut against Heart of Midlothian towards the end of season 1974-75. By the age of nineteen, he was team captain and over his two years with the Dens Park club he was to make eighty-seven appearances, scoring fifteen goals.

In November 1977, a cash plus player exchange - £50,000 and Jim Shirra, saw him move to Aberdeen, with Dons manager Billy McNeill saying "This may not be the biggest signing Aberdeen have made, but it could well be the best". His career at Pittodrie, however, got off to a far from ideal start, going over on an ankle in a tackle during training and ending up in hospital.

McNeill's departure and Alex Ferguson's appointment saw Aberdeen become the top side in Scotland, pushing the ' Old Firm' of Rangers and Celtic into the background, winning the League in 1980 and 1984, the Scottish Cup in 1982, 1983 and 1984 and the European Cup Winners Cup in 1983.

Strachan's performances won him the Scottish Player of the Year award in 1980, a year which also brought him his first Scotland cap, against Northern Ireland in Belfast. His effervescent play was soon attracting much attention outwith Scotland, (Ron Atkinson being keen to sign him for United in August 1983) and in the summer of 1984, a two-way battle for his signature evolved.

With Manchester United poised to sign the flame haired forward cum mid-field player for a fee of £600,000, German side Cologne stepped into the picture, saying that they had a pre-signed letter by Strachan, agreeing to sign for them.

A tense and arguementive debate ensued over whose player he was, with both UEFA and the SFA becoming involved. Eventually, Aberdeen agree to pay the German club £100,000 in compensation and the player travelled south to join Manchester United, signing a four year deal on May 8th.

Strachan marked his United debut with a goal against Watford on the opening day of season 1984-85 and went on to score fifteen (one behind top scorer Mark Hughes), playing in all but one of the forty-two League fixtures. At the end of this season, he also added an F.A. Cup winners

medal to his already impressive hoard. Over the following four seasons, he was to make a further one hundred and thirty-nine appearances, six more as substitute, scoring nineteen goals.

An integral part of Ron Atkinson's attacking team, he became a firm favourite with the Old Trafford support, but he must have suffered mixed emotions upon the arrival of manager Alex Ferguson.

Under his four managers, Gordon Strachan had continued to enjoy his football, but by the time Alex Ferguson had brought his first trophy to Old Trafford, in the shape of the F.A.Cup in 1990, he was a mere memory, having been transferred to Leeds United in March 1989 for £300,000.

At Elland Road, after his latter days at United had turned rather sour, his career blossomed, playing a major role in helping Leeds United out of the Second Division and subsequent First Division Championship success of 1991-92, piping Manchester United at the post.

Season 1990-91 had brought him the Footballer of the Year award and in the New Years honours list of 1993, he was awarded the OBE for his services to football.

With his playing days drawing to a close, his former manager at United, Ron Atkinson, took him to Coventry City in a player-coach capacity, eventually taking over from Atkinson as manager.

Early in season 2001-02, having seen his Coventry side relegated to the Second Division at the end of the previous season, he was sacked following a poor start. After a brief spell out of the game, he took over the manager's job at Southampton.

Arriving at Old Trafford around the same time as Gordon Strachan, in the summer of 1984, was Alan Brazil, a player who had on more than one occasion previously, had come close to joining Manchester United. He had in fact been scheduled to appear for United in Lou Macari's testimonial match against Celtic in May 1984, but had to withdraw due to injury.

Alan Brazil, was born in Glasgow and played for Celtic Boys Club prior to signing for Ipswich Town as an apprentice in August 1975.

At Portman Road, having signed professional forms in

1977, he made steady progress, following his debut against Manchester United, and during the summer of that initial season, 1977-78, having made only two substitute appearances he went to America to play for Detriot Express, quite an experience for a young player. Under the guidance of Bobby Robson, Ipswich became one of the country's top sides, winning the UEFA Cup in 1981 and coming close to winning the First Division title in the following two seasons, finishing as runners up on both occasions.

During this period, the name of Brazil appeared in the full Scotland side, having already represented his country at youth and under 21 level. By this time, he had also formed a deadly striking partnership at Portman Road with Paul Mariner. In his one hundred and forty-three full and eleven substitute appearances for Ipswich, he scored seventy goals. His goalscoring exploits earned him a £450,000 move to Tottenham Hotspur in March 1983, at a time when it was widely thought that he would join Manchester United. However, after an initial spell that produced six goals in ten games, he struggled to find the form At White Hart Lane which had been so evident at Ipswich.

Just over one year later, he was on the move again, this time to Old Trafford, for a fee of £625,000. After signing, United manager Ron Atkinson declared that Brazil was "the player he wanted more than any other, after Bryan Robson". Such a declaration put undue pressure on the player and he once again struggled to discover the form of his Ipswich days. He was to find himself, more often than not, on the substitute's bench and only made seventeen starts in his first season. His confidence was also not helped by some of the Old Trafford support, which not only booed him as he warmed up on the touch line, but also spat at him as well. During the opening months of the following season, 1985-86, he managed to make the starting line up only once and it was obvious that his days as an United player were numbered.

In January 1986, Coventry City rescued him from his hell at Old Trafford in a deal, which saw Terry Gibson and £65,000 go to Manchester. A relieved Alan Brazil was quick to admit, "the pressure of being an United player had become too much to bear. To be honest, neither my move to Tottenham or to United worked out well for me".

At Highfield Road, he only played fifteen times and left at the end of 1985-86 to join Queens Park Rangers, where his bad luck continued, with a back injury bringing an end to his League career.

Not a player to give up easily, Alan Brazil persevered at non-League level, with a variety of clubs such as Witham Town, Chelmsford City (on three separate occasions), Southend Manor and Wivenhoe Town, over a four year period, before finally hanging up his boots in 1991 and moving into media work.

Ron Atkinson added a second F. A. Cup win to his CV in 1985, but the League Championship still eluded him, having finished 4th in three consecutive seasons – 1983-84, 84-85 and 85-86.

The failure to take United onto a higher plain was beginning to take its toll and a poor start to season 1986-87, having opened the previous campaign with ten straight wins and an unbeaten run of fifteen games, saw the knives being sharpened.

An unbeaten run in October, two wins and two draws, seemed to have won Atkinson some more time, but a 4-1 defeat at Southampton, (a team United had beaten 5-1 at Old Trafford on September 13th), in a Football League Cup third round replay on November 4th, saw the sun bed and other effects being removed from the manager's office at Old Trafford.

No sooner had Atkinson cleared his desk, than a new manager was installed, with Alex Ferguson coming from Aberdeen, having guided them too much success north of the border.

Alex Ferguson was born in the Govan area of Glasgow, on New Years Eve 1941, in the shadows of the vast Clydeside shipyards and Ibrox Park.

Upon leaving Govan High School, amid dreams of emulating his Rangers heroes of Waddell, Woodburn and Young, he went to work for Remmington Rand, as a toolmaker, at their factory in Hillington, playing for Harmony Row Boys Club and Drumchapel Amateurs, after having represented Glasgow Schools and Scotland Schools.

With so many Junior and Amateur clubs in the Glasgow area, there was also a large scouting network and Alex Ferguson was soon singled out by a representative of Queens Park, signing forms with the famous old amateur club in the summer of 1958.

Whilst still only sixteen, he was given his Scottish League debut on November 15th 1958, at Stranraer, (a match Queens Park lost 2-1) and he was soon to establish himself as a regular in the side.

Because of their amateur status, Queens Park had difficulties in holding on to players of any promise and in the summer of 1960, Alex Ferguson took his leave off Hampden Park and moved to St Johnstone. This was only as a part timer, as he was determined to finish his apprenticeship at the typewriter factory.

By now, a Scotland Youth international, he made his debut for the Saints on September 3rd 1960 and in a four year career with the Muirton Park club he played forty five games, scoring twenty-two goals. Nothing much in the way of headline making about that, but one game in particular did see the name of Ferguson appearing across the back pages.

On December 23rd 1963, St Johnstone travelled to the Ferguson homeland of Govan to play Rangers. The twenty-one year old was to celebrate Christmas early, with a hat trick in his teams 3-2 win.

Although not a noted goalscorer, he did seem to find the net on a regular basis, averaging a goal every other game and with St Johnstone never likely to be one of the most successful Scottish clubs during the mid-sixties. The possibility of him leaving Perth was always there. So, when the opportunity arose to join Dunfermline in June 1964, Ferguson jumped at the chance, going on to become an almost ever present in the side during his three years at East End Park.

His first season brought a return of fifteen goals from twenty-seven League appearances, as Dunfermline came within a whisker of League and Cup success.

Disappointment came towards the end of this 1964-65 season though, as he was left out of Dunfermline's Cup Final side to face Celtic, having played in the earlier rounds.

Season 1965-66 saw Alex Ferguson top the scoring charts in Scotland, with thirty-one in thirty-one League games, setting a Dunfermline record. Adding to this his Scottish Cup and European goals, he scored forty-five in fifty-two games.

The goals continued to flow during the following season, twenty in the League, but it was to be his last with Dunfermline, as following a world tour with Scotland, having already represented the Scottish League, he returned home to join Rangers in a £65,000 record breaking transfer.

The dream had come true. His sixty-six goals in eighty-eight League outings (with eight hat tricks) for Dunfermline, had made a big impression.

His goals and determination created high expectations upon his arrival at Ibrox, which he was unfortunately unable to fulfil, despite scoring nineteen goals in twenty-nine appearances during his first season with Rangers.

Although not strongly built, Ferguson was not averse to 'putting it about a bit' during games. From time to time, he took the physical side of his game a bit too far and had the privilege of an early bath for his over exertions on six occasions over a sixteen year period.

With Rangers, however, he was only to make seventy-three appearances, scoring thirty-nine goals, not a bad return, but by the opening couple of months of 1969, he was found more in the reserves than the first team, as relations with Rangers manager David White became strained.
The decision was made to continue his career elsewhere, with a £20,000 transfer taking him to Falkirk, in October of that year, scoring on his debut against Dundee in the Dewar Shield and on his League debut against Berwick.

By a strange quirk of fate, White was sacked by Rangers shortly after Alex Ferguson left and the player was left to consider what might have been had he remained at Ibrox just a few weeks longer.
At Falkirk, he began to take an interest in coaching and if it had not been for a change of manager, might have remained at Brockville in such a capacity. Instead he was on the move once again, joining Ayr United in September 1973, at the age of thirty-one, for what was to be his final season as a player, playing his last ninety minutes on April 13th 1974, ironically at Falkirk.
A mention of his search for a management opening by Ayr boss Ally McLeod to an East Stirling director gave him a foot on the bottom rung of the managerial ladder at the start of season 1974-75. Numerous rungs of that ladder were not trod upon as Alex Ferguson climbed to the top in only five years.
The East Stirling appointment lasted only one season, moving to St Mirren in October 1974. Here he took the Paisley club to the First Division Championship in 1976-77 and eighth in the Premier League the following season, before leaving to take over at Aberdeen in 1978, beginning a remarkable eight seasons with the Pittodrie side.
In his first season, as he found his feet, Aberdeen finished a respectable fourth in the Premier League and runners-up in the Scottish League Cup. A year later, they were League Champions and again League Cup runners-up and over the following six seasons, he guided Aberdeen to two further Premier League titles, four Scottish Cup wins, one Scottish League Cup win. In season 1982-83, he reached the pinnacle of his career up to that point, lifting the European Cup Winners Cup.

He was duly rewarded with the CBE for his achievements and in 1986 was given the Scotland manager's job for the World cup in Mexico, following the untimely death of Jock Stein.

Now a highly respected manager, with a talent for bringing young players through the system, Alex Ferguson was Manchester United's number one choice as manager following Ron Atkinson's sacking in November 1986. His appointment received something of a mixed reception from the far flung United support, with many hoping that he could transform the club as he had done at Aberdeen, whilst others thought that although he had done well in Scotland, he would find managing in England a completely different kettle of fish and that the club should have gone for someone with experience of managing a club south of the border.
It was the latter, who thought that they had been proved correct, as under the new manager, Manchester United struggled in the League, after finishing as runners up in his first full season of 1987-88.

Numerous doubts began to be raised regarding Alex Ferguson's ability to be a success with United, but with his future at the club beginning to be questioned, United reached Wembley in 1990 and won the F. A. Cup, beating Crystal Palace in a replay. Ferguson had replied to his critics in the best possible way and United were now set to begin the most successful period in their history.
Alex Ferguson transformed the club, as Matt Busby had done half a century before, creating a team renowned for their attacking flair, introducing numerous players who would capture the imagination of the Old Trafford support. Success followed success, ranging from the European Cup Winners Cup to the Premier League and further F. A. Cup triumphs and following the remarkable treble winning season of 1999, Alex Ferguson emulated Busby when he was awarded a knighthood for his services to the game. A fitting tribute to the man, who had not only transformed Manchester United, but transformed the English game as a whole.

Not content to simply manage the club, he was also to play for it and it will be unknown to many that A. Ferguson once appeared on a Manchester United team sheet.

At the end of November, beginning of December 1987, United played two friendlies in Bermuda, due to a break in the domestic programme. In the second of those, against the Somerset Cricket Club, the boss claimed the number twelve shirt and it was obvious to all, that at some point he would haul someone off, in order to get a game.

Sure enough, off came the tracksuit top, Peter Davenport was called to the touch line and Alex Ferguson made his first and only Manchester United appearance.

There was one other surprise inclusion in the Manchester United line up for that friendly in Bermuda, with the name of **Archie Knox** appearing at right back. Knox, like Alex Ferguson, was well past the veteran stage of his career as a player and was in fact the United manager's first signing upon his arrival in Manchester.

Dundee born Knox, had been Ferguson's number two whilst at Aberdeen and it was only natural that the working relationship continued south of the border.

Upon leaving school, he had played junior football before joining Forfar Athletic as a part timer. After six years playing in the lower regions of Scottish football, he joined St Mirren and then Dundee United, where he came the closest he was to get to any sort of success, with defeat in the Scottish Cup Final of 1974 against Celtic.

With his playing career coming to an end with Montrose, he returned to his first club Forfar in 1976, as player manager, spending four years there before joining Alex Ferguson at Aberdeen, as a replacement for Pat Stanton. During his time with 'the Loons', he took them to the Scottish League Cup semi-finals, only to lose out to Rangers in extra time.

Together, Ferguson and Knox enjoyed three and a half productive years at Aberdeen, before the number two decided to go it alone with Dundee in December 1983. But, he was to resume his relationship with Alex Ferguson two and a half years later at international level for the 1986 World Cup, before returning to Aberdeen at the start of 1986-87.

Before leaving the Dons to join his companion at Old Trafford, he was offered the managers position at Aberdeen, but decided to turn it down and move to Manchester.

In April 1991, with the Final of the European Cup Winners Cup looming on the horizon, he surprisingly quit his post with United, returning to Scotland to become Walter Smith's assistant at Rangers. United quickly claiming some £75,000 in compensation.

When Smith finally gave up the Rangers job, after years of continued success and joined Everton, Knox followed. He also returned to the Scottish international scene as assistant to Craig Brown.

In his performance against the Bermudan First Division side, he outshone the United manager, by scoring with a thirty yard left foot shot in the 86th minute, consolidating a 4-1 win.

THE ALEX FERGUSON YEARS.

Back in 1987, Alex Ferguson saw out his first campaign in charge happy to give the players already at the club a chance to prove themselves. It soon became clear to him what was required, both at senior and junior level and in the summer of 1987, he set about rebuilding the club from grass roots level upwards. Goals, and to refine it a little more, an out and out goalscorer was Alex Ferguson's number one priority and he knew exactly the man he wanted, Celtic's Brian McClair. Ferguson's decision to bring McClair south received instant reward, as "Choocy" scored twenty-four League goals in forty outings, ten more than Peter Davenport had scored the previous season and the best return from a United player since season 1967-68, when a certain George Best scored twenty-eight in forty-one games. McClair also scored a further seven goals in the two domestic cup competitions.

Born in Airdrie, **Brian McClair** played for local sides St. Edwards Boys Guild and Coatbridge Y.M. before moving south of the border as an apprentice, with Aston Villa in 1980, but returned home disenchanted after fourteen months, mainly due a piece of good luck. The then Motherwell manager Ally McLeod, had received a telephone call from his opposite number at Aston Villa, saying that they had a youngster called Mills on their books who was homesick and would Motherwell be interested in signing him? When McLeod eventually got back in touch, he was told another lad, Brian McClair, also wanted to return north. With nothing to lose, McLeod agreed to take the boys north and see what they had to offer.

McClair spent one week training with Motherwell, but had also arranged a similar period with Celtic, who had heard of his plight. However, he only stayed one day with the Glasgow club and returned to Motherwell.

With a doubt in his mind regarding a full time career in football, McClair enrolled in a mathematics course at Glasgow University. His plans for the University degree lasted as long as his Motherwell playing career, just two years, as Celtic renewed their interest in the player, but this time had to pay out around £75,000 to take him from Fir Park, to the east end of Glasgow.

Brian McClair was Celtic manager's Billy McNeill's last signing in June 1983, before joining Manchester City and soon proved to be an excellent acquisition.

Stepping up from part time to full time caused few problems for a player who had already experienced one season in League football, scoring fifteen goals in thirty-nine games.

At Celtic Park, the goals continued to flow, topping the club's scoring chart for the next four seasons, with forty-one in fifty-seven appearances in that initial season. In August 1984, he was credited with scoring one of the 'best ever' Celtic goals, against Dundee United. With Celtic 1-0 down, McClair gathered the ball in his own penalty area and raced the length of the pitch before scoring.

His goals, one hundred and twenty in four seasons brought him the personal accolades of the Scottish PFA Player of the Year and the Scottish Writers Player of the Year in 1986. However, from a team perspective, Celtic only won the League title in 1986 and the Scottish Cup in 1985. It also earned him four Scotland caps.

In November 1985, whilst not a regular first choice in the Celtic starting line up, McClair asked for a transfer, but his request was turned down. Perhaps this was in the back of his mind almost a couple of years later when he turned down £80,00 to resign for the club.

By 1987, Billy McNeill had returned to the Celtic hot seat and did not meet Alex Ferguson's approach for the player favourably, particularly with the latter only offering £400,000. Celtic considered a fee of £2 million was much more realistic.

With neither side willing to budge, or meet a compromise, it was up to a tribunal to set the fee. At the end of the hearing, it was to be a disgusted Billy McNeill who strode out of the room. The transfer fee having been set at £85,000. The Celtic manager complained, "We've lost the biggest asset in Scotland. They have got him for a song".

If asked now, Alex Ferguson would readily agree, as Brian McClair ignored the problems encountered by many previously purchased forwards and the later groans of disapproval which sometimes echoed down the terracing towards him and got on with the job he knew best, scoring goals.

McClair's second season at Old Trafford was never going to compare to his first, as the team struggled at times to find any momentum and at one point he only managed to score once in six games. He did, however, score the only goal at Wembley, (his one hundredth for the club), as United beat Nottingham Forest to lift the Football League Cup for the first time in their history. An F.A. Cup winners medal and another from the European Cup Winners Cup followed. Perhaps McClair was unfortunate in scoring so many goals in his first season, as expectations on him repeating the feat were high. The closest he came to doing so was in 1991-92, when he managed sixteen.

During the 1990's, McClair took on a more deep lying role, but was soon to find himself more of a squad player, with a place on the bench his now normal match day position. Awarded a testimonial against Celtic, to mark his ten years at Old Trafford, McClair was given a free transfer at the end of season 1997-98, having won four League Championship medals, two F. A. Cup, one League Cup (scoring the only goal of the game) and one European Cup Winners Cup medal.

He returned to Motherwell for a short spell, but when Brian Kidd left Old Trafford for Blackburn Rovers, he appointed Brian McClair as one of his coaching staff. Following the former United assistant manager's departure from Ewood Park, he was out of the game for a while, but prior to the start of season 2001-02 he returned to Manchester United as reserve team coach.

If scoring goals was an early headache for Alex Ferguson, then conceding them was equally so. When he arrived at Old Trafford, Chris Turner was the man in charge of the No1 jersey, with Gary Walsh waiting eagerly on the sidelines. Gary Bailey was also there, but played only five games under the new manager before retiring through injury. Walsh played the first sixteen games of season 1987-88, with Turner taking over for the remainder of the season. Ferguson, however, had his sights set elsewhere and in the

close season, returned to Aberdeen to sign **Jim Leighton**, the goalkeeper he called "the best in Britain".

Leighton, had been born in Renfrewshire and played for Paisley and Disrict Schoolboys before joining Dalry Thistle. As a schoolboy, he had played in every outfield position, before settling between the sticks.

In 1976, following an unsuccessful trial with Dumbarton, Alex Ferguson signed him for Aberdeen, but the aspiring goalkeeper had to wait five years to claim the first team jersey from Bobby Clarke. During that time, he was farmed out to Devorndale on loan, during season 1977-78, to gain some experience.

Once established in the Aberdeen first team, Leighton became an important part of what was to become a very successful team, winning two Premier League, four Scottish Cup, one Skol Cup and an European Cup Winners Cup medal.

During 1987-88, he kept thirty five clean sheets in just over fifty games, so it was little wonder that Alex Ferguson felt that this was the man to solve his goalkeeping problems at United.

With other club's beginning to show an interest in the player, Ferguson moved quickly and a fee of £750,000, a

British record for a goalkeeper, took Jim Leighton south. "My dream comes true", said the new signing. "This is the challenge I need at this stage of my career".

Jim Leighton was by now also an established Scotland internationalist, having won his first cap against East Germany at Hampden Park in 1982. Twenty-one months later, however, his career was in turmoil.

Not having the best of afternoons in the F.A. Cup semi-final against Oldham Athletic at Maine Road, it was generally thought that it was simply one of those things, as he had more encouraging display in the replay. However, an even worse display was to follow less than one month later at Wembley in the 3-3 F. A. Cup Final draw against Crystal Palace, giving Alex Ferguson a couple of sleepless nights, deliberating his team selection for the replay.

After much thought, Les Sealey was given the goalkeepers jersey and enjoyed an exceptional evening as United won 1-0. Jim Leighton's Manchester United career was at an end, his playing career virtually in ruins.

Leighton, however, was a strong-minded individual and although severely disappointed by his demise at Old Trafford, was determined to resurrect his career elsewhere. A brief loan spell at Arsenal as understudy to David Seaman was his first port of call and this was followed by eight appearances for Reading, also on loan.

In February 1992, Jim Leighton's luck changed, with a £200,000 move to Dundee, helping them to the First Division title in his first season, but he was to lose his place during the following campaign and make a brief return south with a loan deal at Sheffield United.

In the summer of 1993 he returned to Scotland and joined Hibs on a free transfer and his career once again took off, earning a recall to the Scotland squad at the age of thirty-five, winning his sixtieth cap against Austria in Vienna on April 29th 1994.

Three years later, he was back at Aberdeen, captaining the side, and in 1998 he was once again involved with Scotland in the World Cup, a level he felt he would never again reach, having an outstanding match against Brazil. In October of that same year, he retired from international football, having won his ninety first cap against Estonia. At the end of season 1999-2000, he decided to retire

from playing altogether, taking up a coaching post with the Pittodrie club.

A career of highs and lows, but when asked, whilst with Hibs, if he was given the opportunity of joining Manchester United again would he do so? He replied "yes", without a second's hesitation.

Many players fell by the wayside as Alex Ferguson continued his quest to rebuild Manchester United to their former glory, with others finding themselves drafted into the side in the hope that their contribution would take the team closer to the managers intended target. One of those to find themselves amongst the former, was Jesper Olsen, a slimly built Danish winger, who had moved to Old Trafford in July 1984, around the same time as Gordon Strachan and Alan Brazil.

Olsen's departure wasn't as surprising as some, but it was his immediate replacement that raised a few eyebrows and also the voices on the terracing, as they suddenly questioned Alex Ferguson's ability to take United back to the top. The same voices were also quick to level much unwarranted criticism at the replacement, **Ralph Milne**, a completely different player from the departed Olsen.

Milne was unfortunate in the fact that many had no idea of his previous career details and had simply looked at the club he had been signed from – Bristol City, and no further. Few realised that he was a very experienced individual, having played at the highest level both at home and abroad.

Given a trial by Aston Villa whilst with Dundee Celtic Boys Club, he had failed to impress and returned home to join Dundee United, signing professional in May 1977 as a sixteen year old.

His Tannadice career spanned the best part of ten years and it was no mere coincidence that it coincided with the club's most successful spell in their history.

The League Championship was won in 1982-83 and three

Scottish Cup Finals were reached. It was, however, runners up medals that he collected on each occasion. Dundee United also reached the Final of the UEFA Cup in 1986-87, but by that time Ralph Milne had left, following numerous bust ups with United manager Jim McLean.

Forty-four goals in one hundred and seventy-nine appearances was not a bad return for a winger cum mid-field player and the title of Dundee United's top scorer in European competitions with fifteen goals, (one short of the Scottish record set by Celtic's Jimmy Johnstone), did not look too bad on his CV either.

Upon leaving his home town of Dundee, he headed for London, joining Charlton Athletic for £125,000 in January 1987, but it was to be an injury disrupted spell, which lasted only a year, playing twenty-two games without a goal to his credit.

In January 1988, he went to Bristol City on loan under Joe Jordan and it was a move that was soon to become permanent and also produce the dream move to Old Trafford ten months later.

Upon getting over the shock of United's initial enquiry, one that he felt was "as cover for Gordon Strachan", he was stunned when Alex Ferguson told him " I am going to sell Jesper Olsen and I want you to play on the left wing".

The stocky built Milne signed a three year deal and saw it out, with a loan spell at West Ham sandwiched in between, but made only one substitute appearance outwith his initial season of 1988-89 during which he made twenty-six League and Cup appearances, scoring three goals (his first, a volley from the edge of the penalty area against Charlton), with a further three as substitute.

With the club still going through something of a transitional period under Alex Ferguson, Ralph Milne was an easy choice when a scapegoat was required by the ever-impatient support.

Some unwanted and unmerited press in 1991, something that the player later regretted, followed and he was released on a free transfer, eventually moving to Hong Kong, joining Sing Tao F.C.

Perhaps remembered more fondly in Dundee than in Manchester, the £175,000 paid by Alex Ferguson to Bristol City for his signature, was the last cheque that he would sign for a Scottish born player.

Having seen Manchester United finish as runners up in the First Division at the end of Alex Ferguson's first full season in 1987-88, hopes were high for a continued improvement, but a year later, they had dropped to eleventh and had stuttered along in the early months of 1989-90. A 5-1 defeat at Maine Road against neighbours City raised numerous doubts about the manager's capabilities of being a success in England.

Attendances began to fall, a mere 23,328 had watched Wimbledon at Old Trafford in May 1989 and the average during the early months of 1989-90 was around the 33,000 mark.

The F. A. Cup win in 1990 gave Alex Ferguson some much needed breathing space and any doubts which still lingered over his suitability to be manager of Manchester United were finally erased at the end of season 1990-91 when he guided his team to the European Cup Winners Cup, defeating Barcelona 2-1 in Rotterdam.

Ferguson was now on his way to emulating everything that he had achieved at Aberdeen.

Having expressed an urgency regarding the restructuring of the club's youth policy when he arrived, fresh young faces were beginning to appear in the first team frame. Lee Martin, scorer of the winning goal at Wembley against Crystal Palace was only twenty-two, Lee Sharpe also became something of a regular and Russell Beardsmore had also featured prominently. A skinny legged, slip of a boy called Ryan Giggs had made his initial breakthrough as had Darren Ferguson.

If it had been down to his managerial father, **Darren Ferguson** would not have been at Old Trafford, never mind making his first team debut as substitute at Sheffield United on February 26th 1991.

As a schoolboy, he was eagerly sought by Aberdeen and Rangers and whilst playing alongside his brother Jason for Wilmslow Sports, it was reported that Brian Clough, then manager of Nottingham Forest, had made an approach for the mulit-talented fifteen year old, who had also played in the Manchester United 'B' team.

It was a move that Ferguson senior pondered on, as he felt that it would perhaps be in his son's interest if he tried to make the grade elsewhere and not be constantly under the microscope as the "managers son" at Old Trafford.

Alex Ferguson himself was put under pressure, by his United coaching staff who advised him not to let his son go, as they considered him too good a player to be allowed to leave. With Tottenham Hotspur also beginning to show an interest, Darren Ferguson was signed as an apprentice in July 1988, turning professional two years later.

The United training staff's opinions were proved correct as Ferguson junior made his way through the ranks and followed his Bramall Lane debut in February 1991, when he came on as substitute for Neil Webb, with his full United debut the following week against Everton at Old Trafford. A third appearance followed on the final day of the season at Crystal Palace.

Season 1991-92 saw him back in the reserves, except for appearances in the first and last games of the season, with one substitute appearance sandwiched in between.

The name of Darren Ferguson was to appear in the Manchester United line up for the first fifteen fixtures of season 1992-93, but injuries and the return to form of Lee Sharpe saw him miss out on the Championship run in, as the season reached its climax.

Darren showed many of his father's traits, mixing his ability to pass the ball well, with grit and determination in the tackle.

A place in the Scottish under 21 team was achieved, but unable to secure a United first team place, a £500,000 bid by Wolves took him away from Old Trafford in January 1994.

His career at Molinuex did not really take off, despite playing in well over one hundred games and he was loaned out to Sparta Rotterdam between January and May 1999 before signing for Wrexham, where he finally began to enjoy his football again.

Having eventually broken the twenty-six year Championship duck in 1992-93, Alex Ferguson was

determined to maintain the progress made and with his youth policy bearing fruition, the future did indeed look promising.

From the F. A. Youth Cup winning team of 1992 came the likes of Keith Gillespie, Gary Neville, Ben Thornley, Nicky Butt, Ryan Giggs, David Beckham and Glasgow born **Colin McKee**.

The former Scottish Schoolboy internationalist joined United in June 1989 and made steady progress through the A and B teams, before commanding a regular place in the reserve team during 1993-94, following a brief loan spell at Bury, where he made two League appearances in Division Three.

Compared to some of his previously mentioned Youth team mates, his progress was not as rapid, despite his goal scoring achievements in the Pontin's League (eighteen in twenty-two games) and also after having been voted the reserves Player of the Year during 1992-93. The manager, however, did reward him with his League debut on the final day of the 1993-94 season against Coventry City at Old Trafford. It was obvious, that a regular first team place was beyond him, due to the immense quality of those in front of him in the pecking order – Cole, Sheringham and Solskjaer. So much so that in 1994 he joined Kilmarnock, as part of a double £500,000 signing along with United team mate Neil Whitworth, where he had no problem in securing first team football.

Three seasons at Rugby Park was followed by a brief spell with Falkirk, but at the age of only twenty-four, his career was already on the wane. Loan deals with a variety of club's, on either side of the border, saw him disappear from view following a final attempt to salvage something from such a disappointing latter half to his career, with Ross County.

A player similar to McKee was **Alex Notman**, a stocky built forward from Edinburgh.

In his first season as an apprentice, 1995-96, he scored twenty-one goals in twenty-six appearances playing for the United 'B' team and with three goals from two starts and five substitute appearances in the 'A' team, a favourable future was envisaged.

The following season, he was a member of the Scotland Youth side and a year later was leading scorer in the Reserves with eleven from ten full and seven substitute appearances.

Like his contemporary, McKee, the established international stars blocked his path to the first team, but he never let up in his determination to try and make the grade with United. In August 1998, he proved that he was more than capable of playing on a bigger stage, scoring twice for United in the Munich Memorial match against a World X1. Shortly afterwards, he was given his senior debut as a substitute against Tottenham Hotspur in the Worthington Cup fifth round tie at White Hart Lane, coming on for Nicky Butt. Due to limited opportunities at Old Trafford, he, like many before him, was allowed to go out on loan, joining Aberdeen between February and May 1999. However, he was only to make two substitute appearances during his time at Pittodrie. A further loan period at Sheffield United

followed, during 1999-2000, for what was initially agreed to be for one month, but stretched into two. During this time, he scored his first Football League goal, against West Bromwich Albion after making his debut against Manchester City.

Much to his disappointment, nothing permanent surfaced and with his United appearances going to be few and far between, he was allowed to look elsewhere for a future in the game.

In November 2000, the Scottish under 21 internationalist joined Norwich City, hoping that his luck would finally change.

The initial Premier League Championship of 1992-93 was followed by a League and Cup double in 1993-94 and again in 1995-96, the Championship itself in 1997 and in 1998-99, the ultimate treble of the League, F. A. Cup and European Cup, with the Inter-Continental Cup thrown in for good measure. Seasons 1999-2000 and 2000-2001 saw the League Championship won yet again.

Season 1999-2000 saw the emergence of one young Scot, Michael Stewart, a fiercely patriotic youngster, who spent much of his spare time learning Gaelic.

Born in Edinburgh, **Michael Stewart** began playing with local Boys Club teams and Hutcheson Vale and was invited south by United for trials and training during the school holidays as a twelve year old. He was subsequently snatched from under the nose of Rangers, with whom he trained regularly and played in the Scottish Youth League, signing for United as a trainee in June 1997.

Steady progress ensured his graduation up to the reserve side in 1998-99 and in the final first team fixture of 1999-2000, he was named as substitute against Aston Villa.

A typical fiery Scottish redhead, the under 21 internationalist had to wait until the following season to make his debut, coming on as substitute in the Worthington Cup tie at Watford and on April 28th 2001, he made his League debut at Middlesbrough, replacing Roy

Keane. Season 2000-2001 saw him named as Reserve team Player of the Year and also turn down a loan move to Royal Antwerp, so that he could concentrate on his Old Trafford future.

The signing of Juan Sebastian Veron in the summer of 2001 did not help Stewart's progress, but as season 2001-02 progressed he was appointed captain of the United reserve side.

He is clearly though of by the manager as one for the future at both international and club level.

One other individual made his debut in Manchester United's first team during season 2000-01 and although a Scot through his father and not his birthplace, as a Scottish internationalist, he has to be given space within these pages. The playing career and personal life of **Andy Goram** would fill a book on its own and at thirty-six years of age, when hearing of Sir Alex Ferguson's approach for his services, thought that it was nothing more than a joke.

His arrival at Old Trafford raised perhaps as many eyebrows at Old Trafford as that of Ralph Milne's a number of years before, with Goram at least being better known. He was, however, considered too old to be considered as a replacement for either Fabien Barthez or Raimond Van Der Gouw.

Goram, whose father had played for Hibs and who had given him his Scottish blood, was born in Bury in 1964. As a seventeen year old, he was rejected by West Bromwich Albion, having been signed by Ron Atkinson, and the possibility of joining Bury also evaporated when after turning up for an interview, was kept waiting too long. Father and son simply walked out of Gigg Lane.

His father then approached the chief scout at Oldham, who had shown some earlier interest and the youngster was offered a contract, playing three games at the end of season 1980-81.

His performances and his ability were soon noted by the England set up and the possibility of an under 21 cap materialised, due to an injury to Gary Bailey. Howard Wilkinson, however, did not consider him good enough to take over from the Manchester United man.

Alex Ferguson, had no qualms about the young Goram's ability and in 1986 awarded him his first Scottish Cap

against East Germany. He also went to the World Cup in Mexico, as Scotland's third choice goalkeeper.

In October 1986, after six years with Oldham, he was transferred to Hibs for a fee of over £300,000, where not content with just being a Scottish International goalkeeper, he also turned out for Scotland at cricket. With the Easter road club, he also managed to get his name on the score sheet, scoring against Morton on the last day of season 1997-98.

Up until signing for Walter Smith at Rangers in 1991, his career and personal life could be considered as nothing out of the ordinary, but once at Ibrox, controversy was never far away.

Two years after signing, having already been 'advised' to quit playing cricket and having won the Scottish Player of the Year award for three years in succession and prompted Celtic star Tommy Burns to quip that he wanted "Andy Goram broke my heart" written on his gravestone, he was transfer listed over a dispute regarding training routines. 1995 saw him walk out of the Scottish squad after claiming he was "not mentally attuned" to play against Greece in a European Championship Qualifier. Nineteen months later though, he returned to the Scotland set up against Columbia and was soon Craig Brown's number one choice for Euro '96. Attacked by a Hib's supporter upon one return to his old stomping ground with Rangers, he was not offered a new deal in 1998, following Rangers' failure to win any of the Scottish trophies for the first time in twelve years.

Disgruntled and disillusioned, he announced his retirement from Scottish International football fifteen days prior to the opening World Cup tie against Brazil.

As a free agent, finding a new club was now his main priority and a brief spell at Notts County was followed by a longer two month loan deal with Sheffield United.

Motherwell eventually plucked up the courage to take the wayward star onto their books, but in 1999 the displays between the posts as team captain were overshadowed by bouts of controversy and on one occasion he was linked with Irish terrorist groups.

Nearing the end of a two year deal, a goalkeeping crisis at Old Trafford prompted Sir Alex Ferguson to sign him as emergency cover for three months, paying Motherwell £100,000 in compensation.

The thirty-six year old made two first team appearances for United, against Coventry City at home and Southampton away and was substituted in both. At the end of the season, he became a free agent, eventually joining Coventry City Again it was only a relatively brief stay, being released as a free agent once more.

As season 2001-2002 draws towards its climax, with Manchester United once again challenging for the games top honours, any success will see the continuation of a Scottish connection that has been there for every major triumph in the club's one hundred and twenty four year history.
The preceding pages of this book have told the stories of almost one hundred and sixty individuals who, have either played for or managed Newton Heath/Manchester United in a League match or F. A. Cup tie.
Many others, like Frank McGivern in the early seventies, a prolific goalscorer in the junior sides and who played in the Anglo Italian Cup against Bari during season 1972-73 only to disappear from the scene and John McInally, a goalkeeper from Gatehouse of Fleet, from around the same period, who kept me out of the south of Scotland side, (but that's another story), both failed to make the grade.

You will have noticed as you worked your way through the pages, that the number of individuals from north of the border grew fewer and fewer with each passing decade. It is no mere coincidence that this also coincides with a decline in both the domestic and national game in Scotland.

Ironically, since Alex Ferguson's departure from Aberdeen to Manchester United in the mid-eighties, Scottish football has slowly slid down a steep gradient.
Firstly, an influx of Englishmen helped Rangers reclaim the top spot, but the accents in not only the blue half of Glasgow, but in the green half and also in line up's of most of the other Premier League sides, as well as many lower Division sides, became multi-national.
The standard of play dropped dramatically and home grown talent was few and far between. Raids by English club's across Hadrians Wall for the best of the tartan talent became practically non-existent, as there were very few youngsters and established players worth a second glance. The English club's themselves had now begun to scour the overseas market for improving their teams.
Youngsters today have far more distractions than those of years ago The games of football in any suitable area, with lamp posts or jackets and jersies for goal posts, lasting until darkness set in, are a thing of the past.
It is sad that such productive areas of footballers for Newton Heath/Manchester United, like Ayrshire, Lanarkshire and Dundee are now non-existant, with perhaps the decline in industry in those same areas having more than just a little bit to do with it. However, they will not be forgotten for the parts that they have played in producing some of the players who made Manchester United the club it is today. Had it not been for the "TARTAN REDS", who knows where Manchester United would be today. Not the club it is, of that I am certain.